Language as Cultural Practice
Mexicanos en el Norte

Language as Cultural Practice
Mexicanos en el Norte

Sandra R. Schecter
York University

Robert Bayley
University of Texas, San Antonio

2002

LAWRENCE ERLBAUM ASSOCIATES, PUBLISHERS
Mahwah, New Jersey   London

Lawrence Erlbaum Associates, Inc., Publishers
10 Industrial Avenue
Mahwah, NJ 07430

Cover design by Kathryn Houghtaling Lacey

Library of Congress Cataloging-in-Publication Data

Schecter, Sandra R.
Language as cultural practice : Mexicanos en el Norte / Sandra R. Schecter, Robert Bayley.
    p. cm.
    Includes bibliographical references and index.
ISBN 0-8058-3533-4 (cloth : alk. paper)
ISBN 0-8058-3534-2 (pbk. : alk. paper)
1. Sociolinguistics—United States. 2. Mexican Americans—Languages. 3. Children—Language.   I. Bayley, Robert, 1943– .
II. Title.
P40.45.U5 S34   2002
306.44´0973 —dc21   2001040464
                                                           CIP

Printed in the United States of America
10 9 8 7 6 5 4 3 2 1

"J'ai voulu que les moments de ma vie se suivent et s'ordonnent comme ceux d'une vie qu'on se rappelle. Autant vaudrait tenter d'attraper le temps par la queue."

—*Jean-Paul Sartre (1938)*

"Whence this new literature which works at once by metaphor and by narrative, by the variation of being and by the concatenation of acts."

—*Roland Barthes (1964)*

Contents

     References   201

     Author Index   213

     Subject Index   217

Foreword

Ana Celia Zentella

References to the "Latino population explosion" and "the decade of the Hispanics" became commonplace in the United States in the 1980s. Instead of encouraging attention to Latino concerns, the decade spawned the most restrictive language laws since the post-World War I period of xenophobia. Despite—or because of—the continued increase in the number of Latinos in the 1990s, the "English-only" movement grew stronger and restrictions extended into the areas of health and education. Notwithstanding twenty years of projections, the extent of growth of the Latino presence documented in the first census of the 21st century came as a shock, even to demographers. Between 1990 and 2000 the number of "Hispanics" (the census term) increased by 60%, from 22.4 million to 35.3 million. Approximately 65% are of Mexican origin and large states like California and Texas will become increasingly Mexican, but U.S. Americans in many states beyond the Southwest, such as in Iowa, Arkansas, New York, and Maine, are encountering Mexican neighbors. The diversity of Latin American backgrounds, particularly from Central America, is also increasing throughout the nation.

How will the politicians and the general public react to the changing demographics of the 21st century, and how will they interpret their linguistic, cultural, and racial implications? Will there be a concerted effort to attack the barriers that keep many Latinos from realizing their dreams, particularly in regard to education? Or will the fears of a Latino takeover, fed by metaphors of "immigrant hordes" and "alien floods," lead to further restrictions of the civil rights of Latinos and limit their access to education and social services? Issues of language—Spanish, English, bilingualism—are at the root of these fears. "They speak Spanish" seems to be the only thing that U.S. Americans believe they know with certainty about Latinos. Most do not know that the majority of Spanish speakers also speak English (62% in the 1990 Census). Moreover, most Mexicans (and Puerto Ricans) in the United States are not immigrant members of the first generation, and a significant number do not speak Spanish (22% of all Hispanics were English monolinguals in 1990). But the media persist in highlighting the stories of individuals who cannot speak English fluently after years in the United States, and even go so far as to claim that the earlier immigrant pattern of accommodation to English in the second generation is no longer true. Given the lack of accurate information, it is not surprising that Spanish speakers are portrayed as unwilling or unable to learn English. The academic failure that plagues Latino students is blamed on their Spanish, and Spanish is viewed as a threat to the unity and political stability of the nation.

Where can we turn for clarity on these issues, to resolve the impasse that frustrates the well-meaning efforts of both parents and educators? Who can answer the questions they have about the roles that English, Spanish, and bilingualism should play in the personal and academic futures of Latino children in particular and of the nation in general? Sadly, linguists often are not prepared to deal with these issues because they focus on language as a grammatical system, instead of as cultural practice. For this reason, the cultural practice approach to a comparison of Mexicano families in California and Texas, reported on with such sensitivity in this volume, is so welcome; it arrives not a moment too soon. Schecter and Bayley understand the need to consider the social identities of speakers—including their gender, ethnicity, and racial and class backgrounds, as well as the contexts in which they learn and speak their languages—if we are to understand the complex and diverse ways of "doing being bilingual," to use Peter Auer's (1984, p. 7) terms. As bilinguals, we do not live double lives, with the exact same range of speakers, locales, and discourse demands in both of our languages. For most of us, one language is dominant. As the rich case studies in this book reveal, the dominant language may change as our lives change, and the authors argue persuasively that the deep emotions that accompany these changes are not given the attention they deserve. In addition, if we judge our proficiency in either of our languages against an unrealistic monolingual norm, inevitably we find ourselves wanting. For many members of ethnolinguistic minorities in the United States, whose ability to speak two languages may be the only advantage they enjoy over English monolinguals, debilitating feelings of linguistic insecurity can affect the development of their home language and of English, as well as their academic progress.

The authors take into account varied patterns of language use in a wide range of homes as well as the distinct impact of local educational policies and statewide demographics. Linking language, culture, social space, and geographical space in their analyses of observations and interviews enables them to address the sometimes overlapping and sometimes distinct concerns of children, parents, researchers, and teachers. Regarding the latter, it is important for professional educators to know how Mexicano parents use language to teach their children, how to measure Spanish proficiency, and how Spanish affects students' ability to become proficient in oral and written English. Careful attention is paid to parents' efforts on behalf of their children's education, and to their anxieties about the maintenance of Spanish, poorly explained educational programs and alternatives, and teachers' unclear expectations and contradictory evaluations. Clear guidelines emerge for what teachers and parents can do to help each other for the benefit of the children.

A major strength of the book is the amount of diversity in language practices and skills that it documents, sometimes within one family. This material corroborates the findings of my study (Zentella, 1997) of working-class Puerto Rican children in one New York City *bloque* ("block"). The careful case study treatments suggest that Fishman's (1991) insistence that parents raise children in the minority language in order to forestall language shift may be a necessary—but not sufficient—condition. A working class Latino family may require the help of a village, including the schools, to raise a child with excellent verbal and written skills in Spanish and English.

The good news, Schecter and Bayley show, is that children's skills in Spanish do not impede their progress in English. Children who knew how to write in Spanish could write as proficiently in English as those who did not know how to write in Spanish. Contrary to the view of the Texas judge who accused a mother of "abusing" her child because she was raising her in Spanish, parents who raise

their children in Spanish are not thwarting teachers' efforts or hurt-
ing their children's chances in life; they are not the enemy. Schecter
and Bayley encourage all of us to become activists and partners in
fighting narrow definitions of bilingualism that ignore a diversity of
practices and exclude the views of those most directly affected. I,
for one, am encouraged by their optimism about the possibilities of
positive change because of the directions they chart for us in this in-
sightful study.

Acknowledgments

We are indebted to many for supporting our research and the writing of this book. First, and most importantly, we wish to express our appreciation to the families who allowed us to share a portion of their lives and trusted us to tell their stories from our perspectives. The pilot study was supported by a grant from the National Center for the Study of Writing and Literacy at the University of California, Berkeley, to Sandra Schecter. The main study was carried out with the support of grants from the Spencer Foundation and the U.S. Department of Education Field-Initiated Studies Program to both authors. Lucinda Pease-Alvarez, Frank Davis, and Kenji Hakuta provided useful counsel and encouragement in their roles as external evaluators for these major initiatives, and Guadalupe Valdés advised on the design of assessment instruments. Data analysis and writing were supported by a York University SSHRC Small Grant and Faculty of Education Sabbatical Leave and Minor Research and Development Grant to Sandra Schecter, and a National Academy of Education Spencer Postdoctoral Fellowship and University of Texas Faculty Development leave to Robert Bayley. The authors are grateful to Marianne Alvarez, Miriam Barksdale-Botello, Adriana Boogerman, Gerard Bustos, Martha López-Durkin, Mira Katz, Johanna Meighan, Norma Mendoza-Denton, Elvia Ornelos-García, Rosemary Reyna, Diane Sharken-Taboada, Buenaventura Torres-Ayala, and Manuela Willis for their assistance with case study observations, interviews, and transcriptions. Kate Eichhorn provided extensive assistance in researching the historical context. Our thanks go especially to Robert Chodos and Jim

Cummins for their invaluable feedback and suggestions on earlier drafts, and to Naomi Silverman for her goodwill throughout. Finally, as always, we thank our respective families for their understanding, or tolerance, through the various stages of this odyssey.

Preface

Language as Cultural Practice addresses the important relationship between home language practices and the development of bilingualism and biliteracy among language-minority children. In particular, we examine the roles of Spanish and English in the worlds that Mexican immigrant and Mexican American family members participated in, identified with, and aspired to.

In writing this book we had three main goals. The first was to contribute to the understanding of the relationship between familial patterns of language use and children's development of bilingualism and biliteracy. Because previous research on Latino groups has been carried out in single locations, and the findings applied to other Latino populations, in *Language as Cultural Practice* we attend closely to the diversity found within and across Mexican-background communities. Thus, we explore the language practices of Mexican immigrants and Mexican Americans who live in two distinct regions, northern California and south Texas, with very different sociodemographic profiles. Research in two distinct communities enabled us to establish key relationships among family language patterns and broader societal factors in children's bilingual development.

Our second goal was to articulate a more fully developed model for the study of language socialization, the tradition in which we conceptualized our work. In *Language as Cultural Practice* we argue that language socialization, instantiated in language choice and patterns of use in sociocultural and sociohistorical contexts characterized by ambiguity and flux, is a both a dynamic and fluid process. Through an ethnographic account of language socialization practices within Mexican-background families in California and Texas, we illustrate a variety of cases where language is used by speakers across time and space to choose between alternative identities and where language interacts in different ways with defining categories, such as ethnicity, gender, and class.

Our third goal was to contest the terms of the debate that dominate the educational and public discourse about the needs of language-minority children, which tends to focus primarily on the speed with which children acquire English, to call for a critical reformulation, and to urge our readers to do the same. Such advocacy entails a renegotiation of the current framework, which consigns decisions about minority-language maintenance to the domestic, as opposed to public, domain. It also entails resistance to engaging the discussion of mother-tongue maintenance within a deficiency framework.

To promote such a reformulation of the debate about the educational needs of language-minority children, we designed *Language as Cultural Practice* for a broad audience of specialists and nonspecialists alike. The book is intended to be useful to undergraduate and graduate students and faculty in linguistics, anthropology, applied linguistics, and education. The narrative style is also suited to students and scholars in the humanities and to professional educators. *Language as Cultural Practice* may be used as a primary text in courses in language education programs. The full narrative or selected chapters are appropriate as course readings in sociolinguistics, second-language education, foundations of bilingual education and bilingualism, and language and literacy education, as well as in specialized courses such as language and ethnicity.

In considering the substance and form of the narrative to give voice to the dialectical tensions that both caregivers and children lived in negotiating sometimes irreconcilable choices, we needed to reflect on how we locate ourselves in relation to other voices that could speak with authority about the same or similar sets of subjects and circumstances. Neither of us is of Mexican descent; neither has had to endure an immigration odyssey where language was a crucial issue; and neither has been raised in a wholly Catholic home environment, as were the majority of caregivers we spoke with. And although we both speak more than one language, with at least one variety we have learned with considerable difficulty, we both acquired the socially dominant language from birth. We also want to acknowledge our social and professional privilege relative to most of the families, while at the same time underscoring that we do not consider our research to be primarily about the dilemmas of the "marginal" or "poor." To the extent that the families we were privileged to work with are located along a broad socioeconomic spectrum that is representative of the demographics of Latinos in the United States, our university positions ensured a social status that is relatively elevated as compared with the majority. More influential perhaps than these socioeconomic discrepancies were the roles we embodied as university researchers (as opposed to family caregivers confronted with a similar set of dilemmas and options), which were crucial to decisions we made throughout—about how to organize our observations, about the forms that we would use to represent them, about the interpretive methodologies through which we would understand them (cf. Grumet, 1987). About this aspect of our identities we remained relatively unconflicted, so we believe that we were not disingenuous about our motives.

Nonetheless, these disjunctures—and there may be more—suffice to raise legitimate concerns concerning the relation of our personae and stances (as both internalized and perceived through the ascription of ethnicity and other characteristics) to our capacity for empathy with the experiences of the family members who allowed us to share a portion of their lives and trusted us to tell their stories. Indeed, some have argued that, as outsiders, we have no business representing or interpreting these experiences. To such critics, we can only reply that the relationship between researchers and those their research is about is multidimensional, and shared or differing ethnicity is only one dimension of that relationship. Issues of relative power may arise in any relationship between researchers and members of the communities they research, even when ethnicity is shared. Although it is an important consideration with regard to access and interpretation of data, a researcher's ethnicity does not necessarily guarantee or preclude rapport or *confianza*. In our project, we employed Latina bilingual research assistants, involving them directly in interviewing and observing. Such a strategy proved useful at some junctures and in some circumstances, and an impediment to the research process in others. Where it was not helpful, respondents were somewhat self-conscious about expressing points of view or relating decisions that they suspected might diverge from those of their interviewers who, as members of a language minority, confronted similar choices with regard to Spanish maintenance and the use of Spanish and English in family life.

A final, often asked-about area in relation to issues of authorial stance has to do with the collaborative structure of this narrative endeavor. Starting with perhaps the least complicated of factors, although our professional and disciplinary formations are complementary, they are also somewhat different, predisposing the coordinating of understandings through different interpretive lenses. Also, as individuals we differ temperamentally and sometimes ideologically.

Gender difference is clearly a key factor. The different gender realities we inhabit necessarily constitute us as subjects who see and act in the world differently. We believe that the knowledge imparted to and through gender played a crucial role in our collaboration, although we are not in a position to generalize regarding the constraining and enabling effects of gender in the research endeavor. Sandra's extensive background in ethnography and a temperamental predisposition to observe in the domestic realm were clearly considerations in the decision that she would assume primary responsibility for interviews and home observations. Robert's background in variationist sociolinguistics was the compelling factor in his assuming responsibility for quantitative data analysis (including design of instruments for assessing focal children's patterns of language acquisition and retention). Although the complementary distribution of skills, and corresponding distribution of labor, served to reduce some of the analytic and interpretive challenges arising from the partnership, some important issues remained to be worked out, with greater or lesser success. As a consequence, there are subjects that we cannot adequately address in this particular narrative because our thinking does not converge on the vehicle for the telling, the substance of the telling, or even the need for the telling. We are not distressed by these circumstances. For the more compelling of these subjects there will be other venues for solo reflection. We would be remiss, however, if we did not state that on the whole we found the collaboration to be an additive experience. We both believe we were able to accomplish more as a team—not only in terms of volume of work but also in terms of depth of understanding—than we would have as individuals. And in the final analysis, the story that we each believe most worth telling is the one that has evolved out of our efforts to find common structures that would permit us to coordinate our understandings with principle.

Epistemologist Madeleine Grumet (1987) reminded us that there are "multiple narratives" that could be based on the same set of observations, and social scientist Donna Haraway (1991) cautioned that our positions are situated, and that, therefore, our knowledge must always be partial. We believe that the disjunctures and differences that have called attention to the partiality of both our collaborative and our individual perspectives have made us stronger researchers—more careful in the claims we make, the dichotomies we are prepared to signal, and the social significance we ascribe to these dichotomies. For these differences, therefore, and for the privilege of negotiating them in interaction with those voices we inevitably must construct as Other, we are both, and each, exceedingly grateful.

1

Framing Our Agenda

HOME AND SCHOOL INFLUENCES
ON BILINGUAL DEVELOPMENT

In the early 1990s we began to reflect seriously on the agenda that culminated in this book. At the time, both authors were living and working in geographic regions with significant Latino populations, Sandra Schecter in the San Francisco Bay area of northern California and Robert Bayley in San Antonio in south Texas. The education of language-minority children had moved to the top of the agenda for professional educators, researchers, and policymakers in the United States. It had achieved this prominence because of the significant increase in the rate and volume of immigration from non-English-speaking countries that began in the 1970s and continued unabated through the 1980s and into the 1990s, reaching levels not seen since the 20th century's early years.

By the early 1990s, one in seven residents of the United States spoke a language other than English at home (U.S. Department of Commerce, 1993a). A trend emerging from successive national surveys gave the issue an added urgency: An increasing number of children were learning one language at home and proceeding through preschool and grade-school programs that required them to adopt a different language. At the time, much of the public debate about the education of Latino children centered on the efficacy of bilingual education as opposed to the traditional immersion or "sink-or-swim" approaches that had been

1

the lot of earlier generations of children from non-English-speaking immigrant families (Crawford, 1992; Krashen & Biber, 1988).

Although language educators distinguish between transitional and
maintenance bilingual education programs, the distinction is often lost
on scholars and practitioners in other areas of education as well as the
general public. The essential goal of transitional bilingual education is
to provide children who enter school speaking a language other than
English with sufficient support in their first language so as not to impede
their development of subject-matter knowledge (including initial literacy) while they are acquiring English. Typically, transitional bilingual
education programs last for 3 years, usually not more than 4. Once children are regarded as proficient in English, they receive no additional
support in their first language. The goal of such programs, then, would
seem to be language shift and English monolingualism. In contrast,
maintenance bilingual programs, which in the United States are far less
common than transitional programs, attempt to develop children's language and literacy skills in the first language while teaching English.
The orientation is additive and the goal is bilingualism and biliteracy.
Maintenance programs include two-way programs, in which half of the
students are native English speakers and half speakers of a language
other than English, as well as programs directed exclusively to speakers
of a minority language.[1]

In communities where enough children shared a home language, and
where state or local policy favored bilingual programs, professional debate about which type of program would offer the greatest benefits for
children's linguistic and cognitive development tended to center on
questions of instructional sequencing and structure. Researchers, educational policy-makers, and practitioners debated what proportion of instruction should be in English and what in the home language, whether
the two languages should be kept entirely separate or whether code alternation should be permitted and encouraged, and at what age children
should be transitioned to all-English classrooms.[2]

In the first stage of our collaboration, a climate of public opinion that
seemed to threaten hard-won gains in the education of language-minor-

---

[1]See Baker (1996) for a discussion of various types of bilingual programs.

[2]See Arias and Casanova (1993), August and Hakuta (1997), Hakuta (1986), Padilla, Fairchild,
and Valadez (1990), and Stanford Working Group (1992) for a sampling of such debates.

ity children was a source of concern for both of us. In addition, although we found the curricular issues just outlined deserving of attention, we were wary of the heavy concentration of attention on the formal education of language-minority children. This focus, we feared, could invite the inference that school was the most important arena where bilinguals could flourish. At least in the United States, where the loss of the mother tongue has been viewed by many educators and policymakers as a necessary step toward Americanization (Bayley, in press; Hakuta, 1986; Secada & Lightfoot, 1993), such an inference would have been, and continues to be, erroneous. Overwhelmingly, research in both the sociology of language and the linguistic aspects of bilingual development indicated that dual language development and maintenance could not be achieved without a strong commitment on the part of the home. More contemporary ethnographic studies of Latino communities provided especially compelling evidence for the argument that extensive use of Spanish in daily interactions and in literacy events in the home was necessary to foster complementary development in both Spanish and English (Delgado-Gaitan, 1990; Vasquez, Pease-Alvarez, & Shannon, 1994; Zentella, 1997, 1998). At the same time, in an influential volume on reversing language shift, sociolinguist Joshua Fishman (1991) argued that school-based programs alone were insufficient to prevent first-language attrition. Language practice in the home, Fishman contended, was the most critical factor in predicting whether a language would be maintained across generations: "It is in the family that the peculiar bond with language and language activities ... is fostered, shared and fashioned into personal and social identity" (p. 409).

EVOLUTION OF THE RESEARCH PROJECT

"Bilingual by Choice": The Precursor

When we first discussed the opportunity of a collaboration in the interest of exploring the relationship between home language socialization and the development of bilingual/biliterate abilities, Sandra Schecter was in the process of analyzing findings from an exploratory study that addressed Latino parents' perspectives on language use in the home, with a focus on their attitudes toward Spanish-language maintenance. The aim of this project, entitled "Bilingual by Choice: Issues in the Use of Spanish and English in Family Life," was to uncover a range of perspectives that underlay language-minority parents' decisions to raise their children with two languages. The project probed parental views and decisions on a variety of topics related to language transmission and socialization: language varieties used in the home; parental rationales for decisions regarding the differential uses of the two languages; strategies for maintaining Spanish at home; day-to-day issues encountered in the effort to sustain the use of the minority language; support systems that served to help sustain the use of the minority language; and the personal impact of language policy as experienced by different family members over time.[3]

As is characteristic of exploratory studies, resources for this one were limited, and the project's scope was limiting as a result. Given the constraints of a pilot study, a time- and relatively cost-intensive case-study approach such as we would later adopt was out of the question. Although multiple-choice questionnaires, frequently used in survey research, would have been cost-effective, we decided against using these because of our belief that parental perspectives had not been fully represented in the reports of findings of survey-type inquiries. Normally such surveys are of two types. The first consists of protocols designed by sociologists of language to yield measures that, in various combinations, can be used to characterize distinct speech communities. The reports of Allard and Landry (1992; Landry & Allard, 1992) on the ethnolinguistic vitality of two Franco-Canadian communities in the provinces of New Brunswick and Ontario, respectively, illustrate the strengths and limitations of this approach. The protocol used in Allard and Landry's investigation was not designed to uncover the interviewees' individual perspectives. Its utility lies in facilitating correlation of responses on a variety of topics with patterns of language maintenance and loss. The second type of survey research consists of overviews or syntheses of studies conducted by other researchers (e.g., Fishman, 1991). Although this kind of report provides a useful heuristic for studies of home language use, it is difficult to interpret the reported findings independently without access to

---

[3]See Schecter, Sharken-Taboada, and Bayley (1996) for a detailed discussion of the findings of this study.

the specific contexts and questions that elicited the primary data. In particular, it is often unclear whether such summaries evolved from bilingual family members' perspectives or from a sample of responses gleaned from a broader sample of the population. Similarly, it was not always possible to determine whether the rationales provided by respondents were intended to explicate personal choices and decisions with regard to the use of two languages, or to account for their support for bilingualism as a societal goal.

Given these constraints, the elicitation strategy that appeared most feasible and worthwhile was in-depth interviewing. The issue was resolved by default. The interviews for the pilot were conducted during 1992 and 1993 by Sandra Schecter and Diane Sharken-Taboada, under the sponsorship of the University of California, Berkeley.[4] Ten families participated in the pilot study. In each there was at least one child 2 years or older present in the home, and at least one parent was bilingual in Spanish and English.[5] Interviews were of the standardized, scheduled variety; that is, all respondents received the same questions in the same order (Briggs, 1986).

Because the goal at this stage was exploratory, we cast a wide net. Although the largest number of participants had roots in Mexico, participants also included parents from a variety of other Spanish-speaking countries. Table 1.1 summarizes the social and demographic characteristics of the participants in the first phase.

As the summary of social and demographic characteristics indicates, participants in the first phase represented a wide range of occupations and social circumstances, and their children also varied widely in age. In addition, we made a decision to include both single-parent families and families with a nonparent as primary caretaker. Although such families are often excluded from study because this factor is viewed by researchers as a confounding variable, we reasoned that our attempt at inclusiveness would be defeated if we were to exclude family types that represent a significant proportion of the general population.

---

[4]At the time, Sandra Schecter was Executive Director of the National Center for the Study of Writing and Literacy, a federally sponsored research center based at the University of California, Berkeley; Diane Sharken-Taboada was a doctoral student in UCB's Graduate School of Education.

[5]Bilingualism would not be a criterion for participation in the main study. In the exploratory phase, however, we were interested in respondents' rationales and decisions about language use in contexts where some choice figured, and where explanations would not necessarily be of a pragmatic nature.

TABLE 1.1

**Social and Demographic Characteristics of Participating Families:
Pilot Study**

Case	Parents: Birthplace	Parents: Occupation	Children: Gender, Age	Children: Birthplace
1	M, Colombia (single parent) F, Colombia	M, office worker	m, 17; f, 13	United States
2	M, Los Angeles F, Ecuador	M, student F, accountant	m, 11; m, 9; m, 7	Ecuador (two older children); United States (youngest child)
3	M, San Francisco F, Peru	M, student F, computer programmer	m, 18 months	United States
4	M, Oakland (single parent) F, Mexico	M, teacher	m, 13	United States
5	M, Los Angeles F, Mexico	M, secretary F, mechanic	f, 5; f, 15 months; m, 6 months	United States
6	M, Los Angeles F, Panama	M, homemaker F, professor	m, 15; f, 13	United States
7	M, New York F, Guatemala	M, professor F, teacher	f, 10; m, 19 months	United States
8	M, Miami F, United States, raised in Peru and United States	M, government analyst F, administrator	f, 13; f, 2	United States
9	M, Florida F, Mexico	M, teacher F, teacher	f, 17; m, 14 m, 4.5	Mexico (two older children) U.S. (youngest)
10	M, Mexico F, Tucson	M, administrator F, student	f, 9; m, 3.5	U.S.

Note. M, mother; F, father; m, male; f, female; ages in years unless otherwise specified.

Although we were conscious of the limited scope of the preliminary study, we were nonetheless skeptical of basing interpretations solely on individuals' responses to elicitation protocols because analyses of attitudinal factors based on self-reports are especially vulnerable to two criticisms. First, respondents' recollections and opinions are colored by their need to make favorable impressions on the people who are questioning them. Second, self-report data are constrained by the social, cultural, and political influences of the time the study is being carried out. We therefore took care to construct our protocol so as to elicit the kind of narrative accounting that would permit multiple checks on reported attitudes and practices. And indeed, phrases such as *reconstruct your decision* and *family history,* which we embedded in our protocol, ensured that respondents volunteered chronologies of their own and their children's minority-language maintenance odysseys.

Interestingly, the long-term perspective afforded by the life-history accounts revealed a significant number of shifts reported in language orientation and in minority-language maintenance strategies. In fact, 7 of the 10 families interviewed reported changes in their patterns of language use in the home; more than half of these reported two or more such changes. These shifts tended to co-occur either with a critical juncture in the child's formal education (such as transition from home to preschool) or with a time of flux on the home front causing changes in enabling or constraining forces (e.g., a geographic move, separation or divorce of parents, or arrival of a new sibling). Moreover, it appeared as though these circumstances, experienced frequently as traumas by both adults and children, caused respondents to reevaluate their goals and attitudes with regard to language use in the home (Schecter, Sharken-Taboada, & Bayley, 1996).

As we engaged in intensive discussion over the articulation of a research proposal for a major study that would explore in depth the relationship between family language environment and bilingual development, we were struggling simultaneously with interpretation of the pilot study's findings. Among the most striking of these were the concerns that parents expressed about intergenerational language shift. Clearly, parents viewed their children's language behaviors in terms other than those that motivated language researchers, policymakers, or even teachers. They experienced events associated with language use in day-to-day life as enablers of (or constraints to) the maturation of their children's identities as social and cultural beings. However, these identities were not necessarily stable.

On the contrary, they tended to be reconfigured as circumstances shifted and people struggled to accommodate the continuities and discontinuities that defined their lives.

The relationship between changes in language use and shifting life circumstances can be seen vividly in the testimony of Nilda Quintana, (a pseudomyn, as are all the names of family members) whose story we tell in chapter 7. The authenticity of respondents' testimonies regarding their shifting locations, as it were, was reaffirmed as they returned frequently to the disjunctures that had arisen in their endeavors to raise their children bilingually, even when the interview protocol did not call for them to revisit these issues. Our problem would be in reconciling the meanings embedded in these accounts with a body of research on language maintenance and shift among members of immigrant minority communities, a corpus to which we looked for the conceptual framing of our work.

Minority-Language Maintenance and Shift

A growing body of evidence suggests that the majority of the approximately 6,500 human languages spoken in the world today will be extinct by the end of the 21st century (Nettle & Romaine, 2000). In the view of many anthropologists and linguists, such a loss would represent an intellectual catastrophe of unprecedented magnitude. And yet, the probability that half or more of the world's languages will not survive this century is only one of several motivations for attempting to understand the processes of minority language maintenance and shift. Studies of language maintenance and shift have the potential to contribute to our understanding of linguistic processes and, more generally, of social structure—whether they deal with speakers of very small endangered languages such as Taiap in New Guinea, spoken by fewer than 100 people, or with immigrant speakers in the United States of languages such as Chinese or Spanish, whose vitality on a global scale is unquestioned.

In recent years, problems of language maintenance and shift have engaged the attention of researchers in a variety of disciplines, including anthropological linguistics (e.g., Crago, Annahatak, & Ningiuruvik, 1993; Dorian, 1981; Hill & Hill, 1986; Kulick, 1992; Schmidt, 1985), demography (e.g., Veltman, 1983, 1988), psycholinguistics (e.g., Hakuta & D'Andrea, 1992), sociolinguistics (e.g., Fishman, 1991; Gal, 1979; Silva-Corvalán, 1994), and sociology (e.g., Portes & Hao, 1998). The range of disciplinary perspectives from which scholars have examined language maintenance and shift has led to studies that have emphasized different aspects of the phenomenon. We first present a broad view of language maintenance and shift in the United States, drawing on large-scale demographic surveys. We then focus on a different research tradition, language socialization, which, in large part, informed many of the decisions we made in designing our study. Ironically, this research tradition both enabled us to understand the complex dynamics involved in minority-language maintenance and shift in a way that demographic surveys could not and circumscribed our understandings in a way we would later come to find too limiting.

Immigrant Bilingualism and Shift to English

Although linguistic diversity has been part of national life since Colonial times (Heath, 1981), immigrant bilingualism in the United States has traditionally been a transitory phenomenon. Typically, immigrant communities shifted from their original language to English within two or three generations. In most cases, members of the immigrant generations were monolingual or at least strongly dominant in their language of origin. Their children were usually bilingual, although their literacy skills were often less fully developed in the immigrant language than in English (Wiley, 1996). Most often, the second United States-born generation has been strongly English dominant or monolingual in English. In recent decades, however, traditional patterns of immigration have changed. During the period 1981–1991, the United States received more immigrants than in any decade since 1900–1910 (U.S. Department of Commerce, 1993a). Moreover, unlike the massive immigration that characterized the last decades of the 19th century and the first decades of the 20th, recent immigrants have come not from Europe but primarily from Latin America—especially Mexico and the Spanish-speaking Caribbean—and Asia. In 1997, the total "foreign-born" population of the United States numbered 25.8 million, of whom 51% were from Latin America and the Caribbean (Schmidley & Alvarado, 1998). Approximately 7 million of these people, or 27% of the total non-United States-born population, were born in Mexico. From 1980 to 1990 the number of people 5 years of age and older who claimed to speak Spanish at home rose from 11,549,000 to 17,339,000, a 50.1% increase (U.S. Department of Commerce, 1993a).

Given such remarkable increases in the number of Spanish-speakers in the United States, it may appear strange to be concerned about the problem of minority-language loss among Latino populations. A walk through any of the many vibrant Latino neighborhoods in the San Francisco Bay Area, or even a brief visit to the supermarket in many parts of San Antonio, gives the impression that Spanish has become a stable part of the U.S. scene. Indeed, the impetus behind movements such as U.S. English, which seek to make English the sole language of public life and education, stems largely from the perception that Spanish is gaining at the expense of English. Advocates of "English Only" often express fear that the traditional three-generation pattern of shift from immigrant languages to English described earlier no longer obtains, particularly among Spanish-speaking populations. However, despite the ethnic revival movements of the 1970s and 1980s and the best efforts of advocates of maintenance bilingual education, evidence from research suggests that the traditional pattern of intergenerational loss of immigrant languages continues even in areas of the country where the immigrant language would be expected to have the greatest chance of long-term survival. In a study of Spanish language use, for example, demographer Calvin Veltman (1988) concluded that were it not for continuing high levels of immigration, the number of Spanish speakers in the United States would decline rapidly.

That conclusion is supported by the findings of other studies. López's (1982) study of linguistic preferences of language-minority groups, although conducted before the large-scale immigration of the 1980s and 1990s, provided evidence that immigrants from Spanish-speaking countries were shifting to English at a very rapid rate. López studied three Latin American and four Asian-origin groups. In every group, English was the preferred or only language for the great majority of 5- to 17-year-olds. For example, although young Mexican-background speakers exhibited less preference for English than did young Japanese- and Filipino-background speakers (for whom a shift to English monolingualism was nearly complete), 78% of the young speakers from the largest language-minority ethnic group reported using only English or mainly English. Moreover, in every case, 5- to 17-year-olds reported much more use of English than speakers over 18 years old.

López's conclusions are supported by a more recent study based on 1990 census data. Bills (1997) examined the numbers of people who claimed to use Spanish at home in five states with traditionally large

Mexican-origin populations: Arizona, California, Colorado, New Mexico, and Texas. Table 1.2 shows the results by state and age group. These 1990 census data are consistent with the general trends shown by López (1982) and Veltman (1988), although the actual numbers are quite different. In all five states that Bills studied, far more adults (18 years and older) claimed to use at least some Spanish at home than did the 5- to 17-year-olds. That is, despite the impressive percentages of Spanish-language claimants in some states, the census provides yet another illustration of the gradual replacement of Spanish by English. Moreover, as Bills pointed out, the home is usually the last domain of an ethnic language to undergo shift. The 1990 census data do not provide information about language use in domains outside the home, such as the workplace or neighborhood stores, but it seems reasonable to infer that many of those who report using Spanish at home use English in most of their interactions outside the home. In addition, the census data tell us nothing about the character of Spanish used at home. Recent work on language practices in Latino families (e.g., Schecter & Bayley, 1997; Vasquez et al., 1994; Zentella, 1997, 1998) reveals considerable variation in both the quantity and quality of Spanish used. In fact, in some of the families whose language practices we studied, parent–child interactions in Spanish, which are critical for minority-language maintenance,

TABLE 1.2

Spanish Home Language Claimants as a Percentage of the Hispanic Population in Five Southwestern States

	Total	*Age 18+*	*Age 5–17*
Arizona	79.6	87.1	62.4
California	81.7	84.9	73.3
Colorado	54.5	63.2	32.3
New Mexico	74.7	84.6	49.4
Texas	89.9	95.0	77.9
Total	83.1	87.4	72.0

U.S. Bureau of the Census (1993b), as adapted by Garland Bills, "New Mexican Spanish: Demise of the Earliest European Variety in the United States," *American Speech*, 72:1 (Spring 1997), table 2, p. 157. Copyright 1997, American Dialect Society. Reprinted by permission of Duke University Press.

were restricted to occasional endearments or to specific times that the parents had set aside in an attempt to revive Spanish.

If the large-scale studies exemplified by Bills (1997), López (1982), and Veltman (1988) can provide only the broad outline of changing patterns of language use among U.S. Latinos, how do we go beyond such an approach to get at the day-to-day home language practices that are so crucial to understand if language-minority children are to become proficient bilinguals? A number of approaches are possible. These include traditional sociological approaches, exemplified by Fishman, Cooper, and Ma (1971), in which Puerto Rican residents of an east coast *barrio* were asked, among other things, what language they would use in speaking with different interlocutors and in different situations and locales. Other studies have taken different approaches. Hakuta and D'Andrea (1992), for example, administered language use and attitude questionnaires in tandem with a variety of language proficiency measures to a group of Mexican-background high school students in rural central California. Their results illustrated the complexity of the phenomenon of minority-language maintenance and shift in that they showed that there was not a one-to-one relationship between language proficiency and reported patterns of language use. However, although they asked a variety of questions about participants' language preferences at home, Hakuta and D'Andrea's study did not include any actual observations of the students in their homes or any other out-of-school environments. Recently, Kondo (1997) took a social-psychological approach in studying language maintenance and revival by *shin Nisei* (new second-generation Japanese) university students in Hawaii. Kondo explored a range of background factors through intensive interviews with six bilingual and semibilingual focal students and extensive interviews with numerous other *shin Nisei* students. Her conclusions indicated that mothers play a major role, although not a determining one, in their children's bilingual maintenance, especially with regard to oral skills. Other factors, however, also play a role. In particular, social identities, which are subject to change over time, interact with maternal patterns of language use.

The types of studies just outlined, based on questionnaires about language use (including use in hypothetical situations), measures of language proficiency administered at school, and retrospective interviews with university students enrolled in language courses, have contributed to our appreciation of minority-language maintenance and shift as a complex phenomenon that is influenced by a wide range of factors that may vary both within and between communities. However, if home, particularly maternal, patterns of language use are indeed the major factor influencing children's bilingual development, studies such as these all suffer from a major lacuna. They contain no data drawn from actual observations in the home. However, another research tradition, language socialization, does focus closely on interactions between children and caregivers. In designing our study, we saw research within this framework as providing a promising approach to understanding the complexity of these processes of minority-language maintenance and shift and the ways in which these processes influence the role of language in cultural context. Crucially, the perspective afforded by language socialization research allowed for study of the pragmatic and symbolic roles of different languages in language-minority families, as well as the implications of changes in these roles for language acquisition, maintenance, and shift.

Starting With a Language Socialization Perspective

Researchers in language socialization have conceptualized the process of language acquisition broadly.[6] They have tended to view language acquisition as a composite phenomenon of cognitive-linguistic and sociocultural factors (Gaskins, Miller, & Corsaro, 1992; Ochs, 1988; Ochs & Schieffelin, 1995; Rogoff, Mistry, Göncü, & Mosier, 1993; Schieffelin & Ochs, 1986). The process by which children become socialized into the interpretive frameworks of their culture, moreover, includes not only the period of primary language acquisition, from infancy to the age of 5 years; it extends throughout childhood and into adolescence (Goodwin, 1990; Heath, 1983). Researchers working within this framework see both the context of interaction and the culturally sanctioned roles of the participants as major determinants of language forms and strategies used in given situations.

---

[6]See, for example, Crago, Annahatak, and Ningiuruvik (1993), Crago, Chen, Genesee, and Allen (1998), Eisenberg (1986), Goodwin (1990), Heath (1983), Kulick (1992), Ochs (1988), Philips (1983), Schieffelin (1990), Scollon and Scollon (1981), and Watson-Gegeo and Gegeo (1986).

Recently, a number of scholars have extended the tradition of language socialization research to study the linguistic development of children in bilingual and multilingual communities (Sommer, 1997). In general, this research has documented the difficulties of maintaining minority languages, whether Inuktitut in the far north of Quebec (Crago, Chen, Genesee, & Allen, 1998), Taiap in rural Papua New Guinea (Kulick, 1992), Dyirbal in northern Queensland, Australia (Schmidt, 1985), or Spanish in U.S. cities (Bayley, Schecter, & Torres-Ayala, 1996; Pease-Alvarez & Vasquez, 1994; Schecter & Bayley, 1997; Schecter et al., 1996; Vasquez et al., 1994; Zentella, 1997). Language socialization research in U.S. Latino communities has examined children's developing competence in various speech and literacy events, for example, teasing and other forms of verbal play (Eisenberg, 1986), reading Spanish-language advertising flyers (Bayley et al., 1996), and simultaneous translation (Pease-Alvarez & Vasquez, 1994). This line of research has also documented the wide range of linguistic resources available to children in bilingual communities and the ways children learn to choose among these resources for their symbolic value. For example, standard Puerto Rican Spanish, popular Puerto Rican Spanish, English-dominant Spanish, Puerto Rican English, African American vernacular English, standard New York English, and Hispanized English were all spoken by various residents of the New York *barrio* block studied by Zentella (1997, pp. 41–48). Moreover, a speaker's choice of one or another variety represented not only a linguistic decision, but, perhaps more importantly, a choice of identity. Indeed, Zentella's 14-year longitudinal study showed how, for children and adolescents of a community such as *el bloque,* language socialization includes becoming competent in many of the varieties spoken in the community and learning to switch from one variety to another according to the image of himself or herself that the speaker wishes to present.

Research in bilingual and multilingual communities is now beginning to focus on the dynamic nature of language practices, particularly in societal or situational contexts where individuals have choice with regard to the use of the minority or the dominant language (Kulick, 1992; Schecter & Bayley, 1997; Schecter et al., 1996). By adopting a long-term perspective, language socialization research, in addition to evaluating children's developing competencies in various speech and literacy events, is able to elucidate changes in the symbolic associations of the use of different language varieties. It is also able to document changes in family and community ideologies concerning the importance of different languages. We envisioned our own inquiry as contributing to this growing body of work that explores choice of language practices in fluid social contexts.

In the early stages of our collaboration we were not overly concerned with this dimension of flux. We concentrated on designing an agenda for a major study that would examine in detail the relationship between family language environment and bilingual development, with special attention to the issues that arise among parents, children, and schools when a minority language plays a significant role in language socialization. Thus, we began our inquiry into language choice, maintenance, and loss on the part of Mexican-descent primary school-aged children residing in California and Texas. (In the next chapter, we discuss our reasons for choosing these two particular geographic locales.) Over the years, as a direct result of the at once destabilizing and edifying effects of our ongoing inquiry on our understandings of the issues surrounding bilingual development in societies such as in the United States, our agenda has broadened to include a theoretical commitment to exploring the relationship between socialization processes involving language choice on one hand and the role of language in cultural practice and social action on the other. In *Language as Cultural Practice,* we attempt to make this theoretical journey transparent. Indeed, although in our ethnographic telling our overriding concern is with the actors' viewpoints, our narrative may also be read as an account of our own evolving struggle to understand the multifaceted role played by language in how, in the words of Fox (1991), "individual lives are culturally lived."

"Family Language Environment and Bilingual Development": The Main Study

On the basis of the findings from the exploratory study, we narrowed the criteria for participation and broadened the geographic and linguistic reach in the second, more elaborate stage of the investigation. Forty families participated in this stage of the study, 20 in California and 20 in Texas, representing a broad range of social and economic backgrounds, occupations, neighborhoods of residence, and immigrant generations. In selecting participants, we attempted to reflect the population differences in the two areas. Thus, because there is a greater proportion of recent immigrants in the general Mexican-origin population in California than in Texas (Solé, 1995), the California families included many more parents born in Mexico than the Texas sample. The social and demographic characteristics of participating families are summarized in Table 1.3 (California) and Table 1.4 (Texas).

All participating families had at least one parent of Mexican background and all had at least one fourth-, fifth-, or sixth-grade child who served as the focal child for the study. The decision to focus on families with children in the fourth to sixth grades followed from the nature of the investigation—the role of home language use in children's bilingual development. By the time children are in the fourth or fifth grade, those who have been in bilingual classes are usually transitioned to all-English classes. When children are no longer receiving support from the school for minority-language development, home language practices become even more important if the minority language is to be maintained.

For each of the 40 families we conducted two interviews with one or both parents or other primary caregiver(s) and two interviews with the "focal" child, and we collected samples of the focal child's writing in English. We also collected Spanish writing samples from children who were literate in Spanish. In addition, as one measure of language proficiency, we collected English and Spanish oral narratives based on two wordless picture books, Mercer Mayer's (1969) *Frog, Where Are You?* and Mercer and Marianne Mayer's (1971) *A Boy, a Dog, a Frog, and a Friend*. The "Frog" stories have been widely used in studies of language development, and thus provided a convenient way to investigate within a comparative framework one aspect of children's bilingualism (cf. Berman & Slobin, 1994). In contrast to previous studies using the "Frog" stories, we used two different stories because we wished to avoid the impression that we were testing the children. At the same time, we wished to obtain comparable data in each language. Finally, because siblings often play a key role in language-minority children's adaptation to the linguistic and cultural requirements of schooling, where possible we interviewed the focal children's siblings.

In the third stage of the investigation, we selected 8 of the 40 participating families—4 at each site—for intensive case study. Our aim was to choose a representative sample on the basis of the family language-use profiles distilled from interviews and preliminary observation. Thus, we included families where both parents were monolingual in Spanish as well as families whose members had shifted to English for most purposes. In addition, because in this stage, as in the previous stages, our aim was to explore the diversity of language socialization practices represented in the two communities, we included families that differed greatly in socioeconomic status, length of time since immigration, and life mode. Thus, case-study families in the San Francisco area included two working-class families (one with a steadier income and more prospects for mobility than the other), one middle-class family whose relatives were part of the small Mexican professional elite, and one marginalized family subsisting on welfare. The San Antonio case-study families consisted of a working-class family that lived in a *barrio,* a rural working-class family, and two middle-class families that lived in comfortable modern subdivisions. The diversity of backgrounds represented in all stages of the study is crucial to the design. Heath (1983), in a study of language and literacy practices in English-speaking communities in the Piedmont Carolinas, has shown that members of different ethnic groups and social strata differ greatly in their language socialization practices, even when all speak the same language and reside in the same general geographic area. Given the diverse socioeconomic backgrounds of the participants in this study, the diversity of their places of origin in Mexico, their differing experiences with schooling in Mexico and the United States, and the differences in the linguistic and social ecologies of northern California and south Texas (see chap. 2), we expected to find a range of language socialization practices and orientations toward literacy.

In the case studies, the primary focus of attention was on patterns of communication in the home—for example, who spoke which language to whom—and on the relationships among language choice and dimensions of language use such as topic, register, mode, and speaker age. To capture a range of family interactions, including those focusing on school and literacy activities, at least 12 home observations were conducted at four different times during three separate weeks when school was in session. Weekday observation periods, which normally extended

TABLE 1.3

California Families: Social and Demographic Characteristics

Case	Caregiver(s): Birthplace, Age	Caregiver(s): Occupation	Children: Gender, Age	Children: Birthplace, Age of Arrival in United States
1	M, New York F, Quintana Roo Stepfather, Minnesota	M, ESL teacher F, fisherman Stepfather, physician	m, 12*; m, 3	Child 1, Quintana Roo, 6 Child 2, Bay Area
2	M, Michoacán (single parent) F, Michoacán	M, homemaker F, gardener	m, 14; f, 12; m, 10*; m, 7	Bay Area
3	M, Jalisco F, Jalisco	M, homemaker F, factory worker	m, 15; m, 10*	Bay Area
4	M, Nayarit (single parent) F, Mexico	M, factory worker (unemployed)	f, 9*; m, 8	Bay Area
5	M, Mexico City (single parent) F, Texas	M, community college student F, engineer	m, 12*	Bay Area
6	M, Sinaloa F, Sonora	M, factory worker F, construction worker	f, 10*; m, 2	Child 1, Sinaloa, 3 Child 2, Bay Area
7	M, Guanajuato F, Guanajuato (Mother's two adult brothers also live in the household)	M, homemaker F, gardener	f, 9*; f, 7	Child 1, Guanajuato, 3 Child 2, Guanajuato, 1

#	Origin	Occupation	Children	Location
8	M, Jalisco F, Baja California	M, homemaker F, cleaning company worker	m, 20; f, 16; m, 11	Bay Area
9	M, Guanajuato F, Guanajuato	M, domestic worker F, restaurant worker	m, 10*; f, 8; f, 4	Bay Area
10	M, Northern California F, Ecuador	M, dance teacher F, engineer	m, 12; m, 10*	Ecuador
11	M, California (rural) F, Bay Area	M, bank teller F, civil servant	m, 12*; m, 9	Bay Area
12	M, Guanajuato F, Michoacán	M, factory worker F, baker	f, 18; m, 15; m, 9*	Bay Area
13	M, Sinaloa F, Michoacán	M, food service worker F, ironworker	f, 18 m, 12; f, 12*	Bay Area
14	M, Jalisco F, Jalisco	M, radio announcer F, manager, janitorial service	m, 11*; m, 5	Bay Area
15	M, Jalisco F, Jalisco	M, teacher's aide F, graduate student	f, 10*; m, 4	Child 1, Guadalajara; 2; Child 2, Bay Area
16	M, Michoacán F, Michoacán	M, homemaker F, plumber	f, 11*	Bay Area
17	M, Michoacán F, Michoacán	M, cashier F, auto mechanic	m, 13; m, 11*	Bay Area

continued on next page

TABLE 1.3 (continued)

Case	Caregiver(s): Birthplace, Age	Caregiver(s): Occupation	Children: Gender, Age	Children: Birthplace, Age of Arrival in United States
18	M, San Luis Potosí M's partner, Mexico	M, beautician F, domestic work	f, 11*; f, 1	Bay Area
19	M, Michoacán F, Michoacán	M, homemaker F, iron worker	m, 17; m, 15; f, 11*; f, 8; m, 6	Children 1, 2, 3, Michoacán; Children 4, 5, Bay Area; focal child arrived U.S. at 1 year old
20	M, Guanajuato F, Guanajuato (raised in San Francisco)	M, F, have small landscaping business	m, 10*; m, 9; m, 6	Bay Area

Notes. Asterisk indicates focal child. Ages given in years. M, mother; F, father; m, male; f, female.

TABLE 1.4

Texas Families: Social and Demographic Characteristics

Case	Caregiver(s): Birthplace, Age	Caregiver(s): Occupation	Children: Gender, Age	Children: Birthplace, Age of Arrival in United States
1	M, Coahuila F, Nuevo León	M, homemaker F, laborer	m, 10*; f, 5; f, 3	San Antonio
2	M, San Antonio F, San Antonio	M, cafeteria worker F, factory worker	f, 12; f, 11*; f, 10	San Antonio
3	M, Coahuila F, Coahuila	M, homemaker F, auto painter	m, 12*; f, 9; f, 8	San Antonio
4	M, Tamaulipas F, Tamaulipas	M, homemaker F, construction worker	m, 20; m, 18; f, 10*; f, 8	Child 1, Laredo, Texas; children 2, 3, 4, San Antonio
5	M, San Antonio F, San Antonio	M, cafeteria worker F, hospital worker	f, 9*; f, 9; f, 2	San Antonio
6	M, San Antonio F, San Antonio	M, community college student F, truck driver	m, 13; m, 11; m, 10*; m, 8; f, 6	San Antonio
7	M, southwest Texas (rural) F, southwest Texas (rural)	M, telephone service representative F, high school teacher	f, 18; m, 16; m, 10*	Child 1, southwest Texas; children 2, 3, San Antonio
8	M, Coahuila F, Durango	M, homemaker F, carpenter	f, 12*; f, 8	San Antonio

continued on next page

TABLE 1.4 (continued)

Case	Caregiver(s): Birthplace, Age	Caregiver(s): Occupation	Children: Gender, Age	Children: Birthplace, Age of Arrival in United States
9	M, F, Texas (rural)	M, F, migrant workers	f, 11*	San Antonio
	Grandmother, Texas (rural)	Grandmother, homemaker		
	Grandfather, Texas (rural)	Grandfather, security guard		
	(grandparents are primary caregivers)	(grandparents are former migrant workers)		
10	M, San Antonio	M, university student	m, 12*	San Antonio
	F, San Antonio (Anglo)	F, sales		
11	M, San Antonio	M, homemaker	m, 13; f, 11*; f, 8; f, 4	San Antonio
	F, San Antonio	F, city worker		
12	M, San Antonio	M, university student	m, 10*	San Antonio
	F, San Antonio	F, law enforcement		
13	M, San Antonio	M, homemaker	f, 14; m, 10*; m, 7	San Antonio
	F, Coahuila	F, construction		
14	M, Coahuila	M, homemaker	m, 11*; m, 9; m, 5	Child 1, Texas (rural); children 2, 3, San Antonio
	F, Coahuila	F, laborer		

	Parents	Occupation	Children	Location
15	M, Coahuila F, Chicago (raised in Coahuila)	M, homemaker F, ranch worker	m, 11*; m, 10*; m, 5	Child 1, Coahuila, 6 months; Child 2, Texas (rural); Child 3, San Antonio
16	M, San Antonio F, San Antonio	M, customer service representative F, engineer	f, 12; f, 10*; f, 6	San Antonio
17	M, Texas (border) F, Texas (border)	M, F, family real estate management business	m, 10*; m, 8; m, 6	Children 1, 2, Texas (border); child 3, San Antonio
18	M, southern California F, San Antonio	M, F, own and work at a small construction business	m, 16; f, 12*; m, 9; m, 4	San Antonio
19	M, West Texas F, San Antonio (deceased)	M, social worker	f, 24; m, 19; m, 10*	San Antonio
20	M, San Antonio F, San Antonio	M, manages housecleaning service F, utility company (white collar worker)	m, 14; m, 10*	San Antonio
21	M, San Antonio F, Nuevo León	M, F, transportation (white collar)	f, 9*; f, 7	San Antonio
22	M, Texas (border area) F, San Antonio	M, clerk F, security guard	m, 19; m, 10*	San Antonio

Notes. Asterisk indicates focal child (in case 15, the Gómez family, both older children participated in a full schedule of interviews and observations). Families 7 and 12 did not participate in the full schedule of interviews. Hence, families 21 and 22 were added. Families 1, 2, 3, 4, 5, 6, 8, 11, 13, and 22 live in predominantly or exclusively Latino neighborhoods. Families 14 and 15 live in a rural area. Families 7, 10, 16, 17, 18, 19, 20, and 21 live in ethnically mixed areas. M, mother; F, father; m, male; f, female. Ages given in years.

shortly after the children returned from school, and three early morning periods, from the time the children awoke until they left for school. Weekend observations included three mornings, usually Saturdays, and three Sunday evenings from the time the family returned from their weekend activities until the children's bedtimes. In addition to these planned observations, we also took advantage of a variety of other opportunities that arose. For example, Robert Bayley and project associate Buenaventura Torres-Ayala accompanied one of the Texas families on one of their biweekly trips to visit relatives in a neighboring Mexican border city. In addition, because two brothers in this same family exhibited very different patterns of academic achievement, after a series of observations of the older child, a sixth grader, we arranged to conduct a similar series of observations of a younger brother, a fourth grader. On another occasion, Sandra Schecter was called on by one of the California families seeking an appropriate placement for their young son to investigate programs in the local schools. She was also honored with an invitation to a semiformal family function celebrating the eightieth birthday of a great aunt of one of the Bay Area focal children. (Although with family members the aunt spoke both Spanish and English with frequent code switching, her pet parrot, curiously, was a monolingual English speaker.) Finally, because the need for communication with Spanish-monolingual grandparents and other relatives was often an incentive for children to use Spanish, where possible we observed and recorded such interactions and conducted interviews with relatives. These additional observations, interviews, and interactions not only sometimes proved useful to participants, but also provided further insights into families' concerns, particularly in the ways that they conceived their own roles in their children's education, and in the role of extended family members in fostering children's bilingual development.

In all three stages of the study, all interviews were recorded. During observations in the case studies, children wore belts designed for joggers containing small professional-quality tape recorders. They also wore lapel microphones. Although recorders were occasionally turned off accidentally when children engaged in vigorous physical activity, the combination generally worked well, giving us access to a great deal of relatively unmonitored speech. Microphones picked up all utterances of the focal children, including *sotto voce* self-regulatory remarks, as well as nearly all the speech of others in the immediate vicinity. Finally, approximately a third of the observation periods were videotaped as well.[7]

LANGUAGE AS CULTURAL PRACTICE

Language as Cultural Practice does, indeed, address the important relation between home language practices and the development of bilingual and biliterate abilities among linguistic minority children. However, in constructing an analytic narrative that makes our findings relevant, not only for language educators and linguistic ethnographers but also for those who would identify with family members who, by participating in our study, also participated in the interpretation of their needs, we have expanded this research agenda. Perhaps we have been undisciplined, but we think not. We believe, rather, that as ethnographers we were compelled to go beyond a frame of reference that would have circumscribed an interpretation grounded in a concern for how home language practices efficiently or less efficiently orient children to school literacy to examine more broadly the role of language—of Spanish and English—in the worlds that family members both participated in and aspired to. True, for participants these worlds may have been linked to definitions of academic competence and the qualities that children need to acquire in order to develop successful text-based identities, but just as often they were not. Over time these worlds became transparent through dialectical processes revealed in respondents' narratives and observed lived experiences, in tensions surrounding issues of individual, peer, and ethnic identity, with language almost always a crucial component.

Nor could we separate these tensions either from the texture of the social spaces in which important, formative scenes in participants' narratives unfolded or from the geographic canvases on which these scenes

---

[7]To prepare the data, audio recordings of interviews with family members were transcribed in full in standard orthography. In addition, selected portions of the home observations, containing informal interactions between focal children and siblings, parents, and other relatives, were also transcribed, as were conversations concerning schoolwork and other aspects of literacy. Standard procedures for analyzing qualitative data were employed (e.g., Bogdan & Biklen, 1992; Miles & Huberman, 1984; Spindler & Spindler, 1987). That is, all data relating to the same family—interview transcripts, recordings of home interactions, field notes, children's written products, videotapes of interactions—were grouped to yield case studies of different families' experiences with bilingualism. Behaviors and responses of individual family members were compared, and further comparisons were made across families, social categories, and regions.

played out. For such social spaces and geographic canvases, we discovered, had everything to do with the symbolic meanings that family members attached to the uses of Spanish and English in daily life as well as the ideological values that they attached to these language practices both on a societal level and in asserting their own social competence. Thus, in uncovering patterns of systematicity and change both in participants' uses of Spanish and English and in their constructions and deconstructions of cultural meanings ascribed to these processes, we followed an analytic trail that led us to a more comprehensive understanding of the relation among language, culture, social space, and geographical place. In this book, we devote some attention to describing and illustrating the processes that resulted in this critical reformulation. We hope it is evident that the implications of this relation for the struggle to secure the political status of educational and other policies that address the needs of language-minority groups and individuals remain our central concerns.

2

Mexicanos in California and Texas

SOCIOCULTURAL ECOLOGY
AND LANGUAGE MAINTENANCE

The Mexican immigrant and Mexican American families whose language decisions and practices we explore in *Language as Cultural Practice* live in two geographically distinct areas, the San Francisco Bay Area in northern California, and San Antonio in south Texas. With our initial research focus on the relationship between minority-language maintenance and the development of bilingual and biliterate abilities, these two locales were attractive to us because they differed in ways that previous research had identified as crucial for minority language maintenance (see, e.g., Allard & Landry, 1992; Giles, Bourhis, & Taylor, 1977; Landry & Allard, 1992, 1994). The most important of these differences concern:

1. Concentration: San Antonio has a Latino majority, whereas Latinos constitute a minority in the San Francisco area.
2. Composition of the Latino community: The San Antonio Latino community is overwhelmingly composed of persons of Mexican descent; the Latino community around San Francisco is more diverse in terms of ethnic origin and includes many immigrants from Central America as well as other Spanish-speaking countries.

3. Ethnic mix: Latinos and Euro-Americans are the two main ethnici-
ties in the San Antonio area. The San Francisco area is much more
heterogeneous ethnically and racially.

4. Length of residence in the United States: The San Antonio Latino
community has far fewer recent immigrants than does the San Francisco-area community. Many Texas Latino families have maintained Spanish across generations of residence in the United States.

5. Distance from the Mexican border: San Antonio is much closer to
Mexico than San Francisco, and residents of San Antonio have the
opportunity to visit a Spanish-speaking country significantly more
often on the average than do their San Francisco counterparts.

6. Language policy: San Antonio is in a state that has not adopted official language legislation, whereas on an official level California is
an English-only state.

All of these factors have consequences for what sociologists Allard
and Landry (1992) term *ethnolinguistic vitality* and for Spanish-language maintenance. Indeed, all except factor 4 would suggest greater
Spanish-language maintenance in San Antonio than in the San Francisco area. As we show, however, general societal factors that favor language maintenance are insufficient to explain the day-to-day and
moment-to-moment language choices that result in children's maintenance or loss of the minority language. By locating the research in two
distinct communities, and by employing a variety of research strategies
and methods, we were able to provide insights into key relationships
among family language patterns and broader societal factors in the bilingual development of children.

POPULATION PROFILE

The San Francisco Bay Area, although it is home to a rapidly growing
Mexican-background population, is one of the most ethnically and lin-
guistically diverse areas in the United States. Indeed, in California as a
whole, no single ethnic group constitutes a majority of the population.
Even among the Latino population, people of Mexican background are
one group, albeit the most numerous, among many. In addition to people of Mexican origin, substantial numbers of Guatemalans,

Salvadorans, Nicaraguans, and Spanish speakers from a variety of South American communities contribute to the San Francisco Bay Area's multicultural mosaic.

San Antonio, Texas, has a very different population profile. The eighth largest city in the United States, it has a majority Mexican-origin population, and many areas of the city are almost exclusively Latino. Moreover, in contrast to northern California, which tends to draw immigrants from central Mexico, most people of Mexican background in San Antonio trace their origins to the northern Mexican border states of Coahuila, Nuevo León, and Tamaulipas, as well as to Mexican Texas.

Length of Time Since Immigration

The communities differ in other important ways as well. Although San Francisco, like San Antonio, was founded before the U.S. annexation of California and the Southwest, the Mexican-origin community in the northern California towns in which we worked tends to be of fairly recent origin. Lincoln City (a pseudonym), for example, located on the San Francisco peninsula approximately halfway between San Francisco and San José, had almost no residents of Mexican origin in 1960.[1] However, by 1990, Mexican-origin children made up the largest group in the school system. In California as a whole, one recent study (Solé, 1995) reported that approximately 70% of Mexican-background adults were born in Mexico.

Again, the picture in south Texas in general and San Antonio in particular differs from northern California. San Antonio, although located in the northern Mexican frontier, was a well-established town at the time of Texas independence in 1836, and continued to have close ties to Mexico. Throughout the 20th century the Mexican-origin population grew rapidly, concentrated in the west and south sides of the city. Although in recent decades the Latino population has expanded into new housing developments as well as established neighborhoods in the northwest and northeast sections of the city, the west and south sides have remained overwhelmingly of Mexican background. In Texas as a whole, in sharp

---

[1]To preserve the anonymity of the San Francisco-area families, we have used pseudonyms for the towns in which they reside. Differences in population structure and distribution made such precautions unnecessary in San Antonio.

contrast to California, approximately 30% of Mexican-background adults were born in Mexico (Solé, 1995).

Distance From the Border

As we noted in the introduction to this chapter, geography would seem to favor Spanish maintenance in San Antonio to a greater extent than in the San Francisco area. It is possible for most San Antonians with relatives in Mexico to return for visits in less than a day's drive. In fact, one of the families we worked with most closely returned every 2 weeks to the border city where the mother had been born and grew up; to spend the weekend with extended family members. A one-way trip took approximately 2½ hours, far less time than it takes to drive from San Antonio to Houston or Dallas. Mexican immigrants who live in northern California clearly face a far more arduous and expensive journey if they wish to return to visit their places of origin. Not only is the San Francisco area much farther from Mexico than is San Antonio, but Bay Area families who return to central Mexico for visits have, for the most part, only completed half their journey once they reach the Mexican border. In contrast, the places of origin of many San Antonians are close to the Texas–Mexico border, with many families having roots in border cities such as Nuevo Laredo or Piedras Negras, Coahuila, as well as in Monterrey, the largest city in northern Mexico.

Language Policy

Finally, the two regions where we worked differ in their language policies. In 1986 Californians passed Proposition 163 declaring English the official language of the state, and since 1992, voters have approved a succession of ballot measures that seemed aimed at various segments of the Latino community, including a measure effectively banning bilingual education. The overall effect of these measures has been to create an atmosphere where Spanish is threatened and Mexican cultural identity is devalued. Texas, in contrast to California, has never had an official language and state officials have generally opposed attempts to establish English as the official language of U.S. government. Both bilingual and English-as-a-second-language (ESL) programs are common throughout the state, and there have been no serious attempts to limit services to non-English-speaking children to the extent that has characterized California.

MEXICANS IN SOUTH TEXAS

Early History

In 1718 the Spanish established a military base and mission at San Antonio, and by 1731 a civilian population had joined the missionaries and soldiers living there. Both the Spanish and later the Mexican government were eager to populate Texas and offered land grants in the hopes of encouraging such settlement. Initially, Mexicans and non-Mexicans alike benefitted from the land grants (Barrera, 1979). However, as Anglo settlers spread out across the vast territory, Spanish-speaking settlers tended to remain in the southwest part of the territory. Barrera (1979) suggested that by the 1830s "only the area around and south of San Antonio could be said to be distinctly Mexican in character" (p. 9).

After the Republic of Texas was officially established in 1836, the number of Anglos living in Texas continued to increase. Although the transition was difficult for Mexicans living throughout Texas, the most drastic and visible changes occurred in the central and southwest part of the Republic where the majority of Mexicans lived. Even though some Mexicans had fought for independence alongside their Anglo neighbors, including eight Mexicans who reportedly died defending the Alamo, their role in settling the territory and establishing independence was quickly forgotten. Following independence, many Mexicans lost title to their land as the newly formed government required established landowners to produce excessive amounts of documentation to validate title to their own properties (McDonald & Matovina, 1995).

During the second half of the 19th century the Mexican-background population in south, central, and west Texas grew significantly, but as a result of the influx of Anglo-American settlers, it accounted for a decreasing proportion of the population. Exceeded in population, land, and wealth by Anglo-Americans and later other non-Spanish-speaking settlers, the remaining Mexicans in Texas found life extremely difficult during the second half of the 19th century. In San Antonio, Mexicans suffered visible setbacks economically, politically, and socially. In the 10 years preceding Texas's entry into the Union, 57 of San Antonio's 88 aldermen had Spanish surnames. Between 1847 and 1857, immediately following annexation, the number of aldermen with Spanish surnames dropped to 17 out of a total of 99. By the turn of the century, not one city alderman in San Antonio had a Spanish surname (Montejano, 1987). A successful cart trade established by Mexicans in the early 19th century declined, and as Mexican men were forced to accept low-paying positions as general laborers, women and children entered the work force in greater numbers. Stewart and De León (1993, p. 35) noted that between 1850 and 1900 the proportion of child laborers in Texas rose from 4% to 16%. The economic pressures facing Mexican families combined with the heightened racial tensions throughout Texas also had a negative impact on the community's education and literacy levels. The literacy rate for Mexicans over the age of 20 dropped from 25.1% in 1850 to 12.4% in 1900 (De León, 1982, p. 188).

20th-Century Developments

In the early part of the 20th century thousands of Mexicans migrated to the United States. Immigration statistics from the period indicate that 238,527 legal immigrants from Mexico entered the United States between 1925 and 1930, compared with only 2,259 between 1900 and 1904 (Barrera, 1979, p. 65). The newly arrived Mexicans spread out across the Southwest, and some ventured even farther north, but the vast majority of them crossed the border into Texas, with many settling in San Antonio and Bexar County (Barrera, 1979, pp. 65–66). As a growing city with an already established Mexican-origin population, San Antonio was well positioned to accommodate the new immigrants' needs in the areas of employment, culture, and language. Most of the new immigrants found work in San Antonio's growing manufacturing sector, which by 1930 supported more than 300 major manufacturing plants (García, 1991, p. 29). In addition, San Antonio served as a home base for thousands of seasonal workers who typically spent 5 to 7 months working in the northern part of the state and returned to San Antonio between contracts (García, 1991, p. 28). It also served as a place of exile for people displaced by political conflict in Mexico. To mention just the most famous example, Francisco Madera, the first president of Mexico after the revolution of 1910, organized revolutionary activities from exile in San Antonio. By 1930, Mexican immigrants and people of Mexican ancestry accounted for nearly half of San Antonio's population.

In San Antonio, the impact of early-20th-century Mexican migration was far-reaching. García (1991) noted that during this period San Antonio's west side continued to evolve as a distinctly Mexican district "with its own language, dress, religion, customs, and traditions" (p. 25). However, as Barrera (1988) and García (1991) suggested, this period was also characterized by an increased class stratification within San Antonio's Mexican-origin community. Although most Mexican Americans remained highly impoverished, an emerging population of lower- and upper-middle-class skilled and professional Mexicans as well as a small group of exiled Mexican elites began to have a visible influence on local politics (García, 1991, p. 71).

An important consequence of the emerging middle-class Mexican American minority was the formation of several politically moderate Mexican American lobby groups, notably the Order of Sons of America (OSA) and the League of United Latin American Citizens (LULAC). Although the OSA's goals, which included the elimination of racial prejudice and improved educational opportunities, clearly aimed to benefit the Mexican community at large, membership in the OSA was restricted to U.S. citizens, native-born or naturalized. Consistent with its membership policies, the group was a strong promoter of English language and citizenship training (Barrera, 1988, p. 22). LULAC, formed in 1929 as a result of divisions in the San Antonio and Corpus Christi chapters of the OSA, also reflected middle-class Mexicans' aspirations to blend into American society. With English as the organization's official language and an American flag as its emblem, LULAC has often been depicted by Chicano scholars as an organization that aimed to improve the conditions of Mexicans by promoting acculturation over community cohesion (Barrera, 1988, pp. 24–25; Muñoz, 1989, pp. 42–43).

Throughout the early part of the 20th century, Mexican immigration had been highly contingent on labor demands. The mass deportation and repatriation of Mexicans during the 1930s simply confirmed the fact that Mexicans were welcome only as an inexpensive and disposable work force but not as permanent citizens. Despite the thousands of Mexicans who were forced to leave the United States during the Depression years, San Antonio's Mexican population continued to grow marginally. Between 1930 and 1940 the Mexican-origin population in San Antonio rose from 82,373 to 103,000, an increase attributed to a high birth rate (García, 1991, p. 59).

As Mexicans were forced to return to their homeland throughout the 1930s, middle-class Mexicans in San Antonio became increasingly preoccupied with the need for Mexicans to learn English, adopt American cultural norms, and obtain their permanent residency papers. However, as organizations such as OSA and LULAC focused on the need for Mexicans to acquire the language and work skills necessary to adapt to American society, working-class Mexicans became increasingly active in the trade union movement. Blackwelder (1984) documented the extent of Mexican women's involvement in the labor movement in San Antonio, where the severely underpaid pecan shellers unionized in 1934 to demand increased wages and better working conditions. Although they did achieve some initial gains following unionization, by the late 1930s their working conditions had once again deteriorated. Under the leadership of Emma Tenayuca, the pecan shellers launched a second strike in 1938. Middle- and upper-class Mexicans, who had expressed considerable ambivalence toward the pecan shellers' earlier labor actions, by 1938 were publicly expressing their opposition to the strike. When the mayor and the police chief ordered the tear-gassing and arrest of the strikers, the Mexican Chamber of Commerce and LULAC were among the organizations who applauded the extreme actions taken against the workers, many of whom were Mexican teenage girls (Blackwelder, 1984, pp. 141–145; García, 1991, pp. 62–65).

During the Second World War the demand for laborers increased, enabling San Antonio's impoverished Mexican community to return to work. Moreover, as an increasing number of people enlisted, a new group of Mexicans began to stream into Bexar County. However, this time most of the new arrivals came not as immigrants but as *braceros* or temporary workers. In many ways, the Bracero Program, which employed nearly a quarter of a million Mexican men between 1942 and 1947 (Gonzales, 1999, p. 171), did not change so much as confirm the United States policy on Mexican immigration, which had always welcomed Mexicans only insofar as a labor shortage required their presence.

The patriotism that led many Mexican Americans in San Antonio and the surrounding region to enlist was consistent with the goals of San Antonio's middle-class Mexican fraternal organizations. Members of LULAC, for example, were required to take an oath swearing to be "loyal to the government of the United States of America, [and to] support its Constitution and obey its laws" (Márquez, 1993, p. 10). Not surprisingly, LULAC members enlisted en masse, leaving many local chapters inactive throughout the war years (Márquez, 1993, p. 39).

As the soldiers began to return home in the mid-1940s, membership in LULAC increased. With at least some members benefitting from the booming economy and increased access to social services and education provided under the G.I. Bill, the organization grew in both membership and influence. Although LULAC has been dismissed by many Chicano historians in recent years for its arguably conservative and even assimilationist politics, García (1991) and Gonzales (1999) attempted to rethink the organization's strategies in a new light. Both historians suggested that despite LULAC's enthusiasm for the "Democratic Melting Pot," the organization's lobbying was not entirely limited to advancing the status and prosperity of middle- and upper-class Mexicans. LULAC was instrumental in providing Mexican American political hopefuls with the money, support, and credibility to successfully run for political office at the municipal and state level in the 1940s and 1950s when Mexicans remained virtually unaccounted for in elected positions (Gómez-Quiñones, 1990, pp. 57–59). LULAC also played an essential role in school desegregation, which would have profound implications for Mexican children across class locations in San Antonio and throughout the southwestern United States.

For many working-class Mexicans, particularly those who chose not to embrace the politically moderate goals endorsed by organizations such as LULAC, the 1950s would prove to be an extremely difficult period. As McCarthyism penetrated postwar politics in the United States, Mexican Americans, like other perceived "foreigners," were increasingly under attack. "Operation Wetback," initiated in June 1954 by the U.S. Border Patrol, was fueled by the rising anti-Mexican sentiments being felt across the Southwest. This military-style operation, which used many of the same intimidation tactics that had been deployed by officials during the immigration "sweeps" in Los Angeles in the 1930s, apprehended more than 1 million people and returned them to Mexico in 1954 (Gonzales, 1999, p. 177). Given the political climate, one might conclude that the extreme patriotism demonstrated by LULAC members in the 1950s was not a politically naive oversight but instead a necessary political tactic in their bid to establish some degree of credibility with the politicians they sought to lobby.

Education as a Site of Mexican Resistance

In the 1920s, school attendance among Mexican children in San Antonio increased significantly. Factors at work included educational reforms based on the philosophy of John Dewey, emphasizing the need to prepare *all* children to become productive citizens (García, 1991, p. 175). During this period, the San Antonio Independent School Board also demonstrated an increased interest in adapting the curriculum to the specific needs of the city's Mexican community. García (1991) noted that as early as 1920 the school board recognized Spanish as "a living language in San Antonio" (p. 176). In recognition of the important role the Spanish language played in San Antonio and in an effort to improve the educational prospects of young Spanish speakers, the school board authorized schools to offer all subjects in both Spanish and English beginning in Grade 1. Beginning in Grade 5 they also offered Spanish-language classes to English-speaking students, further indicating that the local school board viewed San Antonio as a bilingual city where the future success of Spanish- and English-speaking students would be partially contingent on the ability to work effectively in both languages (García, 1991, pp. 176–177).

Unfortunately, the San Antonio Independent School Board's seemingly progressive policies in the early part of the century did not necessarily work to improve the prospects of Mexican-origin children. At the center of Dewey's educational philosophy and praxis lies the need to prepare productive—in other words, employable—citizens. His emphasis on vocational training, which he did not necessarily suggest should be restricted to students from lower-class backgrounds, was often interpreted, correctly or incorrectly, as support for a carefully tracked form of education. For most of the Mexican children in San Antonio, who were not seen to hold the potential to enter the professions, vocational programs soon emerged as the only option. A series of studies carried out in San Antonio during the 1920s, which sought to account for the "history of slowness" among Mexican children, further worked to reinforce the assumption that Mexican students would not necessarily benefit from sharing an education with non-Mexicans. By the late 1920s, the San Antonio School Board had begun to segregate Mexican American students, channeling them into programs with an emphasis on English-language training, "Americanization," and the acquisition of vocational skills (García, 1991, p. 178). Although one may argue that segregation was, at least early on, often carried out under the guise of a progressive, culturally sensitive package of educational reforms, its impact on the Mexican community was overwhelmingly negative.

Between 1929 and 1941, the Mexican-background student population more than doubled in San Antonio (García, 1991, p. 201), and schools continued to serve primarily the needs of local employers by producing large numbers of English-speaking semiskilled laborers. Although LULAC continued to support the San Antonio School Board's emphasis on English-language training, by the 1940s it had become increasingly frustrated with the board's methods of achieving such goals. In the early 1940s LULAC emerged as a leader in the fight to desegregate Texas schools, a battle that would culminate with the case of *Delgado v. Bastrop Independent School District* in 1948. Along with an earlier victory in California, *Delgado v. Bastrop* would serve as an important precedent for *Brown v. Board of Education* in the mid-1950s (Gonzales, 1999, p. 181).

Throughout the 1950s and 1960s, conditions in San Antonio schools, rates of graduation, and overall literacy rates in the Mexican community continued to improve, albeit marginally, as the influence of Mexican lobby groups and the presence of Mexican American politicians, both locally and at a state level, became more apparent. However, even with Mexican students no longer being officially segregated, most schools in San Antonio remained divided along ethnic and socioeconomic lines, with the vast majority of Mexican-background students attending schools on the west side. As Gambitta, Milne, and Davis (1983) demonstrated in their detailed examination of the Texas educational finance system, San Antonio area schools with the highest numbers of Mexican students, in particular those in the predominantly working-class Edgewood Common

School District, remained severely underfunded throughout the century. Between 1939 and 1949 Edgewood's school population jumped from 1,586 to 6,600 as a result of a large influx of Mexican newcomers on San Antonio's west side. Unfortunately, the massive influx of students was not accompanied by a proportional increase in the district's tax base on which the school relied for core funding (Gambitta et al., 1983, p. 143). In the late 1940s a Congressional committee investigating the need for federal subsidies in needy school districts described Edgewood schools as "the worst we had encountered in any school district in the country" (cited in Gambitta et al., 1983, p. 143). Although per-student funding levels would fluctuate throughout the coming decades, at times Edgewood's students received less than half the amount of funding allotted to students in San Antonio's more affluent school districts, such as Alamo Heights (Gambitta et al., 1983, pp. 154–155).

In the late 1960s San Antonio's schools once again emerged as a central arena of political activism. In the wake of the civil rights movement, the U.S. Congress passed the Bilingual Education Act, Title VII of the Elementary and Secondary Education Act of 1968, sponsored by Senator Ralph Yarborough of Texas. Bilingual education programs were established shortly thereafter in the Edgewood Independent School District and elsewhere in San Antonio. Academic programs to prepare bilingual teachers were established at Texas universities, including the newly formed University of Texas at San Antonio, where Albar Peña, the first director of the U.S. Office of Bilingual Education, returned to found undergraduate and M.A. programs (Cárdenas, 1995; Crawford, 1995).

The lived realities of bilingual education and legal desegregation, however, were not always distinctly different from those of education only in English, when children were punished for speaking Spanish at school (Hurtado & Rodríguez, 1989), and legal segregation. In particular, the unequal distribution of financial resources across school districts, which in Texas have traditionally been derived primarily from local property taxes, served to disadvantage many Mexican-background and other students of color. Indeed, in San Antonio, school districts remained divided largely according to ethnic and class lines. In the 1970–1971 school year, Alamo Heights, the city's wealthiest district, spent $492 per child, versus $356 per child in the Edgewood district on the city's overwhelmingly Latino west side. In Texas as a whole, in

1971, the 162 poorest districts paid higher taxes for education than the 203 richest districts (Acuña, 2000, p. 413). In response to this disparity, in the late 1960s a group of Mexican American parents filed suit, claiming that the Texas system of school finance violated the equal protection clause of the U.S. Constitution by discriminating against students in low-wealth school districts. Although the lower courts decided the case of *San Antonio Independent School District v. Rodríguez* in favor of the plaintiffs, the U.S. Supreme Court rejected the parents' case in a five to four vote (Cárdenas, 1995, p. 93), arguing that wealth was not a suspect classification subject to equal protection and that education was not a fundamental right under the U.S. Constitution (Reed, 1998).

The Supreme Court's decision in the Rodríguez case moved the struggle for educational equity back to the state level, involving the courts, the state legislature, and, in 1993, an unsuccessful election campaign to amend the state constitution to meet state court requirements to equalize school funding. Finally, in 1994 the legislature enacted a solution that marginally improved the situation, but fully satisfied no one (see Reed, 1995, for details of the Texas legislative debates about school financing). Thus, in 1995, the disparity between the per-pupil expenditures of the poorest and wealthiest districts in the state remained as great as ever. For example, in 1988, the poorest district reported an expenditure of $1,308 per pupil, compared to $7,064 per pupil in the wealthiest district, with a statewide median of $1,904.[2] In 1995, the poorest district in Texas spent $1,837 per pupil, compared to $10,941 in the wealthiest district, with a median of $4,084 (Reed, 1998, p. 186).[3]

In addition to suffering from an inequitable system of school finance, Mexican-background students often continued to be streamed into vocational programs where employment prospects remained limited. One recent review of Mexican American education in the Southwest, for example, reported that 64% of Mexican American and other Latino children attended schools with a minority enrollment of 70% or greater. In

---

[2]Reed (1998) provided figures in constant 1995 dollars.

[3]To be fair, Reed (1998) noted that a comparison of per pupil expenditures of the poorest and wealthiest school districts may not be the best measure of financial equity. He also computed scores for equity according to the "Gini coefficient," "a measure of equality that takes in to account transfers from all districts in the revenue distribution, not just those at the top and bottom of the scale" (p. 191). According to this measure, inequality in Texas decreased by 32.5% over the 7-year period that Reed studied.

contrast, 49% of African American students and only 7% of White students attended such schools (Valencia & San Miguel, 1998, p. 380).

The Mexican American Youth Organization (MAYO), founded by a group of students at St. Mary's University in San Antonio, illustrates another aspect of the struggle for equal rights in Texas. MAYO began to organize high school students in San Antonio and other parts of south Texas (Navarro, 1995, p. 80). The organization's first high-profile victory in Texas occurred in early 1968 when it helped organize students at Sidney Lanier High School, who succeeded in convincing the school's administration to agree to 9 of their 10 demands aimed at improving school life for Mexican-background students. Among their gains was an agreement to drop the school's English-only policy. MAYO would go on to organize more dramatic boycotts in other parts of Texas throughout the coming year (Navarro, 1995, p. 118). Although its demands were not always met, the organization at the very least raised the awareness of a new generation of Mexican youth and at least momentarily incited a renewed interest in Mexican nationalism, a position from which previous generations had often sought to distance themselves. This commitment to Chicano or Mexican nationalism was part of a shift to a far more radical political orientation. In San Antonio's Mexican community, with its reputation for being politically moderate, this shift may have been particularly notable.

However, as Sánchez-Jankowski (1999) suggested, the Chicano nationalism spearheaded by the Mexican American youth movement did not necessarily have a prolonged impact on the young people who came of age in the late 1960s and early 1970s. In a longitudinal study beginning in 1976 and ending in 1986, Sánchez-Jankowski surveyed Chicano youth living in San Antonio, Albuquerque, and Los Angeles on their attitudes toward Chicano nationalism. The study aimed to identify the number of young people who called themselves "Chicano nationalist" and displayed at least some "hostility" toward all or part of the existing socioeconomic and political order in the United States (Sánchez-Jankowski, 1999, p. 201). Although the study's author discovered that the nationalist tendencies of the participants had declined in each city, the most drastic declines were reported in San Antonio, where 20% to 30% of youth had identified as Chicano nationalist in the 1976 survey, but by 1986 only 2% of working-class respondents and no middle-class respondents identified with the nationalist movement (p. 205). Sánchez-Jankowski (1999) suggested that the lack of enthusiasm for nationalism among the San Antonio participants might be partially rooted in the fact that the city's "political culture, nurtured by its unique local economy and social demographics, has not been tolerant of any ideologies that challenge the status quo" (p. 220). Another factor might be that San Antonio's Mexican-origin *majority* has not felt threatened to the same extent as their counterparts in other cities in the southwestern United States. By 1986 most of the young people from San Antonio who had identified as Chicano nationalist, albeit never as separatists, believed that their nationalism had simply been a youthful form of extremism. As one participant explained, "I was for being proud of our culture. Now things are different. We don't really need nationalism" (p. 214).

MEXICANS IN NORTHERN CALIFORNIA

Early History

Like San Antonio, San Francisco was originally the site of a Spanish military base and mission. However, although San Antonio grew significantly under Spanish rule and later under Mexican rule, northern California did not attract large numbers of Spanish, Mexican, or Anglo-American settlers in the late 18th and early 19th centuries. Until the 1820s, the settlement near the site of present-day San Francisco was primarily controlled by a small group of military officers and Franciscan missionaries (Camarillo, 1984, p. 3). Mexican independence in 1821, however, had a profound impact on the settlements. Following independence, the Mexican government secularized nearly all the missions in California, including the Bay Area's Mission Dolores, altering the region's class structure and greatly accelerating its rate of expansion. Under Mexican rule an estimated 8 million acres of land were distributed to more than 800 grantees (Pitt, 1966, p. 10). Despite a proclamation promising half the grants to the area's indigenous peoples, the vast majority of grants were given to Mexicans, with a disproportionate number distributed to already well-established *Californios* (Camarillo, 1984, p. 6). In comparison with Texas, where Anglo-American settlers firmly established themselves during the early 19th century, there were few Anglos in California prior to annexation. Gonzales (1999) suggested that many of those Anglo-Americans who did choose to settle in California made at least some attempt to assimilate into Mexican culture, with some even marrying into upper-class Mexican families, learning Spanish, and converting to Catholicism (p. 72).

In the mid-1830s, when the secularization process was already well underway, a trading post was established at Yerba Buena Cove. Despite restrictions on commerce imposed by the Mexican government, the trading post flourished. By the mid-1840s, Yerba Buena, which would change its name to San Francisco in early 1847, was home to a sizable Anglo population. When California was ceded to the United States through the Treaty of Guadalupe Hidalgo in 1848, Mexicans in San Francisco were already experiencing some degree of Anglo encroachment, although there is little evidence of racial tension in the preannexation era (Godfrey, 1988, p. 56).

After annexation, the *Californios'* cultural, political, and economic position, particularly in northern California, declined precipitously. No doubt, the discovery of gold in northern California only a week after the signing of the Treaty of Guadalupe Hidalgo greatly accelerated the racial conflicts in California that would promote their decline (Camarillo, 1984; Pitt, 1966). In the first 12 months following annexation, 80,000 Anglo-Americans, 8,000 Mexicans, and 5,000 South Americans arrived in the state. *Californios* found themselves increasingly outnumbered not only by Anglo-American settlers but also by new Spanish-speaking immigrants for whom they were frequently mistaken. By 1852 another 150,000 American settlers and immigrants from Mexico and other Central and South American countries had arrived in the state (Pitt, 1966, pp. 52–53). Although some *Californios* benefitted from early mining expeditions, most retreated as violence targeting Spanish-speaking and other racial-minority miners heightened. Eventually many miners from Mexico and other countries also retreated from the gold fields as a result of both the violence and the exorbitant "foreign miners tax" requiring "foreign miners"—who included those from Mexico, Central America, South America, and China, but not Europe—to pay a $20 (later lowered to $16) monthly fee (Pitt, 1966, p. 60). In San Francisco, mining-related businesses flourished. With river access to both the northern and southern gold fields, San Francisco soon became an active port and supply center. In the 2 years following 1848, the population of San Francisco grew from approximately 1,000 to more than 20,000 (Godfrey, 1988, p. 58). As in other parts of northern California, Mexicans in the Bay Area were quickly outnumbered not only by Anglos but also by other Spanish-speaking settlers and temporary laborers.

In addition to their dwindling numbers, many Mexicans in the Bay Area began to lose title to their land during the rapid period of growth brought on by the gold rush. The Land Law, introduced in 1851 by Senator William Gwin, was officially an attempt to clarify who could hold title to the highly disputed land throughout the state. However, despite earlier assurances that Mexicans would be entitled to the same rights as other American citizens in the newly annexed state, Gwin's act would serve as an effective means to displace, or at least drastically reduce, the land holdings of California's *rancheros* (Pitt, 1966, p. 85). Although some Mexicans were able to prove title to their land, many were ill-represented by the lawyers they had hired to present their cases to the land commission and were forced to part with large acreages simply to pay their outstanding legal fees (Gonzales, 1999, p. 87). For those Mexicans who had never held official title to their land or could not produce the required documentation, the Land Law proved even more damaging. Although Mexicans across the state underwent similar struggles, those situated in northern California were among the first and most severely affected by the Land Law of 1851.

Although the *Californios* continued to live in San Francisco and were joined by new Mexican immigrants throughout the later part of the 19th century, their numbers remained relatively low, and they left little documented history of their contributions and struggles during this period of California's history. Moreover, in contrast to African American and Chinese residents as well as a range of European ethnic groups who were accounted for in census reports, Mexicans, both California-born and immigrant, were categorized either as Whites or simply as "Others" in census reports, further troubling attempts to examine their work, housing, and education patterns during the century following California's annexation to the United States.

20th-Century Developments

Although the vast majority of Mexicans who entered the United States during the early part of the 20th century settled in Texas, a small percentage settled in California, migrating either directly from Mexico or from other states. Between 1900 and 1920 the number of documented Mexican-born individuals living in California rose from 8,086 to 88,771 (Barrera, 1979, p. 66). Most new arrivals remained in rural areas where work in the cotton and citrus industries was plentiful, but the Mexican population in several coastal cities also grew. Los Angeles, San Diego, and Santa Barbara all experienced significant increases in the years leading up to the Depression (Camarillo, 1984, p. 34). As in San Antonio, California's southern coastal cities supported sizable *barrios* where the majority of Mexicans, often along with other Spanish-speaking immigrants, lived and worked. In San Francisco, where Mexicans and other Spanish speakers were greatly outnumbered by non-Spanish-speaking ethnic and racial minorities, early-20th-century migration was less dramatic but not entirely insignificant. Between 1910 and 1930 the Mexican-born population quadrupled, reaching 7,900 in 1930 (Godfrey, 1988, p. 140). A less significant increase in the number of Central American immigrants also contributed to an increasing presence of Spanish-speaking residents. However, despite the increase in population and the fact that many Mexicans and other Spanish-speaking immigrants were beginning to congregate in the north part of the city's Mission District, there was no area of the city which resembled the *barrios* of Los Angeles or San Antonio (Godfrey, 1984, p. 148). Mexicans and other Spanish speakers continued to live among a range of ethnic and racial minorities, typically congregating in areas of the city where other predominantly Catholic immigrants, such as the Irish, were already well established.

During the Depression, Mexican residents of California were subjected to many of the same pressures as those in Texas. The repatriation and deportation drive, which eventually affected Mexicans across the Southwest, initially focused on southern California. Targeting Mexicans in public places, including shopping areas, movie theaters, and workplaces, immigration officials and the police reportedly confined and questioned thousands of Mexicans. Those unable to prove their citizenship were then forced across the border, in some cases riding in boxcars (Camarillo, 1984, pp. 50–51). Despite the outcry from the Mexican consulate, community organizations, and the Spanish media, an estimated 50,000 to 75,000 Mexicans were deported in 1931 alone (Gonzales, 1999, p. 148). During the height of the Depression in the mid-1930s, when destitute Anglo families began to pour into California in search of agricultural work, the remaining Mexicans were quickly replaced. Although Anglos had accounted for only 20% of the agricultural work force in 1929, by 1936 they made up 85% of California's migratory labor force (Gonzales, 1999, p. 149).

During the Depression, Mexican labor activism in was even more apparent in California than in Texas. Although strike issues typically focused on job security, wages, and working conditions, the issue of racism was never far from the surface in these labor disputes, which in many cases saw Mexican laborers working in solidarity with other racial-minority groups (Camarillo, 1984, pp. 53–57). However, the threat of deportation remained an effective union-busting tactic throughout the Depression, making labor organizing in the fields and the cities extremely difficult for Mexican laborers in particular (Camarillo, 1984, p. 52). In the northern part of the state, where Mexicans were fewer in numbers and influence, repatriation and deportation had a less significant impact, but they did stall the growth of San Francisco's Mexican community. And, as Godfrey (1988) noted, the North Mission district, where many Mexicans resided, was among the hardest hit areas of the city (p. 147).

As an important military center, San Francisco, and the Bay Area generally, experienced considerable population increase during World War II. A growing need for laborers in the city's shipyards and other wartime industries resulted in increased migration of African Americans from the U.S. South as well as increased immigration from Mexico and Central and South America. Although many of the incoming Mexican immigrants reportedly remained in the rural areas surrounding the Bay Area, where there was a high demand for farm laborers, a small number of Mexicans did settle in San Francisco. In 1950 the Mexican-born population in San Francisco represented 4.6% of the total foreign-born population (Godfrey, 1988, p. 150). Following the war, Mexicans and other Spanish speakers continued to carve out a presence for themselves in San Francisco's Mission District. Between 1950 and 1960 the Latino population in the Mission rose from 5,531 to 11,622 (Godfrey, 1988, p. 154). Latino-owned businesses also emerged in greater numbers. However, throughout the 1950s the area was plagued by inadequate and overcrowded housing, lower than average family income levels, and low rates of educational achievement. In many respects, the Mission District during this period reflected the living conditions experienced in *barrios* in cities across the Southwest. However, in contrast to San Antonio's West Side, the Mission District was neither predominantly Mexican nor predominantly Spanish speaking. Thus, the Mission District was not so much an ethnically segregated ghetto but instead an ethnically and racially diverse working-class inner-city neighborhood where many Mexicans, particularly new immigrants, resided.

As in Texas, education of Latinos was characterized by segregation, allegedly instituted in the educational interests of the students but in fact serving to direct Latinos to the low end of the labor market. Although attempts were made in the 1930s to segregate Mexican children legally by classifying them as Indians, segregation never became state law in California. Instead it became a widespread local custom, supported by supposedly "scientific" methods such as vocational testing and psychometrics (Donato, 1997). Mexican American parents eventually challenged the segregation of their children in the courts, and in the landmark *Mendez et al. v. Westminster School District of Orange County* case, a district court judge declared in 1946 that segregation had no legal or educational basis (Acuña, 2000). *Mendez* helped inspire the similar *Delgado v. Bastrop* decision in Texas 2 years later. After *Brown v. Board of Education* in 1954, a series of court decisions through the 1960s and 1970s mandated specific requirements for school desegregation plans. By the 1960s the California State Department of Education was pressing school systems to "ethnically balance" their schools (Donato, 1997). But implementation proved difficult, and most Mexican American children continued to attend schools with high minority concentrations.

A radical student movement, under names such as United Mexican American Students and the Mexican American Student Confederation, evolved at the same time as MAYO in Texas. At a conference in Santa Barbara in 1969, these groups came together under the name El Movimiento Estudiantil Chicano de Aztlán (MEChA), emphasizing the extent to which these young activists favored cultural cohesion and Spanish-language maintenance over acculturation and assimilation. Initially called to develop a plan to facilitate Mexican American access to California's colleges and universities, the Santa Barbara conference became the founding convention of the Chicano student movement. The students rejected the term *Mexican American* in favor of the once pejorative *Chicano* and adopted an ideology of *Chicanismo*. MEChA took positions on broader issues such as the Vietnam War, as well as supporting the struggle of the largely Mexican American farm workers in California led by Cesar Chávez. Although the organization has experienced internal struggles over class and gender issues, in its early history it did bring about several important educational reforms and raised the consciousness of a new generation of Mexicans.

The period between 1940 and 1960 was characterized by rapid growth in California, greater than at any time since the gold rush period of the mid-19th century. Latinos, however, made up only a small part of this growth. After 1970, by contrast, overall growth was much slower, but the Latino component was much larger. Thus, although the state's Anglo population grew by 6.6% between 1970 and 1990, the Latino population grew by 259.5% (Hayes-Bautista, 1992). By 1990 there were 7.7 million Latinos in California, representing 26% of the state's population. This proportion was projected to rise to one third by 2000, and because the Latino population is on average substantially younger than the Anglo population, Latinos are expected to constitute an absolute majority of California's labor force by 2010.

Hayes-Bautista (1992) suggested that Latinos are making a significant positive contribution to California society. For example, they form families at higher rates than other groups, have a strong work ethic, and are not overrepresented in prisons. He also noted that Latinos in California see themselves as bilingual and bicultural. Ninety-five percent of Latino respondents to the 1991 California Identity Project survey felt that Latino children should learn to read and write in both Spanish and English. Large majorities do in fact have at least some command of both languages. In contrast, only 36% of Anglo respondents professed any desire to learn Spanish.

This survey came in the middle of a decade in which Californians reacted at the ballot box to the increasing presence of Latinos in their midst, passing a series of measures in which issues of language, ethnicity, and immigration figured heavily. In 1986, Proposition 163 established English as the official language of the state. In 1994, voters passed Proposition 187, which, among other things, was intended to limit access to education for children of undocumented immigrants, principally Mexicans. Proposition 209, which banned affirmative action in higher education and state employment, was passed in 1996, and the number of Latino students admitted to the flagship branches of the University of California dropped precipitously. The process culminated in 1998 with the passage of Proposition 227, the Unz initiative (named after Palo Alto businessman Ron Unz, its chief sponsor), which effectively banned bilingual education in the state's schools and limited the amount of time children were allowed to receive instruction in English as a second language to 1 year. The overall effect of these initiatives has been to create a sense among Mexican Americans that their language and culture are threatened, especially in northern California where Latino population concentrations are lower than in the southern part of the state.

FROM THE PUBLIC TO THE PRIVATE SPHERE

We began this chapter with an overview of the main factors in California and Texas that previous research suggests are likely to facilitate or impede Spanish-language maintenance or loss. However, as we have seen, in both states, Mexican-background residents have suffered from a variety of forms of discrimination and, especially, from inadequate educational opportunities. And in both states the question of language has remained a key issue, whether in the Americanization campaigns of the first part of the 20th century, in the attempts to improve educational opportunities through bilingual education, beginning in the 1960s, or in the use of Spanish by the Chicano nationalist movements as a symbol of resistance to assimilation in more recent decades. Language has also remained a potent symbol for those who, like Ron Unz, have sought to promote an assimilationist form of education and to restrict the range of educational options available to Latino and other immigrant families by eliminating bilingual education from California's schools.

In the following chapters we move from the public realm and debates about various policies designed to facilitate or to impede Spanish maintenance and examine how members of Mexican-background families in northern California and south Texas position themselves with respect to Spanish and English as symbolic and instrumental capital. We pay close attention to the futures parents envision for their children and to children's developing concepts of their own identities, to the strategies used by families who have chosen to raise their children bilingually, and to the consequences of these decisions for caregivers' and children's relations to institutions beyond the families, particularly schools. These family members' voices, to which we now turn, reveal a diversity of views on the historical experience of Mexicans in the United States and on the role of language. In _Language as Cultural Practice,_ we celebrate these multiple perspectives.

3

Language and Cultural Identification

In this and the following chapters we examine the two constitutive elements informing ideologies about language—beliefs and practices. We recognize, along with others (e.g., Eagleton, 1991; Larrain, 1979), that *ideology* is a term with historically and situationally varying meanings.[1] We see part of its meaning as its attendant practices, conducted by individuals and social groups. In the case of language, these conceptions are articulated both in discourses about what is real and what has value in relation to language acquisition and use, and in language practice, or practices. At times we see these two constitutive elements, attitudes and practices, interacting in ways that appear obvious, or predictable; at other times, these interactions yield dialectical processes that are a good deal less transparent, or intuitive.

This chapter is about family members' *beliefs* about the importance of language and, specifically, the social significance they attach to the uses of Spanish and English in daily life. In chapter 4, we focus on the diverse strategies family members use in their efforts to support minority language maintenance.

CONSTRUCTING LANGUAGE AND IDENTITY THEORY

Recent discussions of cultural identity have distanced themselves from perspectives that view the phenomenon as unified, fixed, and static;

---

[1] See Billig et al. (1988) for a clear discussion of this point.

rather, they have approached the process of identity construction as complex, multifaceted, dynamic, and dialogic (Eckert, 2000; Rampton, 1995). Focusing on the heterogeneity of identity categories, such discussions seek to represent the social phenomenon as a collection of symbolic performances generated by individual choices of practices in fluid societal and situational contexts (Butler, 1999; Faigley, 1994; Foucault, 1977b; McCarthy & Crichlow, 1993).

In the case of minority groups, ethnic identity has been defined additionally as the manifestation of an interaction involving three aspects: the way an individual locates her- or himself within (or at a distance from) a particular social and cultural framework, the orientation of representatives of dominant groups to individuals and groups who display expected (and unexpected) lifestyle differences, and official characterizations, such as those contained in census documents (Garza & Herringer, 1987; Phinney, 1990; Verkuyten, 1995). Writing about cultural identity, Stuart Hall (1995), for example, envisioned "subjectivities" in a perpetual process of being differently positioned, and positioning themselves differently, within the first two of these aspects.

This body of scholarship would eschew "essentialist" conceptions of culture and identity, based on criteria of fixed, observable characteristics such as race or place of birth. Until recently, however, it has lacked substantial work that addresses the role of alternate languages and language varieties in the self-definitions of linguistic minority individuals and groups. This omission is significant, especially in connection with those for whom minority-language transmission is a factor, who grapple with an identity-related issue that has received scant attention in the research on cultural production (but see Bucholtz, 1995; Schecter et al., 1996). In their daily negotiations between dominant and minority groups, and empowered and disenfranchised individuals, they confront questions of discreteness and synthesis of linguistic code at many junctures and levels of self- and other-defining decision making. In modern, diverse societies one may expect to see considerable variation in the manner in which individuals who may align to the same census categories engage these linguistic choices. Because of these variable conditions, broad generalizations about the relationship of language to cultural identity are, arguably, imprudent, and understandings about the continuities and differences yielded by the different interpretations are advisedly generated from analyses grounded in local, particularized historical and spatial contexts.

In this chapter we explore the relationship between language and cultural identity as tied to linguistic and other self-defining practices of members of five families. Although the families represent a range of socioeconomic strata and life modes, we have not privileged these particular criteria in selecting these respondents to inform our discussion here. Rather, each case study constitutes a core narrative in participants' developing views of the relationship between language and cultural identity. We offer five illustrations because we identified five such core narratives. In the conclusion, we take up the implications of each of these texts, as well as the interactions among them, for the status of linguistic minorities in U.S. society.

Our descriptions attend closely to the orientations of family members to the central issues. We consider individuals' views concerning a number of frameworks in which children's identity practices are embedded[2]—the symbolic importance of the two languages, the ways in which cultural transmission occurs, and the role of schooling (and educational resources, broadly defined) in supporting family members' idealized social constructs involving language and culture and their respective places within them. We also look at the patterns of meaning suggested by the use of Spanish and English in the speech and literacy performances of the focal children and the adults and peers with whom they interact. Indeed, we see the texts produced by family members as they are socialized to and through language as embodying "acts of identity" (Le Page & Tabouret-Keller, 1985), the meanings of which are determined not by objective criteria but rather by those criteria that the various actors consider emblematic (Barth, 1970).

Because we hold language as a form of social action (Austin, 1962; Bourdieu, 1993; Searle, 1969, 1975) with social consequences (see, e.g., Blom & Gumperz, 1972; Gumperz, 1982a, 1982b; Heller, 1988; Sacks, Schegloff, & Jefferson, 1974; Woolard, 1985), a privileged strategy in our research has been to configure the ways in which individual

---

[2]We find evidence for these orientations in a variety of places, including attitudinal data contained in self-reports of home language use, rationales offered by parents and focal children for their decisions and stances with regard to Spanish maintenance, and the constructions provided by focal children and their parents in response to the elicitation: "We'd be interested to know how you see yourself. Let's say someone asked you about your cultural identity. What would you call yourself?"

and family ideologies about the role of language in defining cultural identity are shaped through language choice, mixing, and alternation. Also, because an integrated view of the role of language in identity construction acknowledges the relevance of ideological and power relations (Fairclough, 1995; Luke, 1995), we attend to the ways in which representatives of the dominant culture orient themselves to such discursive practices, in addition to, or in comparison with, other salient identity descriptors.

FIVE CORE NARRATIVES

Maintaining Ties With the Mexican Elite: The Villegas Family

> If someone asked me I would say I'm Mexican, I'm from Mexico, I come from a ci- I come from Guadalajara um ... I'd tell them about my ancestors maybe ... what they ate or what they wore ... o:r tell them about my grandpa, how ... he fought in World War II ... I don't know, it's kind of hard.[3]
>
> —*Diana Villegas (age 11)*

Diana Villegas, unlike the majority of children we interacted with, is experiencing discomfort in responding to our queries about how she sees herself. She finds this topic more difficult to negotiate than a myriad of others we (and sometimes she) have initiated—for example, her use of Spanish versus English in oral and literate performances and across various domains such as family life, peer interaction, and school communication. She is, instructively, not as lucid in engaging this area as she is in fulfilling our requests for writing samples in both Spanish and English, tasks that not all our focal children were comfortable performing. We think we understand the reasons why the topic is unsettling for Diana. First, she is a serious girl, who understands the need for diligence in one's commitments. We've asked a serious question for which she was not prepared, and on which she will require more time to reflect. Second,

---

[3]We have kept transcription conventions to a minimum for the sake of readability. The following conventions have been retained: All upper-case letters indicate strong emphasis; a colon following a vowel (e.g., e:) indicates an elongated vowel; an equals sign (=) indicates an overlap; X indicates inaudible text, with each X indicating a syllable; and translations are in parentheses and comments are in brackets.

within Diana's immediate family the issue of cultural identification has not (at least, not until recently) been conceptualized in reference to their experience in *los Estados Unidos*.[4] Although Diana has learned that her cultural heritage precedes her life in the United States, and is ideally to be located in another nationality and place, she is not entirely certain which decontextualized artifacts associated with that other place should be privileged in her self-identification.

Diana lives with her parents, Mariana and Enrique Villegas, and younger brother Luis (age 4) in a small, detached house in Lincoln City (a pseudonym), a town located approximately 20 miles south of San Francisco. The Villegas residence, on the fringe of a middle-class neighborhood and within a short walking distance of commercial activity, is located about half a mile west of the *barrio* that contains Lincoln City's majority Mexican-origin population. By North American standards their rented quarters are modest. The outer structure has not been maintained—large cracks disrupt the surface of the stucco shell—and the front grassy area has gone unattended. Inside, the living room has a barren, almost tentative, appearance, owing to the absence of artifacts or photographs, displays we associate with the homes of the other families we visit. In contrast to the minimalist furnishings, an elaborate home entertainment unit spans an entire wall of the family room. Another TV/VCR/stereo ensemble is found in one of the two bedrooms. A laptop computer occupies a permanent position atop the dining room table, with the remainder of the surface occupied by books and papers associated with the professional activities of Diana's parents. Over the duration of our fieldwork, our descriptions of the children's bedroom evolved from "sparsely furnished" to "cluttered." The summer of 1995 saw the addition of a music keyboard as well as a twin bed to accommodate Leticia, Mariana's 16-year-old cousin, who arrived from Mexico to complete high school in the United States.

Both Mariana and Enrique are from Guadalajara, Mexico's second largest city. Their families, most of whom have remained in Guadalajara,

---

[4]Information pertaining to ethnic and cultural identification was volunteered by respondents throughout the interview conversations, whether such information was explicitly requested or not. Indeed, our ethnographic records support the findings of Ruskin and Varenne (1983) concerning a willingness on the part of participants to engage the topic of individual and group identification and difference.

belong to the small, well-educated, Mexican *profesionista* (professional) stratum.[5] Mariana's father is a medical doctor, Enrique's brother an engineer. The couple moved to northern California when Diana was 2 so that Enrique could pursue a degree in business. Mariana, a Spanish–English bilingual who learned to speak, read, and write both languages at the American School in Guadalajara and in interactions with foreign medical students at the local university, planned to profit from her stay in the United States by taking courses to qualify as a medical assistant.

The couple's early years in the United States were full of financial hardship. In addition to attending classes, both parents worked full-time to support their family. During the daytime, preschooler Diana was placed in professional day care. Mariana and Enrique selected an "all-English" facility because they wished to take advantage of their limited time in the United States for their daughter to acquire a good base in the language. Around the time Diana was ready to start primary school, the couple made the decision to remain permanently in the United States, where Enrique plans to start his own business after completing his studies.

As a result of her parents' decision to immigrate, the selection of a primary school had long-term consequences for Diana's future. The cultural capital the couple brought from Mexico—that is, their knowledge of how the educational system in free market countries worked—allowed them to predict these consequences. Mariana and Enrique were concerned with identifying a school with high academic standards where Diana could receive the best possible preparation for a professional vocation. After researching the schools within close driving distance, they decided that the wisest choice would be St. Mary's Academy, a Catholic school located in the adjacent, affluent town of Oak Grove.

In her first meeting with Diana's kindergarten teacher, the latter firmly counseled Mariana against teaching Spanish literacy to her daughter, and advised the parents to speak English wherever possible

---

[5]It is difficult to estimate the percentage of the Mexican population that belongs to this stratum, particularly in the period following the collapse of the *peso* that occurred in December 1994, around the time we were beginning data collection. However, Nolasco and Acevedo (1985, cited in Valdés, 1996, pp. 175–176), who studied social stratification in Ciudad Juarez and Tijuana, estimated that 8% of the population belonged to this stratum, which also included middle-level executives and business people.

in the home, so as not to "create a conflict" that would cause the child to experience problems in school. The Villegases saw no reason to question this counsel— *"Queríamos ... que la niña se adapte lo más pronto posible al sistema"* ("We wanted ... our child to adapt as quickly as possible to the system").[6] Although initially Enrique, whose English proficiency is not as strong as his wife's, valued the opportunity provided by these unnatural discourse practices to improve his English, eventually all family members came to view these interactions as disorienting: *"Y perdemos el uso de idioma español en la casa. Y con eso perdemos tambié:n un poco la cultura y- y al final están como en un limbo, no están en ningún lado."* ("And we're losing the use of the Spanish language at home. And with this we're also losing some of the culture an- and in the end it's like they're in limbo, they aren't anywhere.")

This theme of a connection between language and cultural identity was strongly reinforced a year or two later at the time of a visit from Diana's paternal grandparents. Sra. Villegas was alarmed at the degree of Spanish-language loss her granddaughter exhibited. Ensuing discussions provoked a major change in attitude on the part of Diana's parents regarding the relation of mother-tongue maintenance to cultural continuity. The Villegases briefly considered transferring their daughter to a bilingual program in a local public school, and Mariana went to look for a Spanish immersion program of the kind she had heard were common in Canada. However, appalled by what they regarded as the poor quality of Spanish they observed in the neighborhood schools, they were disabused quickly of the idea of transferring their daughter to a public school. Mariana reported:

> *Los niños eran de tercer grado y: leyeron un cuento ... y tenían que escribir una pequeña composición de lo que habían entendido ... y no había coherencia ... usaban cosas en español ... "voy pa'trás, te llamo pa'trás."* (The children were third graders and they read a story ... and they had to write a little composition about what they had understood

---

[6]Translations of exclusively or predominantly Spanish utterances and exchanges are provided in parentheses, immediately following the utterance or exchange. Translations of brief Spanish phrases included in primarily English utterances and exchanges are provided in parentheses immediately after the phrase.

... and there was no coherence ... they used things in Spanish ... *"voy pa'trás, te llamo pa'trás."*[7]

It is not only in the public schools that the Villegases encountered what they regarded as *un español muy pobre* (an impoverished Spanish), but all around them—in the community and in the media as well. For example, for the Villegases, mother-tongue input from Spanish-language media has been problematic because they consider the Spanish spoken on the local television and radio stations to be full of errors. Comments Mariana: *"La tele no nos ayuda, porque encontramos barbaridades co:mo la palabra* 'gang,' *'ganga'* [laughs], *eso no existe en español, es 'pandilla.'"* ("The TV doesn't help us, because we find barbarisms like the word 'gang,' *'ganga'* ... this doesn't exist in Spanish, it's *'pandilla.'"*) The couple also express their dissatisfaction with decisions regarding programming for the Spanish media. Mariana continues: *"No hay muchos programas educativos en español."* ("There aren't many educational programs in Spanish.")

However, their reservations about the cultural resources to which they have access extend beyond issues of language, for the Villegases see a direct link between Spanish-language usage in the United States and lower-class Mexican values and mores. According to Enrique, *"La comunidad mexicana son de las personas que vienen de una clase baja ... y muchos de ellos no tienen ni escuela."* ("The Mexican community is made up of people who come from the lower class ... and many of them don't have any schooling.") The Villegases are also careful to distance themselves from specific cultural identities associated with segments of the Mexican community, identities that they find either alienating or disdainful: *"Yo soy mexicano pero el movimiento chicano para mí es desconocido ... No lo puedo entender."* ("I'm Mexican but to me the Chicano movement is unfamiliar ... I can't understand it.")

For the Villegases, the main drawback of living in the United States is, in fact, the absence of the kind of cultural activity they associate with their life in Mexico—museum exhibits, musical concerts that informed them about "the roots of our dances," and media resources where one could depend on *"un buen español, un español estándar"* ("a good

---

[7]The expression *ir pa'trás* (lit. "to go back"), a socially salient variant that is common in popular dialects of U.S. Spanish, is most likely an English calque. *Regressar* ("to return") is the standard form.

Spanish, a standard Spanish"). They regret that Mexican-descent children in the United States demonstrate little or no familiarity with the works of Mexican poets and novelists. They want their children, in the words of Mariana, *"tener conciencia de lo que es TOda la cultura ... que sea más rica la experiencia"* ("to be aware of what the WHOLE culture is about ... so that their experience will be richer").

Given their profound concerns about their daughter's mother-tongue attrition and its implications for the maintenance of Mexican cultural identity, as well as their reservations concerning bilingual programs in the California public schools, the Villegases elected to require the exclusive use of the mother tongue in the home. From the time Diana entered third grade, a Spanish-only policy has prevailed in the household: Diana's parents initiate interaction with their daughter in Spanish, and require the use of Spanish in return. In addition, Mariana has begun a formal program of teaching her daughter to read and write in Spanish.

Although Diana does not consistently use Spanish in her interactions with her parents, she knows that its use is expected, especially by her mother. Sometimes, when her daughter begins an interaction in English, Mariana commands explicitly: *"¡Habla español!"* ("Speak Spanish!"). More often, however, like the mainstream Anglo parents and teachers described by Heath (1982, 1983) and Michaels and Collins (1984), the mother's admonishments take the form of indirect requests, as illustrated in the following example:

Diana:	What do you want that for?
Mother:	Huh?
Diana:	*¿Para qué quieres eso?* (Why do you want that?)

Despite the official Spanish-only policy that governs the Villegas household, Diana uses a fair amount of English, although not normally with her parents or cousin Leticia, who arrived from Mexico midway through the observation period. With her school friends, however, she speaks exclusively English, even though her two closest friends are also Latinas who speak fluent Spanish.

Diana also listens to and watches a lot of English-language media. The family schedule, in fact, is often organized around a televised sports event—the Villegases are avid basketball and soccer fans—despite Mariana's earlier expressed disdain for Spanish sports programming. And Diana uses a considerable amount of English with her brother. The next excerpt, where we find Mariana entering the kitchen as Luis is protesting his sister's choice of main course for his school lunchbox, provides evidence for a parental double standard with regard to expectations for the two children's language use.

Luis: Nah! No peanut butter today.

Mother: Oh. No peanut butter today.

Diana: [to Mother] Are you sure?

Mother: [tying Luis's left shoe lace] Yeah. He's tired of peanut butter today. [turning to face Diana] *¿Dónde está el otro tenis?* (Where is his other tennis shoe?)

Mariana's and Enrique's differential expectations are not gratuitous. Early in our field work, the couple was informed that Luis would not be accepted as a student at the private school which their daughter attended. Mariana recounted: *"De la escuela de Diana nos mandaron a decir que el niño falló el examen de kinder, su puntaje fué SUMAmente bajo, no fué bajo, fué ANORMAL."* ("They told me at Diana's school that the child had failed his entrance exam for kindergarten, his performance was SO low, no it wasn't low, it was ABNORMAL.") Mariana and Enrique's initial response to this devastating news was a composite of anguish and guilt. They wondered whether the home language strategy that they were using to foster their children's sense of Mexican identity was interfering with their young son's cognitive development.

When it came time for a decision, the Villegases enrolled their son in one of the neighborhood schools after Sandra met with the new principal and reported positively on his academic background and professionalism. But family and school got off to a rocky start: Initially Luis was placed in a bilingual education class even though the parents had specified on the registration form that they wished him enrolled in the monolingual English strand. Mariana intervened, insisting that the staff respect the parents' judgment with regard to their son's interests, and the child was transferred to an all-English class.

Preserving Traditional Values: The Hernández Family

I'm Mexican … 'cause I'm from um because my parents are from Mexico and I want to talk like from where I am, um where my parents came from.

—Eduardo Hernández (age 10)

Eduardo is speaking with Sandra on the stoop outside his family residence in the East Bay community of San Ignacio, California, while waiting for his two brothers, Francisco (age 9) and Tomás (age 6), and his next-door neighbor, Jacobo, to join in a game of touch football. His home, a colonial blue bungalow bordered by flower beds and manicured shrubbery, appears at odds with San Ignacio's gritty reputation. Although the economy of the town, populated largely by working-class and economically marginalized families, has received a boost as a result of the two recently opened casinos, this good fortune does not appear to have mitigated the notoriety associated with its name. San Ignacio's streets are still considered unsafe—indeed, a series of gunshots disrupted an interview we were conducting with another of the families participating in the study.

We talk in the doorway, the boys' music (Selena, Boyz II Men), which resounds from the boom box positioned in the driveway, fusing with the sounds of sirens from passing police cars (one in nine vehicles, although not all have their sirens activated). Eduardo's two brothers arrive, and eventually we are joined by Jacobo, age 13, who has brought the football. Safe in numbers, the cohort now moves out into the street in front of the Hernández home. Following is an excerpt from a conversation between Eduardo and Jacobo, as twilight brings closure to their pickup football practice. The conversation, which contains several typical examples of the type of code switching common among the youth of the neighborhood, concerns their schedule for the following day, which is Halloween. Jacobo informs his friend that his plans have been curtailed, because he has to serve a detention for arriving late in school.

Jacobo:	Yeah, *eso es que* if you go late … if you go late to school, if you get three
Eduardo:	uh huh
Jacobo:	you er

Eduardo:	you get suspended
Jacobo:	mm mm
Tomás:	Eduardo, *¡que vengas!* (come on!)
Jacobo:	Wait a little bit, either you get a work detail and you get a hum er sweep the hall or sharpen pencils
Eduardo:	a:h hah
Jacobo:	=or clean the school for one hour *y si no* (and if not), if you don't go, you get suspended for one day ... *Y yo tengo que- y te dan* (and I have to- they give you) work detail *y luego yo tengo que ir en* (and then I have to go on) Halloween.

Inside the house, the brothers' conversations with one another are characterized by frequent code switching, a strategy that Eduardo refers to as *"los dos"* ("both"). The boys' running commentaries during one evening of television watching (they watch mostly English-language TV, largely cartoons and hunting and fishing shows) yields examples such as *"Mataron muchos ducks"* ("They killed a lot of ducks") and *"¿Qué pasó?* (What happened?) It crashed?" However, with his parents, Eduardo speaks primarily Spanish, a strategy dictated both by the pragmatic requirements of communication with his monolingual Spanish-speaking mother and his parents' stance in favor of Spanish maintenance. Raúl begins in English to explain his and his partner's position—"I think that's the only way to keep a little bit of what we used to have," then switches to Spanish—*"el único modo de mantener algo de la cultura que tenemos="* ("the only way to maintain something of our culture"). The conclusion to his sentence is anticipated by his wife, as the two rejoin *"=hablando el idioma"* ("[by] speaking the language").

Both Raúl and María are from the central Mexican city of Guanajuato. Although Raúl speaks, reads, and writes Spanish fluently, he claims English as his primary language. His parents immigrated to the United States when he was 5, and for 7 years he attended an all-English elementary school in San Francisco. Raúl reports that during his formative years he came into contact with few Latinos, so that eventually he actually had to "learn" Spanish. His motive for such learning was decidedly affective: While on vacation in his birth town of Guanajuato he met and fell in love with then 17-year-old María, who confirms that Raúl was strongly English dominant when she met him: *"Cuando yo lo conocí a él, bueno cuando ya nos casamos, no hablaba casi español."* ("When I first knew him, well, when we were already married, he hardly spoke Spanish.") After 10 years of residence in the United States, María still speaks only Spanish: *"Yo, nada más español."* ("I [speak] only Spanish.")

In the following sequence, which takes place in the kitchen in early morning, Eduardo's mother is querying her son about his breakfast consumption. Their interaction takes place entirely in Spanish.

Mother:	*¿Y vas a comer nada?*
Eduardo:	*Yo ya me he comido un pan con leche.*
Mother:	*¿No te has comido un pan con leche?*
Eduardo:	*Sí, ayer.*
Mother:	*¡No, ahori:ta!*
Eduardo:	*¡Ah, sí!*
(**Mother:**	Are you going to eat something?
Eduardo:	I already ate bread and milk.
Mother:	Haven't you eaten bread and milk?
Eduardo:	Yes, yesterday.
Mother:	No, now!
Eduardo:	Ah, yes!)

Because of María's limited receptive capability in English, she often calls on Eduardo to translate important documents, or to act as a broker between her and the outside world. An instance of the latter occurs one intemperate Monday morning after the family has passed the weekend without electricity, as a result of a particularly brutal rainstorm that caused havoc in the area. María asks her son to phone his school to find out if there will be classes that day:

Eduardo:	[looking for telephone number to phone school] Mom, *¿esto es un seis o un cero?* (is this a six or a zero?)

Mother:	*U:n seis.* (A six.)
Eduardo:	[into phone] Yes, erm are we gonna- are we gonna go- have school today? OK. Thank you. Bye. [to Mother] *Dijo que sí.* (S/he said yes.)

Eduardo's father speaks English fluently, and he is comfortable with the boys using a fair amount of English with him when they are horsing around; however, Raúl is firm that "as soon as they finish playing, having their fun, it's back to, to the serious, uh to Spanish." He adds that sometimes the boys need to be reminded to speak Spanish: *"Y muchas veces se les puede olvidar, pero lo más tarde que uno les diga no: hijo háblame en español, tu- tu idioma es español, me gustaría que supieras el idioma de origen tuyo."* ("And many times they can forget, but then later I tell them 'no: son speak to me in Spanish, your- your language is Spanish, I'd like for you to know the language of your origin.'") Eduardo understands this rather complex protocol for communication with his father, as evidenced by his account to the latter of the unhappy events he was party to earlier with regard to his friend Jacobo's rabbit. Although Eduardo code switches in the first turn, his speech thereafter, in line with his father's stern *consejos,* is all in Spanish.

Eduardo:	*Papi, la la coneja de Jacobo se le c- erm co- erm* she broke a leg.
Father:	*¿Por qué?*
Eduardo:	*No lo sé.*
Father:	*¿Porque la estaban correteando ustedes?*
Eduardo:	*No, no es ésa, la que estaba afuera. Estaba- estaba al- adentro y luego fuimos a verla y ya tenía el deste [=eso] cortado y había sangre.*
(Eduardo:	Dad, Jacobo's rabbit ... broke a leg.
Father:	Why?
Eduardo:	I don't know.
Father:	Because you [pl.] were chasing it?

Eduardo:	No, that's not it, it was out [of the cage]. It was- it was in- inside and then we went to look at it and it already had this cut and there was blood.)

Both Raúl and María emphasize their view that parents have a responsibility to "educate" their children for success in school and, eventually, life, by raising them to be respectful and hard-working.[8] An important part of this responsibility, they believe, entails the communication of a set of values through one's actions and interactions in the home, an arena over which parents exercise considerable control. For the Hernándezes, these values are inextricably tied to their identity as Mexicans, and their identity as Mexicans is inextricably linked to the Spanish language. Because Spanish occupies such a central role in both the family legacy and the future trajectories envisioned for their children, the Hernándezes believe that its preservation should not be left to chance, but rather is a goal to be pursued through an aggressive Spanish maintenance strategy.

Outside of the proximity of his mother and father, Eduardo speaks Spanish with some interlocutors (his grandmother, who came to visit from Mexico; a "new" boy on the block, from Peru), English with others (his aunt, several cousins), Spanish, with some code switching to English, with others (his younger brother, Tomás, who prefers Spanish), and English, with some code switching into Spanish, with still others (his middle brother Francisco, who prefers English).[9] His language choices illustrate the principle of accommodation. Asked how he made decisions about which language to use with whom when, Eduardo responds: *"Hablo el inglés cuando cuando no- alguien no sabe hablar en español y en español cuando alguien no sabe hablar en inglés"* ("I speak English when when no- someone doesn't know Spanish and Spanish when someone doesn't know English").

---

[8]After school and on weekends, the boys have chores that they are expected to complete before proceeding to recreation: On one Saturday morning visit, we arrived to find Francisco spraying and cleaning the living room furniture, Eduardo grooming the dog, and Tomás wiping the interior of the van while his mother washed the exterior.

[9]The issue of what the base language is in any conversation involving extensive code switching is admittedly complex. For our purposes here, we adopt Myers-Scotton's (1993) matrix language frame model. According to this model, in a mixed-language conversation, the language that supplies the system morphemes is the base language. The base language can (and does) change as new interlocutors enter into a conversation or as the topic shifts.

All three boys attend the same neighborhood elementary school, and all three are enrolled in English-only classes. When the time came for Eduardo to start kindergarten, his parents were advised that their son would be placed in a bilingual program. Despite his strong belief in Spanish maintenance, Raúl was not happy. From his observations of the school experiences of friends and their children in the area, he was convinced that if his son were placed in the bilingual strand he would not learn English. He went to speak with the school principal:

> *Les dije yo que no, que si le iban a poner en el salón bilingüe yo lo sacaba de la escuela y lo ponía en otra escuela, porque el español estoy yo pa' enseñárselos … yo los mando a la escuela a enseñarles el inglés, no el español, si yo quisiera que supieran el español me los llevo a México, verdad.*

> (I told them no, that if they were going to put him in the bilingual classroom that I would take him out of school and put him in another school, because I'm the one who teaches them Spanish … I send them to school to learn English, not Spanish, if I wanted them to know Spanish I'd take them to Mexico, right?)

Raúl and María are satisfied with the quality of their son's public school education, although they attribute much of the credit for his success to Eduardo himself. From an early age, they inform us, their son was studious, *"un muy buen muchacho"* ("a very good boy"). Although neither Eduardo nor his parents remember reading to him when he was younger, according to Raúl and María the child always showed a strong interest in learning and, before entering school, taught himself to read in both Spanish and English. From their favorable comments, Eduardo's parents know that their son's efforts in school are appreciated by his teachers. Notwithstanding the good rapport that Eduardo enjoys with school personnel, the child has started to have difficulty with school math, and is frequently stumped when attempting to complete his math homework. María became concerned, and expressed the view to her husband that they should get her son some outside assistance. Raúl, however, decided to tutor the boy himself, although later he modified this initial strategy to one that combined tutoring with material incentive: "I told him if he pulled up his grades, I would take him to Disneyland." However, because school learning is a serious topic, he conducts these tutoring sessions in Spanish.

After Eduardo completes middle school, his parents plan for him to attend high school in Mexico, where he would reside with his maternal grandmother. Eduardo is looking forward to living with his grandmother; he speaks warmly about the stories she tells about her childhood, and appreciates the books in Spanish that she sends from Mexico. However, unlike his parents, who plan to return to Mexico eventually in their retirement, Eduardo intends to remain in the United States.

Somos Chicanos: The Pacheco Family

¿Qué eres hijo?
> —Dolores Pacheco, to son Hector, as daughter Nina bursts into
> room

Soy Chicana/o.
> —Nina and Hector Pacheco (aged 18 and 10), in unison

Dolores and Pablo Pacheco and their daughter Nina (age 18) and sons Rudy (age 15) and Hector (age 10) occupy a rented flat in a working-class neighborhood of densely populated East Bay city. The house is a hub of youth social activity: On each of our visits, more than the five family members were present in the home. (We would be pressed to be more specific. We found it difficult to keep track of the many comings and goings of siblings and friends while focusing on the interviews.) The bilingual youth activity, involving both receptive and productive engagements with music and musical instruments, discussions about social plans and dating, communal television watching, and homework marathons, swirls around Sr. and Sra. Pacheco, both monolingual Spanish speakers.

Dolores and Pablo immigrated to the United States 18 years ago, Dolores from a rural village close to the central Mexican city of Guanajato, and Pablo from a small town in the state of Michoacán. Dolores accompanied her maternal grandparents. Her parents followed within the year, and her entire large family eventually immigrated. Most of Pablo's family, however, continue to reside in Mexico.

The two met in the United States soon after arriving. They were married almost immediately, living 4 months in Los Angeles, and a total of four more in several towns located in the northern part of California.

Within the year they settled in the Bay Area. Neither Dolores nor Pablo had completed elementary school in Mexico; nor were they able to continue with their studies in the United States: *"No teníamos suficientes centavos"* ("we didn't have the means"). Hence, neither has had access to an academic environment where they could develop proficiency in spoken and written English.

Pablo works in a bakery, on night shift, returning home at 6 a.m. He sleeps while the children are at school—they know to be quiet in the mornings. Dolores is on disability leave, without benefits, from the job at a factory where she has worked for the past 18 years. In our conversations, she dwells at length on how her lack of access to English has impaired her ability to support her family:

> *Yo necesito un trabajo donde no utilice mucho mis manos ya porque estan acabadas. Entonces si yo hubiera sabido inglés yo hubiera tenido escuela, yo hubiera otra clase de trabajo pero por mí situación de mi limitación de inglés no he tenido escuela. Nada más trabajé viente y un años hasta la fecha. No sé qué va a ser mi futuro.*

> (I need a job where I don't use my hands so much because they're shot. If I had known English I would have had more schooling, I would have another type of work but because of my situation of limited English, I didn't go to school. I just worked 21 years up until now. I don't what my future will be.)

Out of pragmatic necessity, the children speak Spanish with their parents. The majority of sibling interactions take place in Spanish as well, although Nina and Rudy use more English than does Hector. Nina and Hector routinely translate official documents, newspaper articles, and promotional ads for their parents' benefit. Hector, who spends more time at home than do his older brother and sister, handles phone calls from monolingual English speakers as well. Rudy, his parents volunteer, does not appreciate being asked to perform these functions; Dolores and Pablo are not even certain that he would be able to at this point. Both Sr. and Sra. Pacheco find it curious that of their three children it is their youngest, Hector, who is most committed to maintaining Spanish. They hypothesize that this state of affairs came about as an extension of Hector's love of reading. From an early age the child devoured books in both Spanish and English. Also, as a preschooler he insisted on being read to all the time, a request that his monolingual parents could fulfill only in Spanish.

Hector views his oral production and reading abilities in Spanish and English as more or less equivalent, although he indicates a preference for writing in English. His greatest passion, however, is his artwork. He regards demands for written production as excuses for drawing, and therefore welcomes writing assignments in both Spanish and English.

The Pachecos elected to send their children to Miraflores School, the local, bilingual elementary school. Sra. Pacheco explains that their decision was based primarily on their commitment to cultural maintenance. A second rationale involved Dolores and Pablo's belief that as bilinguals their children would have access to the broadest possible range of professional opportunities:

> *Necesitamos a ver hacer como un ejemplo verdad- usted es un abogado, y si usted nada más sabe inglés tiene que ocupar un intérprete y si usted es un abogado bilingüe, entonces usted no necesita intérprete. Usted sólo va a su cliente y lo va a atender en español o entender en inglés ... entonces pensamos que tiene más valor un bilingüe que uno [que habla] solo [un] idioma.*

> (We need, let's see, to give an example, right- you're a lawyer, and if you only know English you have to hire an interpreter and if you're a bilingual lawyer, then you don't need an interpreter. You yourself go to your client and you go talk with him in Spanish or understand in English ... so we think that a bilingual is worth more than just one language.)

The preceding arguments notwithstanding, the Pachecos view the acquisition of standard spoken and written English as the highest priority for their children's formal education. They believe that mastery of the dominant idiom is a sine qua non for advancement within U.S. society and that this capacity will ensure that their children do not experience the same estrangement from mainstream culture as their parents. However, they do not believe that such mastery need come at the expense of their children's cultural identity or their home language. Dolores comments:

> *Principalmente yo pienso que lo que se debe de tener en los niños es que respeten su identidad- su idioma de ellos y que los hagan sentirse cómodos como cualquier persona, que no los hagan sentirse menos*

porque también es el hecho que les hace sentirse rebeldes y que no tengan en sus corazones esa cosa de ser menos y lo que son igual que todos. Sea cualquier raza pienso que es la misma.

(First I think that that what needs to be instilled in children is that they respect their identity- their language and that they are made to feel as comfortable as anyone, one needs to be sure that they don't feel themselves to be inferior because this is the thing that makes them rebellious, and that they don't have in their hearts this feeling of being inferior and that they are equal to anyone. Regardless of race, I think that one race is the same as any other race.)

Moreover, they are acutely aware of the costs—both material and psychological—of their own monolingual immigrant status. Dolores here launches into an attack on systemic racism as revealed in the practices of schools and other societal institutions: *"En las escuelas hay discriminaciones contra los- contra los chicanos ... tratan de tenerlos siempre más abajo."* ("In the schools they discriminate against Chicanos ... they always try to keep them down.") Asked to provide specific examples of such discrimination, the Pachecos recount how initially school representatives insisted on placing Hector in an ESL program (a common story among the families in our study), and that only after considerable advocacy on behalf of their son did they succeed in enrolling him in the bilingual program. Dolores expresses her outrage at this injustice: *"[¡Mis hijos] son chicanos, son nacidos aquí!"* ("[My children] are Chicanos. They were born here!")

The Pachecos move on to elucidate the significance that their Spanish monolingualism holds for mainstream society. Here, again, Dolores takes the lead, expanding the frame of reference to encompass other societal institutions beyond schools. In the following account, for example, she describes the response of a clerk at a local pharmacy to her inability to speak English:

> *... le dijo a mi hija por qué sea qué los Mexicanos nada más llegan aquí y no aprenden inglés, nada más quieren ganar dinero ... porque yo estaba hablando español entonces le dijo a mi hija.*

> (... she asked my daughter why the Mexicans just come here and don't learn English, they only want to earn money ... because I was speaking Spanish she spoke to my daughter.)

Although Hector does not have complete access to his parents' (and to a large extent, Nina's) ideological vision of the relation between Spanish and English, there is no question that he views speaking and learning Spanish as a high priority. As an illustration, he volunteers that he chooses to speak Spanish with his friends at school, even during recreational periods. Interestingly, in his articulation of the importance that he attaches to the Spanish language, he makes it clear that he sees Spanish maintenance in oppositional tension with the acquisition of the societally dominant code: "If I use English too much I'm gonna forget about Spanish." Why, we ask, does he not wish to forget? "Cause if I wanted to talk to my mother about something, I would- I want to know exactly how to say it .... And my father *también*."

English as a Fast Track to Americanization: The Esparza Family

> I still call myself Mexican American ... *pero* you know *es más fácil para mí en inglés* (but ... it's easier for me in English).
>
> —Marcella Esparza, age 11

Teresa Esparza immigrated to northern California as a young adult, after a highly mobile childhood during which she spent varying periods of time in four different central and northern Mexican states. In Mexico, she completed 6 years of elementary schooling before hiring herself out as a housemaid to wealthy local families. After immigrating, she settled in Lincoln City. Teresa later obtained a general educational development (GED) certificate and completed a beauty course while working as a domestic and caring for her daughter Marcella.

A single mother, Teresa, who at the time of Marcella's birth spoke virtually no English, radically modified her lifestyle to prepare her daughter for a school program that she felt would allow the child to obtain the social opportunities that she had lacked. Early on, Teresa, influenced in some degree by an educator whose house she cleaned, determined that Marcella would attend an English-medium school. She believed that the sooner Marcella learned to function fluently in English, the sooner she would gain access to the numerous opportunities American society had to offer. Hence, she saw it as her responsibility to prepare her child for a school environment where she would be expected to compete with native speakers of English: *"Yo quería cuando ella fuera a la escuela que se sintiera cómoda ... con poder leer y escribir en inglés."* ("I wanted her to feel comfortable when she went to school ... with the ability to read and to write in English.")

But Marcella faced an obvious quandary with regard to her goal of fast-tracking her daughter's assimilation into mainstream U.S. society. Her own English proficiency fell far short of what she believed was necessary to give Marcella the head start she desired for her daughter. Moreover, during her daughter's early years, she lived with her Spanish monolingual mother and other relatives in a Spanish-speaking environment. Teresa, however, devised an ingenious strategy to compensate for her own limited English and to prepare her daughter for the type of school she wished her to attend:

> Cuando Marcella era baby, yo no hablaba inglés pero yo tenía cassettes y compraba los libros. Yo nunca le leí en español. Yo tenía los cassettes, [y] yo me acostaba en la alfombra y ponía el cassette y como si yo me estuviera leyendo con ella ... hasta que yo aprendí a leer ... libros de baby pero yo siempre le leí en inglés.

> (When Marcella was a baby, I didn't speak English, but I had cassettes and I bought books. I never read in Spanish. I had the cassettes and I used to lie down on the rug and put on the cassette as if I were reading with her ... until I learned to read baby books, but I always read in English.)

Teresa, whose English proficiency has improved considerably in the years since Marcella was a baby, concludes the narrative of this simultaneous language and literacy acquisition odyssey in English: "And *I* learned a lot that way."

Marcella, aged 11 at the beginning of our study, learned a lot as well. She recalls listening to recordings of English books, and later recites from memory one of the Dr. Seuss books that she listened to as a young child:

> Como ella [Sra. Esparza] no sabía cómo leer en inglés entonces me compró esos, esos tapes y los libros ... you can read along you know. So that's pretty much how I learned ... me enseñaron el Dr. Seuss. Oh, I loved those books.

> (Because she [Mrs. Esparza] didn't know how to read in English she bought me those, those tapes and books ... you can read along you

know. So that's pretty much how I learned ... they taught me Dr. Seuss. Oh, I loved those books.)

When it came time to enroll her daughter in school, Teresa considered a neighborhood public school, but opted instead to send Marcella to St. Mary's Academy (the same school attended by Diana Villegas), where the language of instruction is English. She explains this decision by pointing to *"el nivel educativo bien bajo"* ("the very low educational level") in the public system, especially in the schools serving Latino children.

Predictably, although Marcella's verbal and literacy skills in English have developed to the point where her speech as well as her uses of reading and writing are indistinguishable from those of native speakers, her Spanish literacy, which was never reinforced, lagged considerably behind. When asked about her favorite books and her current reading, she names a number of well-known English-language children's books and provides detailed plot summaries of several. Although she expresses some regret at her inability to read age-appropriate books in Spanish, she also voices a strong preference for reading in English. Teresa provides a differently nuanced articulation of Marcella's literacy practices, stating her impression that her daughter is able to read and write *only* in English: *"Para hablarlo sí los dos pero para escribirlo solo inglés o leerlo también solo inglés."* ("She speaks both, but she only writes in English and only reads in English also.")

Teresa describes herself as "Mexicana," underscoring the contrast with the identity category she has chosen for her daughters: "Americana." Even with regard to her own identity, however, she is quick to clarify that her referent selection is based on place of birth, as opposed to affective criteria: *"Yo no tengo muchas amistades con la comunidad."* ("I don't have a lot of friendships in the community.") Daughter Marcella, who describes herself as Mexican American, volunteers her own disclaimer: "I still call myself Mexican American ... *pero es más fácil para mi en inglés*" ("but I'm more comfortable in English").

Nonetheless, recently, Spanish has acquired increased prominence in the Esparza household: Teresa's new partner is a monolingual speaker of Spanish. This change in the household linguistic environment has not, however, had a noticeable effect on Marcella's motivation to learn Spanish—she indicates that she may take it up at a later date in school although her first choice would be French—nor has it led to a change in the language of mother–child or sibling interactions. Teresa continues to use mostly English with her young child Kimberly, and Marcella uses only English. Moreover, unless the dynamic changes drastically, Kimberly is likely to display even less productive competence in Spanish than her sister. At 3 years of age, "Speak English" is a marked staple of Kimberly's rapidly developing linguistic repertoire.

Cultural Maintenance and Minority-Language Awareness: The Baez Family

> [I'm] Tex-Mex. Po'que mi background [is from] *México, pero YO 'sta de Tejas.*
>
> —*Alysa Baez (age 10)*

Roberto and Luisa Baez and their daughters, Linda (age 12), Alysa, and Liliana (age 6), live in a new middle-class subdivision on the predominantly Euro-American north side of San Antonio. A college graduate, Roberto is an engineer with a local firm; Luisa, who completed 2 years of college, works as a customer service representative.

Luisa speaks, reads, and writes Spanish fluently; Roberto, although not as fluent as his wife, is also proficient in Spanish. Because they feared punishment if overheard using Spanish on school premises, each reverted to the use of English in their youth and then continued this pattern with their offspring. "What we tried to do was," Luisa hesitates, the subject clearly painful, "we tried to act Anglo." In the Baez family, English has always been the language of parent–child interactions, with Spanish reserved for endearments [*"mi 'ja"* ("my daughter")], formulaic phrases [*"¿Tú crees?"* ("You think so?")], and isolated vocabulary items denoting objects that hold special significance for the children [*"caballito"* ("little horse")]. The girls attend the local public schools and, as might be expected in a majority-Anglo neighborhood, English is the first language of nearly all their friends. However, they do have occasion to use Spanish in weekly visits with their maternal grandparents, who live in San Antonio, and Roberto and Luisa have attempted to motivate their daughters to learn Spanish. They see Spanish as playing an important role in an overall strategy aimed at cultural awareness. Says Luisa:

Yo pienso que todos que vivimos aquí venimos aquí de otros países y ...
cuando vinieron los ALEMANES hicieron colonias, ellos siguieron
enseñando a sus niños las costumbres de su país. Cuando hay aquí
gente polaca también hicieron lo mismo. Y nosotros mucho dejamos
esas costumbres y yo pienso que 'hora ya reconocimos qué importante
es. Y yo quiero seguir las costumbres, quiero seguir las leyendas que me
dijeron mis abuelos, yo quiero seguir todo eso. Aunque sea que
hacemos tamales una vez por año. Son costumbres que nosotros
queremos que vivan.

(I think that all of us who live here came here from other countries
and ... when the GERMANS built colonies, they continued to teach
their children the customs of their country. When the Poles were
here they also continued to do the same. And we're abandoning
these customs, and I think that now we have recognized how important it is. And I want to follow the customs, I want to pass on the stories that my grandparents told me, I want to follow all this. If nothing
else we make tamales once a year. They are customs that we want to
keep alive.)

For Luisa especially, it has been important that the children be
aware of their Hispanic heritage, and able to appreciate the significance of events and artifacts that in her view have played an important
role in the evolution of the Mexican people, at least in the United
States. She reviewed carefully with Alysa the ingredients that go into
the *caldo* (soup) that she and her own mother prepared lovingly for
their families. She explained the difference between Mexican music,
for which she displayed a special fondness (judging from her station
selection on the van radio), and Tejano. She found books in the library, written in English, that addressed Hispanic cultural themes,
and read these to her daughters as they were growing up. Alysa still
remembers, and cites with fondness, a children's story entitled "Too
Many Tamales."

Alysa is a member of a volleyball team consisting primarily of Mexican-origin girls and a church congregation consisting primarily of Mexican-origin families. She is also an aficionada of Tejano music. Like the
overwhelming majority of girls among the Texas participants, she
names Selena as her favorite performer, and memorabilia commemorat-
ing the late singer's accomplishments dominate the decor of her bed-

room.[10] The Baezes approve of their daughters' musical preferences, and are happy to support their related habit. They feel this is a good way for the girls "to learn more words in Spanish."

Luisa Baez describes her children's Spanish proficiency as resembling a "staircase," a result of the differing lengths of time they spent when they were young with their nearly Spanish-monolingual maternal grandmother, Sra. Vela. Linda, the oldest, essentially grew up in her grandparents' home while Luisa and Roberto worked. Through third grade, she attended a private school nearby and would be bussed or picked up and taken to Sra. Vela's home after school. As a result of regular, constant exposure, she was able to acquire much Spanish in her early childhood years. Alysa, however, although she stayed with the Velas during her infant years, was thereafter cared for by her paternal grandparents when her *abuela* became ill. Following Sra. Vela's recovery Alysa returned periodically to her grandmother's home for day care, but Mrs. Vela believed that the paternal grandparents' derogatory attitude toward the heritage language discouraged the child from using Spanish. Although Alysa reported speaking Spanish "*como* when *yo 'sta a mi, mi 'buelo*'s house," Sra. Vela documented a pattern of regression with her middle granddaughter, claiming that the youngster was a stronger Spanish speaker as a young child than at the time of the study. Liliana, the youngest daughter, spent even less time with her maternal grandparents than the two older siblings. By then the family had moved to their current home in suburban northwest San Antonio, across town from the Velas, and it was more convenient either to leave the child with her paternal grandparents nearby or to place her in a day-care facility attached to the neighborhood elementary school. Of the three girls, Liliana is the least proficient in Spanish and, unlike her sisters, evidences no receptive ability. We noted the near-monolingual Sra. Vela scrambling to accommodate the child when the latter was thrown off by her grandmother's situationally appropriate greeting: "*¿Fuiste al paseo?*" After several seconds of blank look and silence, Sra. Vela followed up: "Did you went to see the parade?"

---

[10]Selena, originally from Corpus Christi, Texas, was among the first Tejano music stars to achieve widespread popularity among a broad audience. Although she achieved a great deal of general popularity, she was particularly idolized by young girls, who often sought to imitate her mannerisms and style of dress. In the spring of 1995, Selena was murdered in Corpus Christi by her former manager.

That intergenerational communication is impeded by the fact that she and her granddaughters do not share a common language is a source of much sorrow for Sra. Vela. It is not the lack of linguistic proficiency in English and Spanish on either her part or her granddaughters' parts that she regrets, nor is she especially concerned with issues of cultural continuity, as are Alysa's parents. Rather:

Sería muy bonito que ... mis nietas me entendieran bien lo que yo les quería decir porque era una forma de, acercarme más a ellas pa' conocerlas, o que ellas me conocieran a mí ... Porque yo podía expresarles mis sentimientos, mis sueños con ellas, aconsejarlas, y ellas me entendían ... Y se me hace que en español es más DULCE ... emotiva más: la conversación de una abuelita con su ... nieta. Y en inglés pos no podría ... hablarles con el corazón ... en español yo podía hablarles ... decirles mis sueños que puedo tener yo con ellas. Pero pos ellas no me entienden en, en español pos ¿cómo se los voy a decir?

(It would be beautiful for ... my granddaughters to truly understand what I wanted to say because it was a way of, getting closer to them and knowing them, or for them to know me ... Because I could express my feelings, my dreams with them, to advise them, and they could understand me ... And it seems to me that it's SWEETER in Spanish, more emotional: the conversation of a grandmother with her granddaughter. And in English, well, I couldn't ... speak to them from the heart ... in Spanish I could speak to them ... tell them the dreams that I have for them. But, well, they don't understand me in, in Spanish, well, how am I going to tell them these things?)

Clearly, Alysa is comfortable in the presence of Spanish, as the following interaction across three generations in her grandmother's home reveals. "It's just that, " as Alysa explains her own communication strategy while in the presence of monolingual Spanish speakers, "sometimes I don't know the words so I get confused and I use English words and try to go back to Spanish when I know the words":

Alysa: *O. Es bueno* [eating her caldo]. (It's good.)

Grandmother: *¿Está sabroso? ¿Um:?* [chuckles] (It's tasty?)

Mother: *Dile a qué hora te levantaste para hacerlo.* (Tell her what time you got up to make it.)

Grandmother: *A las, a las* fi:ve, forty. Um? The morning.
¿Oíste? (Did you hear?) I wake up at five, f- fo-
forty minutes.

Alysa: *¿Po'qué?=* (Why?)

Grandmother: Five in the morning.

Alysa: *¿Por qué?* (Why?)

Grandmother: *Para que estuviera temprano, pronto, pa' cuando
viniera porque ya sé que ustedes quieren comer
luego* [laughs]. (So that it can be ready early, for
when you come because I know that you want to
eat then.)

Alysa: And *yo* woke up a *como a la* eight. (And I woke
up like at eight.)

Alysa attended Spanish classes in the summer "College for Kids" offered by the local community college district. Although our proficiency
measures—along with the examples given here—show that she is not
proficient enough to converse with Spanish monolinguals outside the
family, Alysa exhibits considerably more receptive than productive
ability. Luisa's instructions to her daughter regarding food preparations
are full of Spanish vocabulary—such as *pimienta* (pepper), *un poquito*
(a little)—all of which Alysa interprets appropriately. Another example
of Alysa's receptive ability was provided en route to a hairdresser's ap-
pointment across town, when Luisa, without a pointing gesture, made an
appreciative reference to the passing scenery: *"Mira. Teresitas."*
("Look. Impatiens.") Responded Alysa: "I like the pink ones the best."
Alysa regularly assists her maternal grandfather with gardening chores;
not surprisingly, she has developed an extensive receptive repertoire in
Spanish related to horticulture.

Alysa is popular with her peers and displays a well-rounded character,
playing the clarinet and participating on a number of sports teams, and the
Baezes exude a sense of confidence about their daughter's future. Although they believe that knowing a second language is good for personal
development and can be advantageous in the workplace, they have at no
point expressed the view that their daughter's well-being is tied to her recovery of Spanish, and they have never been observed to insist on its use.

Toward the end of our field work, however, the cause of cultural maintenance in the Baez family received a boost from an unlikely source. Alysa herself reported liking to speak Spanish more frequently, especially with her grandmother, and she has plans to take more Spanish-language courses in school. Her main motivation is to be able to communicate more easily with her maternal grandparents and help them translate important documents from English, but there is also something else. To a greater extent than her parents, she makes an explicit link between minority language maintenance and cultural continuity, stating categorically: "*Yo quiero* talk more *en español po'que ese es mi* background *y* that's it."

POSITIONS AND POSITIONINGS

Like the overwhelming majority of family members associated with our research, Diana, Eduardo, Hector, Alysa, and Marcella, as well as their parents, all define themselves in terms of allegiance to their Mexican heritage, although their stances toward this relation vary, as do the terms they use.[11] Most (but certainly not all, in deference to the ambivalence displayed by families such as the Esparzas) view bilingualism as a positive attribute, and accord an important role to Spanish in the formation of cultural identity. However, the Villegas, Hernández, Pacheco, and Baez families are differently oriented to the *use* of the Spanish language as a vehicle for affirmation of this commonly articulated identity. In the former three California families, parents view Spanish as a necessary social resource for maintaining cultural tradition and ethnic identity. Even in the families where English is an option, parents insist on the use of Spanish in many parent–child interactions. However, this is not to suggest that the Villegases, Hernándezes, and Pachecos share the same vision of their cultural tradition or ethnic identity. In fact, the Villegases' vision stands in stark contrast to that of the Pachecos. The Villegas' definition of cultural continuity involved reading and performance of "classical" pieces rendered in a standard Spanish cultivated by the Mexican elite classes. In contrast, in their own lives, Sr. and Sra. Pacheco maintain continuity with the populist traditions of the rural Mexican laboring class, including the *norma rural,* the language variety characteristically

---

[11]Although the majority of adult and child respondents used a variant of Mexican (Mexican, *mexicano*, Mexican American, Tex-Mex) in conjunction with their self-assigned identities, a significant number described themselves as *Hispanic*. No one we interviewed used the term *Latino,* although it is the privileged nomenclature among U.S. academics and required usage in journalistic texts.

spoken by the members of that class. The Pacheco children, like their parents, wish to challenge inequitable, class-based differentiations. However, unlike their parents, they adopt a bilingual Chicano self-definition to do so. This self-definition, of course, sharply distinguishes the Pacheco children from the Villegases, who, as we have seen, find the notion of Chicano culture foreign to their experience.

In contrast to the California families, the Baezes, the relatively well-off Texas family residing in an ethnically mixed neighborhood, use English almost exclusively in parent–child and sibling interactions. Spanish is reserved for occasional directives and for endearments. Luisa and Roberto, Alysa's parents, describe the discrimination they experienced as Americans of Mexican origin as a vivid historical memory, drawing the contrast with their current status. Although the Baezes—unlike, for example, the Esparzas—do not endorse an assimilationist position, their integration within U.S. mainstream institutions, coupled with their material circumstances, provides day-to-day assurances that dramatic steps to preserve their cultural traditions are not called for. In this family, strategies aimed at cultural maintenance for the most part do not involve use of Spanish. Alysa and her sisters participate in enrichment activities or church groups consisting of Mexican-descent children, addressing themes related to Mexican culture, and meeting in predominantly Latino parts of the city. All of these activities, however, are carried out in English.

With regard to sibling interaction, in the Villegas family, siblings converse largely in Spanish, although code alternation, constrained by topic junctures, is not uncommon. In the Hernández and Pacheco families, sibling interactions are characterized by frequent code switches (much of it intrasentential code switching in the case of the Hernandez family) as well as by longer stretches of both Spanish and English. All the focal children exhibit similar patterns of language use with peers: With classmates and neighborhood friends, they normally use English (although Eduardo Hernández and Hector Pacheco frequently code switch with bilingual peers); with relatives, they generally accommodate their interlocutors' language preferences.

With respect to the envisioned role of schools, only one among the four families that expressed a commitment to cultural maintenance relied on the schools to assist with cultural transmission and minority-language maintenance. On the whole, the families (including the Pachecos, who enrolled their children in bilingual programs) believe that the public school is a place to acquire academic competence in the dominant societal language, and that responsibility for cultural continuity essentially rests with the family.

A final observation about the role of minority-language maintenance: We have seen that the parents and children of the families whose orientations toward ethnic identity we have compared share a sense of belonging to a larger Mexican or Mexican American culture and that most have expressed the view that Spanish maintenance is tied to participation in that identity; however, the ways in which families choose to pursue their goal of intergenerational transmission of Spanish language and culture vary widely. Less accessible to family members than their understandings of language and other identity practices associated with cultural continuity are the ways in which their lived experiences of Spanish maintenance differ. In fact, large discrepancies among family members' representations of practices associated with the notion of minority-language maintenance render the meaning of the notion problematic from an etic perspective. We have seen, for example, how for Enrique and Mariana Villegas, from an upper-middle-class background in Guadalajara, Spanish maintenance is equated with preservation of the cultivated Spanish of the educated Mexican elite, a social dialect that is never spoken by the adults in the other California families whose narratives we have highlighted. Alysa Baez, on the other hand, was happy, when given the choice of language, to "do" the child interview in Spanish ("mi background [is from] *México, pero YO 'sta de Tejas*"), where other focal children with a similar level of Spanish proficiency elected English, asserting that they speak "no Spanish." Interestingly, Luisa and Roberto Baez, two of whose three daughters speak hardly any Spanish, answered positively when asked if they adopt strategies to maintain the minority language, whereas both Teresa and Marcella Esparza, who must use Spanish to communicate with Teresa's monolingual partner, claim not to use any strategies in support of Spanish maintenance. In the next chapter, we turn our attention to the different *specific* meanings of Spanish maintenance our ethnographic inquiry revealed as well as to the generative potential of these different emic representations for our understanding of the contextual bases for minority-language acquisition, retention, and loss.

4

Enacting Spanish Maintenance

This chapter is about the diverse strategies that parents and other caregivers pursue in their efforts to transmit a minority language to their children. By focusing on individual cases of Spanish maintenance, we would not wish to foster the impression that all the families we worked with are dedicated to the goal of maintaining Spanish, either as a personal goal or as an idealized societal construct. To be sure, an overwhelming majority of families expressed a commitment to maintenance of Mexican culture and traditions. However, for reasons explored in chapter 3, some of these do not view active support for the Spanish language as a necessary strategy in pursuit of this goal.

This notwithstanding, we have found it worthwhile to identify the different meanings that participants ascribe to the idea of minority-language maintenance as well as the different roles that they envision for home, and sometimes school, in achieving that goal. Specifically, we want to create a space for caregivers' perspectives and voices on the important issue of minority-language maintenance and, in so doing, to add these emic representations to the normative definitions that have characterized the terms of debate heretofore engaged in by linguists, educators, and policymakers.

In this chapter, we describe six distinct strategies used by families to enact their understandings of Spanish maintenance. As with the preceding chapter, we identify these as core templates, although we admit multiple variations on each theme. And, as in the previous chapter, the six families whose language practices serve as our illustrations are diverse in their places of residence, socioeconomic status, and modes of life. The Texas families include a rural working-class family living on a south Texas ranch, a south Texas urban working-class couple raising a granddaughter, and a professional family living in a middle-class San Antonio housing development. The California families include two working-class single mothers and their children and an upper-middle-class Euro-American mother and stepfather who are endeavoring to maintain the language of their son's father in home interactions. The diversity of environments in which participating parents and caregivers are attempting to transmit the minority language enables us to explore the effects of geographic and social space, conceptualized not only in terms of the differing linguistic ecologies of California and Texas but also in terms of distinctions among rural, urban, and suburban environments in the different communities.

MAINTAINING SPANISH IN A RURAL ENVIRONMENT

Spanish Only in the Home

Ernesto: *Vamos a llevarla y te llevo ahí por donde te gusta/*Antonio: *no/andale, si?*

Antonio: *OK.*

Ernesto: *A ver yo te doy te doy te doy te doy. Dale por el zacate. 'hora dale.* [Antonio begins to move in the other direction.] *A no por aquí.*

Ernesto: [to Carlos] *A ver ... vamos a darle la vuelta.* [to Antonio] *Ya sabes correr a subirte, ¿verdad? Mira pasa aquí mira/*Antonio: *¡espérate!/por aquí mira. ¿OK?*

Antonio: *Ya me cai[go], ya me cai[go], ya me cai[go].*

Ernesto: *Andale.*

Antonio: *Pos me voy a caer./*Ernesto: *¡ay!/*

Ernesto: *Mira le pegamos allá.*

Antonio:	*Estamos en- me voy a subir allá.*
Ernesto:	*Orale, dale otra vez por ahí. A ver otra vez. Esta vez sí te voy a subir aunque no quieras.*
Antonio:	*Ay me voy a caer, me voy a caer, me voy a caer.*
Ernesto:	*A ver, ahora bájate por ahí otra vez.*
(Ernesto:	Let's take it [the tractor toy] and take you down by where you like to go /Antonio: no/c'mon, let's do it.
Antonio:	OK.
Ernesto:	Go by the side of the grass. Now go ahead. [Antonio begins to move in the other direction.] Not that way, this way.
Ernesto:	[to Carlos] Let's see … let's take him around. [to Antonio] So you know that you have to run to the top [of the hill], right? Look go this way, look./Antonio: wait!/This way, look. OK?
Antonio:	I'm falling, I'm falling, I'm falling.
Ernesto:	Come on.
Antonio:	But I'm going to fall/Ernesto: ay!/
Ernesto:	Look, we'll end up over there.
Antonio:	We're in- I'm going to go up over there.
Ernesto:	Yeah, try it one more time over there. Let's see, try it again. This time I'm going to get you up there whether you like it or not.
Antonio:	Ay I'm going to fall, I'm going to fall, I'm going to fall!
Ernesto:	Let's see, now go down that way one more time.)

This extended excerpt from interaction between Ernesto Gómez, age 12, our focal child, and his younger brother Antonio, age 5, is taken from a weekend observation where we find the brothers playing together in front of their house. Young Antonio is riding a tractor toy when Ernesto begins to push him toward a large hilly area to the side of the house. When they arrive at the hilly area, Ernesto repeatedly pushes Antonio, still riding his tractor, up a slope. Throughout the procedure, Antonio protests, only half seriously, and repeatedly expresses his fear that he will fall off the tractor toy. Indeed, as he feared, Antonio does fall off a number of times on the bumpy ride down the hill, and the tape is punctuated by loud noises of protest and occasional thumps. However, each time he gets up ready for another ride.

The interaction, which takes place entirely in Spanish, dramatically illustrates the degree to which the Gómez children maintain Spanish in their ordinary conversation. Clearly the boys are not using Spanish to please their parents, who are not in the area where they are playing. Rather, the brothers interact in Spanish because Spanish is the language of daily communication in the home.

Esteban and María Gómez and their three sons, Ernesto, Carlos (age 10), and Antonio, live in a small bungalow on a cattle ranch in the southwest quadrant of San Antonio, where Esteban has worked as a ranch hand for more than 10 years. Although the ranch is within the city limits, the environment is rural. Only two other families, also immigrants from northern Mexico, live within easy walking distance. Both Esteban and María were raised in northern Mexico, Esteban on a cattle ranch and María in a small border city. In Mexico, both completed 9 years of schooling. Over the course of several interviews, María, who also completed a secretarial course and later worked as a secretary, evidenced considerable pride in her own proper use of Spanish, as well as concern that her children acquire standard Mexican Spanish, as distinct from the local Texas variety.

Of the families whose language maintenance strategies are represented here, the Gómezes have maintained the closest ties to Mexico. Nearly all of their relatives live in a neighboring Mexican state, and most members of María's large family continue to live in the border city where she grew up. During the period of our study, the family made the short journey to the border approximately twice a month to spend the weekend with family members. The Gómez children also regularly spend parts of their school vacations with their father's family, which owns a small ranch in the state of Coahuila. They thus have ample occasions to use Spanish with their non-English-speaking relatives.

Unlike Mariana and Enrique Villegas or Luisa and Roberto Baez, whom we met in chapter 3, neither Esteban nor María Gómez has sufficient proficiency in English to choose whether to raise their children with Spanish, English, or both languages. Most of Esteban's working days at the ranch are spent performing tasks alone or with other Spanish-dominant workers. María took English classes in the local adult school and has achieved the basic proficiency necessary to obtain a part-time position in a school cafeteria. However, she has never gained sufficient proficiency to be able to engage in sustained English conversation.

Even though they did not have a choice as to which language their children would acquire first, the Gómezes do have a clearly articulated vision of the language proficiencies that they desire for their children and a clearly developed strategy for achieving that goal. After considerable discussion, they decided that their children would have ample opportunity to learn English at school; their role as parents would be to ensure that their sons did not lose Spanish. In our first interview with her, María outlined the family's language decisions:

> *Mi esposo y yo siempre hemos platicado de eso y queremos que aquí en la casa sea el español. Y queremos aprender inglés para cuando salimos. Pero aquí en casa primero- lo primero queremos que los niños aprendan bien el español.*
>
> (My husband and I have talked a great deal about this and we want Spanish to be the language of the home. And we want to learn English for when we go out. But here at home the first- the first thing we want is for the children to learn Spanish well.)

Somewhat later in the same interview, María clarified her idea of the conditions necessary for her children to become proficient bilinguals. She has no doubt that the children will acquire English. Both of the school-age children have been enrolled in all-English classes since the first grade. Her role in helping her sons to become bilingual is to make sure that they keep up with their Spanish. As she put it, "[*Los niños*] *van a ser bilingües porque el español aquí lo van a tener.*" ("They [the boys] are going to be bilingual because they are going to have Spanish here [at home].")

The insistence on the use of Spanish in the Gómez home is applied to children and visitors alike. For example, during a visit by Robert and a research assistant to arrange an observation schedule, the assistant,

whose father works on the ranch with Sr. Gómez, made a comment in
English while Sra. Gómez was in the next room. Sra. Gómez, however,
overheard the comment, and rebuked the assistant, remarking, *"Aquí
hablamos nomás español."* ("Here we speak only Spanish.") The household ban on English does not, however, extend to television. During
weekend observations, one or more of the Gómez children can often be
found watching English-language programs, usually wrestling or some
other sporting event.

María and Esteban's decision, constantly reaffirmed, to insist on
Spanish in family interactions has proved effective for minority-language maintenance. Indeed, although the two older boys are both fluent
in English and the youngest attended a predominantly English-speaking
preschool for 2 years, the Gómez children are among the few in the study
who regularly use Spanish in their conversations with one another.
Moreover, the Gómez brothers' use of Spanish is not restricted to informal activities, but extends to their discussions about school assignments, a theme we explore in some detail in chapter 6. Despite her lack
of proficiency in English, Sra. Gomez is also highly involved with her
children's schooling, monitoring their progress and participating in
many of the boys' school projects. Such interactions occur exclusively
in Spanish, notwithstanding that the boys attend an English-curriculum
school.

The success of Esteban and María's strategy is reinforced by the relative isolation of the ranch, by frequent and sometimes prolonged visits
to Mexico, and by close ties with monolingual Spanish-speaking relatives. In contrast to many of the other children in our study, Ernesto has
retained native-speaker proficiency in Spanish and, in large measure as a
result of his mother's efforts, has learned to read and write in Spanish as
well. Nor has his English suffered as a result. Rather, as indicated by his
superior performance in all-English classes and by his performance in
an extended English interview with one of the English-dominant members of the research team, he has developed native-like proficiency in
English. However, notwithstanding their satisfaction with Ernesto's academic success, María and Esteban's primary concern is that the boys
maintain Spanish, which they view as a prerequisite for maintaining
their own parental authority and for participation in extended and easily
accessible family networks in Mexico.

MAINTAINING SPANISH IN AN URBAN ENVIRONMENT

Speaking Spanish at Home, Learning to Read and Write Spanish at School

Prefiero español. Se me hace mas fácil. (I prefer Spanish. It's easier for me.)
—*Emma Castillo (age 9)*

Emma Castillo is indicating to a project researcher that she prefers to continue in Spanish for the remainder of the interview. Although she claims that she is more fluent in Spanish than in English, we actually find her to be equally proficient, and equally impressive, in both languages. Her teachers concur with our view: Emma is a star student at Miraflores, the bilingual public school where she attends fourth grade.

At home, Emma and her brother Rodrigo, age 8, speak only Spanish, between themselves and with their mother, Berta Castillo. In fact, because the Castillos' secondhand, borrowed television set has remained *"quebrada"* ("broken") for going on 2 years, there is even less English input into this home language environment than into that of the Gómez family.

Berta Castillo, now a single mother, immigrated from the Mexican state of Nayarit to northern California when she was 15. Berta explained her decision to use only Spanish in home interactions with her two school-aged children:

> *Es mas fácil porque yo tengo la amplitud de utilizar todas mis ideas y ponerlas en- en voz, ¿verdad? Y en inglés tengo que limitarme, estoy marginada …. Pero en español puedo decirles cuando juegas, brincas, y esto, tú no puedes aprender bien como debes …, no puedes enfocar.*
>
> (It's easier because I can use all my ideas and put them in- and verbalize them, right? And in English I have to limit myself, I'm marginalized …. But in Spanish I can tell them when you play, jump, and so on, you don't learn well like you should …, you can't focus.)

However, for Berta Castillo, as for most caregivers who choose to pursue an aggressive Spanish maintenance strategy, related decisions involve an important ideological component. Indeed Berta, whose children have subsisted on welfare checks, associates mastery of both English and Spanish with *"una mejor vida"* ("a better life") that she is determined her children will enjoy. Conversely, she associates loss of Spanish with the low social status and poverty that they have been forced to endure. The association of mother-tongue loss with impoverishment emerges clearly in Berta's account of the vision that led to her conversion, as it were, to a stance that seeks to maximize her children's exposure to and use of Spanish:

> *Anteriormente yo les hablaba en inglés y me respondían en inglés, y en una ocasión ... miré un programa en la televisión ... un jovencito Mexicano, que trató de hablar en español y lo habló TAN mal, ¿verdad? ... Entonces me- me- hice en mi imaginación que eso sería el reflejo que- que- van tomando mis hijos en el futuro ¿verdad? ... entonces sentí una gran necesidad de que tenían que ser bilingües. Y allí comenzamos a hablar español todos los días y prohibirles completamente el idioma inglés en mi casa.*

> (Before I used to speak to them in English and they answered me in English, and one time ... I saw a television program ... a Mexican youth, who tried to speak Spanish and who spoke it SO badly, right? ... Then I conjured up in my imagination an image of my children in the future, right? ... then I felt a real need that they had to be bilingual. From then on we began to speak Spanish every day and to ban English completely from the house.)

Berta Castillo's awakening occurred well in time for her to identify a local public school that offered a "primary language" program, where Spanish–English bilingual teachers provided instruction simultaneously in both languages, for Emma, her older child, to attend. As Emma described the program, *"Allí se mezclan- mezclan el idioma en inglés y español* so *todos pueden entender y pueden escribir en el idioma que quieren."* ("There they mix- mix the language in English and Spanish so everyone can understand and can write in the language that they want.")

Although Berta Castillo did not have the opportunity to continue her studies beyond sixth grade, she can read and write in Spanish (although she is not confident about her writing ability). Thus, to a limited degree she is able to assist Emma and Rodrigo with their Spanish homework. However, her daughter reports few occasions of such assistance being provided to her personally— *"unas veces cuando no tiene que ayudarle a Rodrigo"* ("a couple of times when she didn't have to help Rodrigo"). Indeed, during much of her interview Berta expands on Rodrigo's history of learning difficulties and the different remedial strategies that she and school personnel have tried to improve his academic performance. By the same token, Berta considers herself fortunate that Emma is an independent and motivated learner who requires little in the way of educational scaffolding from either her mother or her teachers.

Notwithstanding Emma's stellar profile as a student, Sra. Castillo both acknowledges and appreciates the support she receives from Miraflores personnel in promoting Emma's use of Spanish and hence in fostering her daughter's mother tongue maintenance. She is aware that the time she has for her daughter is limited, given the resources she feels she must invest in tutoring her son and in struggling with her own emotional issues. Although Berta's ex-husband, a Spanish monolingual, lives not far away, rancorous relations between the estranged couple have resulted in minimal communication with the children's father. Nor do Emma and Rodrigo have access to extended family members with whom they can speak in Spanish: *"Tenemos familia pero con esas familias no estamos en comunicación."* ("We have family but we have no contact with them.") Moreover, notwithstanding that there are other Latinos living near by, there is no opportunity for Emma to converse in Spanish with them. In fact, the Castillos have not made the acquaintance of any of their "neighbors" (nor do they use either English or Spanish equivalents of *neighborhood* in referring to the location where they live). This unincorporated slice of East Bay City, sandwiched between a row of dilapidated warehouses and the railroad track, is home for a disproportionate number of transients and, given the area's reputation for unsavory goings-on, the children are not permitted to walk home alone from school or to play outdoors in front of the house. According to Berta, inviting Emma's several Spanish-speaking school friends over to the house is also out of the question: *"Mí condición no está cómoda para invitar niños, ¿verdad?"* ("My circumstances aren't convenient for inviting children, right?")

Yet among the California cohort Emma is without equal in her oral Spanish proficiency and in her mastery of Spanish literacy. At school, she converses in Spanish with her friends, even during recreation and lunch. At home after school, when her homework is completed, she is found reading Spanish books she gets from the library or in the thick of creative projects—collages, letters to pen pals, coordinating the music for skits she has written for her *"muñecas"* ("dolls") to perform—involving original Spanish texts which she has composed. Although Berta Castillo does not consider Miraflores to be responsible for Emma's giftedness, at the same time she accords school personnel full credit for her daughter's advanced bilingual development. She considers parent and school to be partners in the dual mission of fostering *mexicano* children's pride in their cultural heritage and promoting their mother tongue maintenance, and she is grateful that, for their part, school personnel have lived up to their side of the bargain.

Promoting Spanish Maintenance

Interviewer:	*Ahora te voy hacer una pregunta ... tú hablas español y ¿por qué cuando yo te pregunto en español me contestas en inglés?* (Now I'm going to ask a question ... you speak Spanish and why is it that when I ask you a question in Spanish you answer me in English?)
Gabriela:	[laughing] Hmm *porque* (because) hmm sometimes I don't know the, some of the words in Spanish.

The unidirectional character of code switching by Gabriela Valdez (age 11) of San Antonio provides a lens on the nature of her bilingualism. As the foregoing excerpt shows, Gabriela often resorts to English when circumstances would seem to call for Spanish. However, when she is addressed in English, she always responds in English, without any switching to Spanish. Although, as we show, she can manage a variety of interactions primarily in Spanish, and certainly has no trouble understanding questions or comments addressed to her, Gabriela clearly prefers English.

Gabriela lives on the overwhelmingly Latino west side of San Antonio, the city's historic *barrio,* with her grandparents, Socorro and Pedro Valdez, both in their sixties, who have undertaken the responsibility of raising their granddaughter. Sr. and Sra. Valdez, who both claim Spanish as their first language, were born in rural south Texas to parents who had immigrated to the United States as young adults. Married as teenagers, they spent the early years of their marriage following the crops, moving from Texas to Florida and as far north as New Jersey. Gabriela's mother and father followed a similar path, and the family decided that the child would have a more stable environment and better opportunities for education if she were raised by her grandparents, who had been settled in San Antonio for several decades when we first met them. Except for a period of a few months, Gabriela has lived her entire life with her maternal grandparents, who formally adopted her when she was 9.

The Valdezes live in a modest bungalow. Throughout the neighborhood, both Spanish and English, often mixed, can be heard on the streets and in the local markets, and billboards and other advertising signs are common in both languages. Several of the most popular radio stations in the area broadcast in Spanish and English, with frequent code switching, even within the same sentence (Bayley & Zapata, 1993). Many members of the Valdezes' large extended family, consisting of 9 children and spouses, 27 grandchildren, and 9 great-grandchildren, live nearby. At the time of our study, Sr. Valdez was working as a security guard, a position he had held for several years.

According to Sra. Valdez, although all of her children were born in the United States, all are bilingual. Gabriela's grandmother made the decision to maintain Spanish because she was appalled by the number of young people, especially girls in her view, who could not speak Spanish, although their surnames clearly indicated their Latino heritage:

> ... a mis hijas no les va a pasar eso. También tienen que enseñarse y así eso fue con mis hijos ... y es lo que estoy haciendo con Gabriela también.

> (... that is not going to happen to my daughters. They also have to teach themselves and that is what happened with my children ... that is what I am doing with Gabriela too.)

Maintaining Spanish is important to Sra. Valdez, not only for communication within the community and extended family, but also for its symbolic value. Even though she herself has never been a Mexican national, Sra. Valdez evidences great pride in her cultural heritage, which she believes can best be represented in Spanish. This concern with traditional culture led Sra. Valdez to teach eight of her nine children at least basic literacy skills in Spanish, so that they could learn more about Mexican history from books. The youngest, age 25, learned to read and write in Spanish by attending a bilingual program. Moreover, although she herself did not have the opportunity to complete high school, her experience teaching her children to read in Spanish was not Sra. Valdez's first experience as a teacher. Early in her marriage, she taught her young husband to read and write in Spanish and later assisted him to acquire English as well. She commented, *"y a pesar de que no fue a la escuela lo aprendió porque yo misma le enseñaba como escribir"* ("and since he didn't go to school he learned because I taught him how to write").

When it came time for her to raise her granddaughter, Sra. Valdez insisted that Gabriela acquire Spanish and become literate in the language as well. However, she has found the task of intergenerational transmission of Spanish more difficult with her granddaughter than it was with her own children. Despite the difficulties, however, she is determined to persevere:

> ... *pero no vamos a olvidarnos el español. Y todos mis hijos—to's saben tanto escribir como leer el español. Con Gabriela estoy llevando el mismo sistema pero como ahora ya casi todos los niños en la escuela ya no te hablan español—ya no te hablan español y ya viene ella y estaba hablando en inglés y todo eso y yo le contesto en español.*

> (... but we're not going to forget Spanish. And all my children—they all know how to write as well as to read Spanish. With Gabriela, I'm carrying on the same system, but because now almost all the children in school don't speak to you to Spanish—they don't speak to you in Spanish and she comes [home] and she's talking in English and everything and I answer in Spanish ...)

Sra. Valdez's "system" was reinforced early in Gabriela's school career by 2 years in a transitional bilingual program, where she acquired basic Spanish literacy. However, as indicated during our first interview with her, conducted by a Spanish-dominant member of the research team, Gabriela is more comfortable using at least some English than only Spanish, even in a case where English is clearly the interviewer's weaker language.[1] Nearly all of the questions were asked in Spanish and Gabriela answered all appropriately. When she responded entirely in Spanish, however, the responses were generally very brief, as in the following exchange about her daily use of the two languages:

Interviewer:	*¿Cuándo y dónde hablas español?*
Gabriela:	*En la casa y poquito en la escuela.*
Interviewer:	*¿Y cuándo y dónde hablas inglés?*
Gabriela:	*En la escuela y en la casa.*
Interviewer:	*¿Y cuándo ... no estás en la escuela ni en la casa sino vas a lugares qué idioma hablas?*
Gabriela:	*Inglés y español.*
(Interviewer:	When and where do you speak Spanish?
Gabriela:	At home and a little bit in school.
Interviewer:	And when and where do you speak English?
Gabriela:	In school and at home.
Interviewer:	And when you're ... not in school or in the house but you go places, what language do you speak?
Gabriela:	English and Spanish.)

As we saw in the opening excerpt, when more than a brief response is required, Gabriela often shifts to English, even where her own comment suggests that Spanish would be the more appropriate language for a response:

Interviewer:	*¿Cómo sabes cuándo usar español y cómo sabes cuándo usar inglés? ¿O sea cómo sabes pues ahora tengo que hablar español?* (How do you

---

[1]At the San Antonio site, children were first interviewed by Spanish-dominant members of the research group. We wished to obtain as much Spanish as we could from each child, and we reasoned that children would be more likely to accommodate to the linguistic preferences of an adult Latina than they would to one of the non-Latino members of the research team. Although, as shown in some of the examples from Gabriela's interview included in this chapter, the procedure did not always result in the elicitation of extensive stretches of Spanish without English, we suspect that it did elicit more Spanish than would otherwise have been the case.

know when to use Spanish and how do you know
when to use English? Or let's say how do you
know ah well now I have to speak Spanish?)

Gabriela: I know when to talk Spanish when somebody else is
talking Spanish to me and I know how to talk English when somebody else is talking English to me.

Like many of the participants in our study, Sra. Valdez is an enthusias-
tic viewer of *telenovelas,* the soap operas that enjoy great popularity
throughout Latin America. Her granddaughter joins her in her daily
viewing of *Marimar,* one of her favorites and the only Spanish-language
television program that Gabriela regularly watches. She and her grandmother often talk about the details of specific episodes and speculate
about the actions and fates of the leading characters. Despite this interest
in the show and its characters, however, when Gabriela recounted the
most recent episode to the interviewer, she switched to English before
concluding her account:

Interviewer: *¿Qué programas te gustan ver en el cuarenta y
uno* [the most popular of the local Spanish-language television stations]?

Gabriela: *Marimar.*

Interviewer: *¿Nada más Marimar o hay otros programas?*

Gabriela: *Nada más Marimar.*

Interviewer: *Cuéntame de Marimar. Oye, ¿viste el último
capítulo?/sí/cuéntamelo porque yo no lo vi.*

Gabriela: [laughs]

Interviewer: *¿Que pasó con el famoso Chuy y el ingeniero que
se iba a casar con ella? Cuéntame el último
porque no lo vi el anterior. ¿Que pasó con Chuy-
le quitó el dinero?*

Gabriela: *No le a- puso en un banco porque el creía que ah
Marimar iba a perder todo su dinero y luego ... y
luego Antonieta no a- Inocencia* she got the tumor
out or whatever ...

Interviewer:	*¿La operaron?*
Gabriela:	... and then she stayed bald ...
(Interviewer:	What programs do you like to watch on channel 41 [the most popular of the local Spanish-language television stations]?
Gabriela:	Marimar.
Interviewer:	Only Marimar or are there other programs?
Gabriela:	Only Marimar.
Interviewer:	Tell me about Marimar. Listen, did you see the last episode?
Gabriela:	Yes.
Interviewer:	Tell me about it because I didn't see it.
Gabriela:	[laughs]
Interviewer:	What happened with the famous Chuy and the engineer who was going to marry her? Tell me the latest episode because I didn't see the last one. What happened with Chuy- did he get rid of the money?
Gabriela:	No ah he put it in a bank because he believed ah that Marimar was going to lose all his money and then ... and then Antonieta no ah Inocenica she got the tumor out or whatever ...
Interviewer:	They operated?
Gabriela:	... and then she stayed bald ...)

As this excerpt illustrates, Gabriela has no difficulty in understanding Spanish utterances addressed to her, and she takes obvious pleasure in at least one regular Spanish-language television series. Moreover, the fact that she code switches from Spanish to English is not surprising. She lives in an area, the west side of San Antonio, where, as we noted, code switching is a prominent feature of everyday discourse among a large segment of the population, and where alternation between Spanish and English characterizes local media as well. Even her grandmother used

English discourse markers in responses concerning the importance of Spanish maintenance.

In sum, Gabriela thinks of herself as bilingual and she articulates clearly the advantages that she has been taught that bilingualism conferred. For the most part, however, she describes these advantages in English. In addition, with the exception of some major gaps,[2] Gabriela has acquired basic Spanish morphology and syntax. Thanks to her grandmother's efforts and her brief introduction to Spanish literacy in first grade and to a much lesser extent in second grade, she is able to read at a rudimentary level in Spanish. Like the other children of United States-born mothers in our study, and like many of the children of Mexican-born mothers as well, Gabriela's receptive abilities in Spanish surpass her productive abilities. Finally, English has come to occupy an increasingly important role in her life. As early as second grade, English became the dominant language of her bilingual program, and by third grade she was transitioned to an all-English program. Her interactions with peers are conducted entirely in English. In fact, even many of her conversations with her grandparents are asymmetrical with respect to language use. Although both grandparents always address her in Spanish, more often than not Gabriela responds in English.

A Weekly Attempt at Language Revival

Mother:	What's today if it's Tuesday Alicia?
Alicia:	M:mh [for I don't know].
Mother:	You don't know?
Marta:	Why what is it?
Mother:	No don't don't tell her if she don't know then she don't participate and she won't get all the extras. What's today?
Alicia:	Spanish day.

---

[2]Somewhat later in the same interaction with which we opened this section, Gabriela's response to a question in Spanish showed that grammatical form is sometimes a problem. She regularized the very common irregular verb *saber* ("know") and said *"a veces no sabo las palabras"* ("sometimes I don't understand the words") instead of *"no sé las palabras."*

Mother:	Why? Why is today Spanish day?
Marta:	I don't know. 'Cause we have it every Tuesda:y.
Mother:	OK, that's why 'cause it's Tuesday.

Elena Torres is seated at the kitchen table with her two younger daughters, Marta (age 11) and Alicia (age 10), shortly after the girls have returned from school to their small, detached home on San Antonio's predominantly Latino south side. Her oldest daughter, Liliana (age 12), is due home shortly. Elena, who works in the cafeteria at a nearby school, has arranged her work schedule so that she can be home when the girls arrive. She believes that it is particularly important that she be home on Tuesdays because that is the one day of the week that she has selected to try to work with the girls to prevent a drift to English monolingualism. However, often, after the failure of repeated attempts in Spanish to elicit a response from her youngest daughter, she feels the need to resort to some not so subtle coercion in English.

Elena Torres and her husband José, who works at an aircraft maintenance facility, acquired Spanish at home from their parents, who immigrated from northern Mexico as young adults, and both continue to use Spanish with their mothers. Although both are literate in English, neither learned to read or write in Spanish. José and Elena speak both Spanish and English with each other. As is the case with many Texas-born Latinos, their speech with each other and with other bilinguals is characterized by frequent code switching. Outside of the home, they accommodate to the language preferences of their interlocutors or to the demands of the situation.

In their daughters' formative years, José and Elena spoke only English in the home to ease their daughters' transition to formal schooling. Elena commented, *"Yo quería enseñarles en inglés porque no les sería difícil cuando ellas fueron a la escuela que aprender en inglés."* ("I wanted to teach them in English so that it wouldn't be difficult for them when they went to school to learn in English.") Education has always played an important role in the Torreses' aspirations for their daughters' futures—both parents are determined that their girls will go to college—and at the time José especially was concerned that if the girls spoke Spanish at home, they would not succeed in school. In recent years, however, José and Elena have become increasingly concerned about the lack of Spanish proficiency of their three children, noting a direct link between a trend of mother-tongue attrition and loss of cultural identity. "I think we're losing it already," explains Elena. "I think it [loss of culture] is already in process and I think that my mother's generation knew lots of Spanish- her kids did not get to learn how- or I did not get to learn to read and write it and I think that's a shame. Because now I can't teach my children that." She continues in Spanish: *"A crecer siendo mexicanas y no saber español- no está bien eso ... Yo cuando miro una mexicana pues yo pienso que ella sabe español. Y muchas no saben."* ("To grow up being Mexican and not know Spanish- that's not good ... When I see a Mexican well I think that she speaks Spanish. But many don't know it.") Their concern, shared by many Tejano parents, arises from not only cultural considerations, but from instrumental ones as well. According to Mrs. Torres, *"En el trabajo vas a necesitar que saben español y si estas niñas no saben español van a tener un problema."* ("At work you're going to have to know Spanish and if these girls don't know Spanish they're going to have a problem.")

To avert the loss of Spanish by their daughters, the Torreses have adopted two main strategies. Mrs. Torres's mother provides weekly Spanish "lessons," which primarily involve the retelling of familiar Mexican stories and pointing out the names of various objects in the house, as well as commentaries on the *telenovelas* the grandmother is so fond of. And in the home, José and Elena attempt to have their daughters speak Spanish one day a week, a practice they have maintained for a year prior to our home observations.

The language revival strategy involving Mrs. Torres's mother is non-problematic. These interactions feel natural for the girls, particularly Marta. Her grandmother speaks Spanish with all her *nietos* (grandchildren) and has done so since they were little, notwithstanding the intervening generation's initial reservations about the use of the heritage language. Marta is fond of her *abuela* and does not, in fact, characterize her visits with her, which sometimes involve sleepovers, as "lessons." Asked what she does when she's over at her grandma's, the child responds, *"Hablamos ... about escuela, y la past."* ("We talk ... about school, and the past.")

With regard to the Torreses' strategy of speaking Spanish one day a week in the household, their goal has been at least partially fulfilled: Unlike

Alicia in the excerpt with which we opened this narrative, Marta did attempt to use Spanish when we recorded the family interactions on several "Spanish days," as illustrated in the following exchange with her mother:

Marta:	Mom, *ya hicimos* vacuum. (Mom, we finished vacuuming.)
Mother:	*Está bien, prontito. ¿Ya barrites cuarto?* (Good, now quickly. Have you swept your room?)
Marta:	*Sí.* (Yes.)
Mother:	*¿Y todo lo barrites?* (And you swept it all?)
Marta:	*Sí, bien ...* (Yes, [I swept it] well ...) *Yo tieno* [regularized 1 sg. present form], *no yo tienes* [2nd sg. present form]. I don't know how you say "have." Mom, how do you say "have"?
Mother:	Half? What? *Medio.*
Marta:	"Have," like "you have to close the door."
Mother:	*"Tienes que."*
Marta:	OK, what about "I have homework"?
Mother:	*"Tengo tarea."*
Marta:	*Tengo carea* [sic].

From this example, we see that Marta's receptive ability outpaces her productive capacity, and that her Spanish exhibits early interlanguage features (e.g., highly unstable verbal morphology as in *yo tieno/yo tienes*). Yet despite her rudimentary command of oral Spanish, Marta's Spanish has surpassed her mother's in one respect. Unlike her mother, Marta has acquired minimal Spanish literacy and sometimes is called on to read Spanish-language leaflets and shopping coupons. Elena Torres commented on her daughter's ability: "A lot of times I get the [shopping] coupons in Spanish and it's like, *'OK Marta, ven a decirme qué dice aquí.'*" ("OK Marta, come and tell me what it says here.")

This encouraging sign notwithstanding, José and Elena's effort to reverse the process of intergenerational language attrition has proved difficult. Although she loves to read, and is an avid consumer of children's literature in English, Marta will not read in Spanish other than for the purely pragmatic purpose of helping out her mother. And getting her to speak Spanish, even on Spanish days, is sometimes trying, as illustrated in our initial excerpt of a conversation among Marta, her mother, and Marta's younger sister.

Marta's parents both appear solidly committed to the goal of Spanish-language revival, yet the degree of conscious effort involved in reversing the household "habit," as Elena describes it, of speaking English is depleting for them. In Elena's words, "It is draining for me that I have to repeat or that I have to make myself clear in what I said because they are so used to me speaking to them in English." What the Torreses find most disheartening, however, is that the burden for Spanish-language input rests almost exclusively on their (and, of course, Elena's mother's) shoulders. Like Enrique and Mariana Villegas (chap. 3), José and Elena have found the selection on the local Spanish-language television and radio channels to be wanting—in fact, they claim there is no children's programming on Spanish TV—and outside of the occasional Spanish-language movie, the family chooses to bypass these resources. Marta is aware of the Spanish-language television channel, *"porque yo* play with the remote"; however, she is not tempted by it *"porque hablan muy* fast ... *y poquito entiendo."* ("because they speak very fast ... and I don't understand much.") Marta does have Latina friends who speak some Spanish, but as in the case of Diana Villegas and her friends who attend school together in English, the girls are more comfortable communicating in English. On the other hand, the family does attend an evangelical church with Spanish-language services, and their involvement in this church congregation has been a source of strength and renewal. But support from the children's schools, which the Torreses view as key to effective language maintenance, is noteworthy for its absence.[3] Once again, Elena:

---

[3]Several Texas-born parents discussed their attempts to enroll their children in bilingual programs. The children, who were all proficient in English, were denied admission on the grounds that the bilingual programs were intended solely to provide assistance for limited-English-proficient students, rather than to assist children with some Spanish to develop their abilities in the minority language. In the late 1990s, however, the situation began to change. Partially as a result of the growing recognition that the city's prosperity is linked to ties with Mexico and other parts of Latin America, and partially as a result of the increasing demand by local businesses for bilingual employees, a number of schools started two-way bilingual programs and one school in an affluent neighborhood began a Spanish immersion program for its predominantly Euro-American student body. Students in the two-way programs are normally evenly divided between English-dominant and Spanish-dominant students. The goal of such programs is to produce graduates who are literate in both the minority and the majority language.

I would think that a class, even just 30 minutes a day, where they can go in and speak only Spanish and the correct Spanish. And learn spelling and writing it and reading it. I think that would be a great impact on the children. I think as long as it's consistent that it would be wonderful.

MAINTAINING SPANISH IN SUBURBIA

Thus far, the families we have described live in areas where Spanish is widely spoken, either by the two other families who live and work on the same ranch as the Gómez family, or in San Antonio's west and south sides, or in the Castillos' mixed northern California neighborhood. In cases such as these the efforts of parents and other primary caretakers to maintain Spanish are reinforced at least to some extent by others in the environment. In the case of Gabriela Valdez, for example, many of her relatives of her mother's generation address the child in Spanish, although her cousins of her own age, like other United States-born children in the area, tend to interact in English. In addition, Spanish can be heard regularly in neighborhood stores and Spanish-language advertising is prominently displayed in shop windows and nearby billboards. However, when we move from the relative isolation of a south Texas ranch or the overwhelmingly Mexicano west side of San Antonio to more affluent middle- and upper-middle-class neighborhoods, whether in Texas or California, the factors outside the home that favor minority-language maintenance become correspondingly fewer, even though the financial and educational resources of the families are considerably greater. In the absence of external support, either from the schools or from nearby relatives, neighbors, and community, the role of the home becomes correspondingly more important.

In this section, we look at the language maintenance strategies of two families who live in English-dominant suburbs, the Trujillos in northwest San Antonio[4] and the Pollack–Pearson family in an affluent northern California neighborhood.

---

[4]Unlike many cities in the United States, San Antonio has relatively few independent suburbs. Rather, the city tends to annex unincorporated areas as they are developed.

Combining Home Interaction and School Spanish as a Second Language

Aunt:	*Ana le dices por favor a Cristina que no carguen a Freddy porque está muy pesado y se pueden lastimar.* (Ana, tell them they shouldn't carry Freddy because he is very heavy and they can do something they will regret.)
Ana:	*Bueno. Oye Cristina.* (Good. Listen, Cristina.) OK you guys Tía Rosa said not to carry Freddy because he's too heavy and if y'all drop him he'll hit his head and he'll hurt himself.

On a hot midsummer Texas afternoon, 9-year-old Ana Trujillo is attending a binational gathering hosted by her parents for relatives from Monterrey, Mexico, and from San Antonio and other Texas cities. The heavy beat of the Tejano group Culturas resounds from the backyard speaker system. The adults at the gathering all speak Spanish, and those from Texas speak English as well. The majority of the Texas children, however, particularly those whose mothers were also born in the United States, speak little or no Spanish. Ana is therefore delegated to translate her monolingual Tía Rosa's concerns about 2-year-old cousin Freddy.

Ana and her 7-year-old sister Sandra live with their parents Angel and Anita Trujillo in a middle-class neighborhood on San Antonio's predominantly Euro-American, but increasingly mixed, northwest side. The Trujillos' modern development home, which dates from the late 1980s, is typical of the neighborhood with its well-trimmed lawn, two-car garage, basketball net, and minivan parked in the front driveway, which is sometimes cluttered with children's bicycles and miscellaneous sports equipment. This section of the city typically has well-funded schools and offers a safe environment where children play in their own yards or with friends in the neighborhood. Local schools and churches offer a range of recreational activities, chiefly but not exclusively organized sports, for children of various ages.

Anita Trujillo was born in San Antonio, as were her own parents, and has lived her entire life in the city except for a brief period after she finished high school when she attended school in Dallas. Angel was born and raised in Monterrey, where he attended the public university for 3 years. The Trujillos met and were married in San Antonio, where both of their children were born. Both Mr. and Mrs. Trujillo work in the airline industry, and their jobs allow them considerable flexibility in scheduling. Mrs. Trujillo has time in her day to drop off and collect her children at St. Martin's, the local Catholic school, and participates regularly in school events as a homeroom mother or volunteer chaperone on school trips. Mr. Trujillo is often home early enough to coach his younger daughter in soccer or to watch his older daughter in a basketball or volleyball game or practice.

Although the Trujillos live in an overwhelmingly English-speaking area of the city, Spanish plays an important role in their household, particularly when Angel is present. At least one television was usually on whenever we visited. Mr. Trujillo, although he speaks English with ease (a requirement of his job), prefers Spanish. When he is home, the television is usually tuned to a Spanish station, often a news program. Ana also evidences interest in Spanish media. Like many young Latinas, she was devoted to the music of the Tejana star Selena, who was murdered several months before we met the family. The local Spanish stations devoted a number of specials to the late singer, all of which Ana watched avidly. Ana owns a copy of every CD that Selena recorded, and, after school, she often occupies herself by playing her CDs and singing along with the Spanish lyrics while looking through books, magazines, or posters of the Tejana star, whom she decided to portray in costume at her school's Halloween party.

In addition to its presence in the media that household members watch or listen to, Spanish is also a factor in day-to-day interactions, both between household members and with others. Many of Anita and Angel's conversations with each other are conducted entirely or mainly in Spanish. Spanish is also the language of the household during visits by Angel's parents, who recently moved from Monterrey to San Antonio, or during the relatively frequent visits by other relatives from Mexico. In addition, both Anita and Angel often use Spanish when talking on the phone to friends or relatives.

The important role of Spanish in the home, combined with the presence of monolingual Spanish-speaking relatives nearby, influenced the Trujillos' choice of a Spanish maintenance strategy. The Trujillos delayed introducing English until they became concerned that Ana might have difficulty adjusting to school and enrolled the child in an English-medium preschool program:

> Oh people compliment me left and right you know- first of all how did I get her to do it? I tell them she didn't really have a choice in the matter. We started it before she could- she was opinionated so uhm she just loved Spanish- and I think that the trick was when she learned Spanish before she learned English. So when we got her- when we enrolled her in that preschool we enrolled her with the intentions of getting her into an English-speaking environment because then we had a live-in maid who was Spanish-speaking, my husband's Spanish-speaking, my in-laws don't speak any English, so she was just in an atmosphere where Spanish was her primary language.

The Trujillos, like María Gómez, are concerned not only that Ana be able to communicate in Spanish, but that she speak the standard language. Indeed, Anita speaks with considerable pride about a compliment she received from one of Ana's teachers about the child's use of standard Spanish, which lacks most of the features commonly associated with Texas Spanish:

> Pues a- todos nos han dicho la ventaja que las niñas son bilingües y que lo hablan bien y correcto. No de TexMex ... Este maestro nuevo señor Baroja que entró y habló con Ana y se quedó tan sorprendido que me mandó una carta y el siguiente día hablé con él. Que no podía creer que una niña que ... una criatura tan chiquita hablaba tan bien. Que no es de México ... Pero siendo de San Antonio no lo- es que casi no se ve.

> (Well everyone tells us that it's an advantage that these girls are bilingual and that they speak well and correctly. Not TexMex ... This new teacher Sr. Baroja who came and spoke with Ana and was so surprised that he sent me a letter and the next day I spoke with him. He couldn't believe that such a young child spoke so well. A child who isn't from Mexico ... But being from San Antonio it isn't- it's almost unheard of.)

Mrs. Trujillo's concern for standard Spanish, however, does not include using the resources of the home to develop her children's literacy in the minority language. Given the area of the city in which they live and the educational aspirations they have for their children, the Trujillos are

concerned above all to help the children develop literacy skills in English, and they read to them only in the dominant language. Indeed, Anita
commented, with frequent code switching, on the decision to focus only
on English literacy:

> *Siempre siempre ... en inglés desde chiquitas pero sí saben las
> canciones ... en español. De los patitos* and stuff like that. They learned
> when they were little./aha/*Pero* we never read to them in Spanish.
>
> (Always, always ... in English since they were little, but yes they know
> songs ... in Spanish. About the little ducks and stuff like that.)

Anita's comment was echoed by her daughter Ana when we asked the
child to retell a wordless picture book in Spanish. Ana became rather
nervous at the prospect of being asked to read a Spanish book and
strongly advised us, "I can't read in Spanish." Moreover, although she
was accustomed to being recorded as she went about her activities, and
although she was assured that the book contained only pictures, on this
occasion Ana asked that we stop the tape so that she could prepare. She
rehearsed her narrative for 5 minutes before she determined that she was
ready to be recorded.

Despite her inability to read in Spanish, Ana has maintained a high
level of oral proficiency. And although she has not learned to read Spanish at home, the Spanish class that she attends as part of her regular
school program was scheduled to begin literacy instruction later in the
year. Her oral proficiency is evidenced not only by the comments of her
teacher, Mr. Baroja, and by her often demonstrated ability to sing along
with popular Tejano songs, but also by the ease of her interactions in
Spanish with her father and at family gatherings, where, as we have
seen, she sometimes acts as a translator between older family members
and several of her English-monolingual cousins.

In the broader perspective of the family's overall aspirations for their
children's future, the Trujillos view their maintenance strategy as successful, but it represents only one of many goals the parents have for
their older daughter. Ana is an avid participant in sports, a pursuit both
parents, but especially her father, encourage. With respect to schooling,
the Trujillos are concerned that their daughters receive an education that
challenges their abilities. In June, before we started working with them,
they took their children out of the local public schools and enrolled them

in Catholic school. Mrs. Trujillo voiced both parents' concern that Ana, in particular, was getting straight A's without ever seeming to study. Although the child has been experiencing some difficulty in her new school, both parents believe that having to work to earn the good grades to which she had become accustomed will serve her better in the long run. Finally, as concerns language maintenance, both parents emphasize the possible economic advantages that they expect knowledge of standard Spanish to provide for their daughters in the future. Although it is clear that both Angel and Anita value the fact that their children—especially the older daughter—can communicate effectively with Spanish-speaking relatives, their main interest in language maintenance reflects their concern for their daughters' educational and economic futures. Concerns with the possible economic benefits of standard Spanish have also influenced the Trujillos' choices about how and when Ana should learn to read and write in Spanish. They reason that she could learn best to master the written form of the standard language at school rather than in the more informal atmosphere of the home.

Maintaining Spanish Without Native-Speaking Adults

Interviewer:	*Bueno OK y ... ¿entonces hablas español con Tommy y con quien más?*
Alfredo:	*Y con mi mamá, como no siempre pero como um cuando acordemos de algo de como en México/ um hum/como cuando mi mama dijo ... vamos a ir a México en- en dos semanas/ah hmm/y- y siempre es- y como yo no sé, cuando ella dice eso um lo dice en español y- y así hablamos un poquito de español.*
(Interviewer:	Good OK and ... then you speak Spanish with Tommy and with who else?
Alfredo:	And with my mom, not always but like um when we remember something about how in Mexico/um hmm/like when my mom said ... we're going to go to Mexico in- in two weeks and- and it's always- and like I don't know, when she says this

um she says it in Spanish and- and so we speak a
little in Spanish.)

Alfredo Villafuerte, age 12, of northern California is describing the
occasions for Spanish-language use in his English-dominant home. The
Pollack–Pearson family presents the most unusual case of minority-language maintenance in our study—maintaining the language of a former
spouse in the overwhelmingly English-speaking environment of the affluent section of a northern California university town. Despite the obvious challenges involved in such a venture, Alfredo exhibits a generally
high level of both oral and written Spanish, as well as a very positive attitude toward the language combined with pride in his Mexican heritage.

The commitment of Louise Pollack, Alfredo's mother, to her son's
Spanish maintenance has precipitated a substantive reorganization of
her parenting practices. Although Louise is a fluent bilingual, her
mother tongue is English. With the dissolution of her marriage to
Alfredo's biological father, a Mexican national, and her remarriage to a
Minnesota-bred Euro-American, speaking English seemed the most
practical strategy for communication in the home. Notwithstanding the
reconstitution of her household, which by 1994 comprised Alfredo,
Louise's current partner Jeffrey, and the couple's 3-year-old son
Tommy, mother and firstborn Alfredo remain committed to the goal of
Spanish maintenance, a goal they link to a kinship they both feel with
Alfredo's Mexican "roots." Jeffrey has proved supportive of the goals of
language maintenance, and when Alfredo was ready to begin his formal
education, the family sought out a local public school that would provide instruction in Spanish during at least part of the school day. "I
looked for bilingual schools for him and bilingual programs," Louise related, "and we both visited the bilingual program at Oak View School
twice, and we weren't impressed. We didn't think it was very good, and I
continued looking into it, at the one in Hamilton and the one at Twin
Pines." Although Alfredo's mother and stepfather noted Mexican
themes, such as *ballet folklórico,* addressed in the classes they observed,
they were dissatisfied with the quality of language instruction provided.
"I believe in bilingual programs, but it seems to me that they're not
working well, " Louise explains. Her comments about the language
proficiencies of the bilingual teachers, most of whom were United

States-born Latinos, reveal highly normative attitudes that are reminiscent of the comments of Mariana and Enrique Villegas early in their U.S. sojourn: "They're [the teachers] not very good in their language [Spanish] ... and they're not very good in English."

So Alfredo was enrolled in a regular English program, while his mother and stepdad undertook a deliberate strategy of using Spanish at home. Although such interactions felt somewhat unnatural in the case of the Euro-American Jeffrey, the awkwardness was minimized by the well-timed arrival of two young adult Mexican cousins in Alfredo's early elementary school years. The pair, who had come to attend adult night school in California, were Spanish monolinguals, a condition that ensured both Alfredo's and his mother's predominant use of Spanish. At the same time Jeffrey, who was finding knowledge of Spanish increasingly useful in his medical practice, registered for classes in Spanish as a second language so that he could better accommodate, or at least not inhibit, the flow of family conversation. The cousins have since returned to Mexico; however, the frequent use of Spanish in home interactions has continued, reinforced by Alfredo's frequent trips to Mexico to visit his extended paternal family. Indeed, as we have seen, planning for such visits and other conversations concerning Mexico provide occasions for renewing the use of Spanish at home.

MAINTAINING A MINORITY LANGUAGE
IN A MAJORITY CULTURE

The strategies for Spanish maintenance that families have adopted differ in their motivations as well as in the responsibilities ascribed to schools and homes. Despite the differences, however, several commonalities emerge that unite the six highly disparate families profiled here. First, in all of the families that feel that they have achieved any degree of success in fostering proficiency in the minority language, Spanish is used frequently, or even exclusively, in parent–child interactions. The cases reported here add to the growing body of literature that indicates that successful intergenerational transmission of a minority language requires extensive use in the home (Bayley et al., 1996; Crago et al., 1993; Fishman, 1991; Hakuta & Pease-Alvarez, 1994). Although schools can provide support for such efforts, our observations over an extended period confirm that the home remains the critical arena for minority-language use.

A second conclusion emerging from our research is that participants' ideas about language maintenance have been developed in response to the role that Spanish and English play in their social and familial networks and in the different communities where they live. In this chapter and the preceding one, we have described in some detail and (as much as is possible through written text) using the voices of participants the roles of Spanish and English in family members' social worlds—both the worlds they inhabit and those they aspire to. Here, however, we would underscore that as concerns geographic space, we found the nature of the local community as important for minority-language maintenance as the particular state—California or Texas—in which participants live. Thus, the relative isolation of the Gómez family facilitates Spanish maintenance because María Gómez has greater control over the environment in which her children live. The distances between the Gómez residence and surrounding rural homes serve not only to limit the children's access to English but also to protect María and Esteban's desire that their children acquire a standard Spanish by ensuring that the parents are the main source of linguistic input.

However, the urban centers present more fluid language environments for the Castillo, Valdez, and Torres children. Thus, Gabriela Valdez and Marta Torres, whose homes are situated within the *barrios* that constitute the south and west quadrants of San Antonio, are constantly in the company of other children whose oral and literacy abilities in Spanish span the entire bilingual continuum (from monolingual Spanish to monolingual English, including a myriad of code-switching patterns in between). Moreover, in these environments, the conditions favoring or impeding minority-language maintenance are constantly in flux. For example, the relocation of one or several block families, instigating changes in Marta's, Gabriela's, or Emma's social networks, could cause any of the children's extended linguistic environments to change from Spanish- to English-dominant, or the reverse. Moreover, for Emma Castillo, whose home is located not in a *barrio* but rather in a poor neighborhood with substandard housing units inhabited largely by transients, this "contact zone" presents exposure to social networks comprising persons who are not Latino as well as some who are. Thus, the linguistic environment outside of her immediate family does not necessarily offer support for cultural main-tenance, let alone minority-language maintenance. Certainly it is Berta Castillo's impression that the entire responsibility for avoiding Spanish-language loss on the part of both Emma and younger brother Rodrigo lies with her.

Families who reside in suburbia face still a third set of enabling and constraining conditions with regard to minority-language maintenance. True, the Trujillos and Pollack–Pearsons are surrounded by a sea of Eng-lish, and therefore they cannot rely on social networks beyond the family to provide support for maintaining the minority language. However, at the same time, with no competing varieties of Spanish in their children's immediate environments, Anita and Angel Trujillo and Louise Pollack find themselves mistresses and masters of their own houses, as it were, with regard to the variety of Spanish used with their children. Thus, Ana and Alfredo have acquired the standard variety of Spanish promoted by their parents, a variety that constitutes their only linguistic input in the minority language.

A final conclusion that emerges is that the decision to maintain a mi-nority language is one that must be constantly renewed in the face of di-rect and indirect countervailing pressures to switch to English. Children are constantly provided with reminders that English is the preferred language, whether from older children in their neighbor-hoods or from the popular media, where the majority of shows directed to children are of course in English. In fact, even the Gómez children, who use Spanish in interactions with one another and who live where there are no English-dominant speakers in the immediate area, prefer English-medium television. And although he can read Spanish, Ernesto Gómez's recreational reading—mostly sports magazines and other materials concerning the National Basketball Association—is primarily in English. Thus, regardless of the general societal con-straining or enabling factors such as population structure or official language policy, successful minority-language maintenance depends on constant effort, a view that was perhaps best summed up by Armando Farias, a parent who works on the same south Texas ranch where the Gómez family lives:

Yo diría que no es un esfuerzo- sino una constancia porque pues sí hace uno un esfuerzo por un momento y lo deja- queda donde mismo- pero pues si es una constancia.

(I wouldn't say that it's a struggle- rather a constant effort because if one struggles for a moment and then leaves it aside- it remains unchanged- but well yes, it's a constant effort.)

5

Narrative Production Across the Bilingual Continuum

Previous chapters have used detailed case studies of bilingual families in California and Texas to describe the various roles and functions that family members ascribed to Spanish and English, the variety of ways in which families that were so motivated attempted to maintain their home language, and the various definitions participants associated with Spanish maintenance. In some families, speaking Spanish was seen as important in preserving intergenerational linkages and literacy was not a concern. In other families, in which parents themselves had experienced significant hardships as a result of their lack of proficiency in English, the concern was that children acquire English—with an emphasis on English literacy—which parents identified with school success. There were, to be sure, some parents who also wished their children to learn to read and write the minority language, and who took steps to achieve this outcome, but they were decidedly in the minority. In addition, the parental goal of Spanish-language maintenance in the home was sometimes in tension with the educational agenda of the schools, and compliance with the schools' agenda was sometimes difficult for minority-language parents.

In this chapter, we turn our attention to a separate but related question: the language proficiency, in both English and Spanish, of children in bilingual families. On the basis of oral and written narratives provided by all the focal children, we examine language and literacy production across the bilingual continuum in order to understand the relationship between minority-language maintenance or shift and children's developing literacy in both the majority and minority languages. This change in focus requires a shift in methodological orientation: Here we add a quantitative dimension to our ethnographic analysis. We examine specific dimensions of oral and written language to achieve a balanced perspective not only on individual children's development in both languages but also on processes of language shift at the level of the community.

For the purposes of this agenda, we perform four types of analysis. First, at the micro level, as a measure of Spanish maintenance or loss, we look at a feature of the children's *grammatical* systems in oral Spanish: tense and aspect. Second, shifting to a more macro, *discourse* focus, we look at children's command of narrative structure as evidenced in both their Spanish and English written production. (Both of these first two dimensions of language production have been extensively studied in first- and second-language acquisition and attrition, and both have been shown to correlate with overall language development.) Third, we look at an array of features associated with the children's writing in both languages, features that practicing bilingual teachers have found important. The use of the Teachers' Assessment Rubric, developed in cooperation with practicing bilingual teachers, enables us to view in more detail the dimensions of children's literacy development that are of concern to educators. Finally, recognizing that language proficiency is a multidimensional construct (Bachman, 1990; Valdés & Figueroa, 1994), we analyze the ways in which children's performances with regard to these multiple means relate to one another and we explore the implications of these relationships.

TENSE AND ASPECT IN FIRST- AND SECOND-LANGUAGE ACQUISITION AND LOSS

In our analysis of the children's oral production in Spanish, we concentrate on the relationship between verb tense and aspect. In recent years, there has been considerable interest among researchers in first- and second-language development in the acquisition (and loss) of aspectual distinctions. This interest is an outgrowth of the concern with the acquisition of morphology (the smallest meaningful units of language) that has been a prominent feature of work in the field since Roger

Brown's (1973) original studies in the late 1960s and early 1970s. In part, the concern with verbal morphology in particular is a reflection of the fact that encoding events and states in time, as well as in relationship to one another, is a basic function of human language. And in part, studies of the acquisition of morphology, including verbal morphology, have been motivated by a desire to determine whether children follow a common path in first- and second-language acquisition. The focus of more recent work in this area has shifted from the concentration on forms that characterized early studies to a focus on meaning (Bardovi-Harlig, 1999). Through the concentration on aspect, models have been developed that allow for a comparison between the linguistic systems of children acquiring first and second languages and children undergoing the process of language shift from a minority to a majority language.

A substantial body of research in language acquisition has shown that children's development of verbal morphology is strongly influenced by inherent verbal aspect, the inherent properties of the verb. The influence of aspect on the acquisition of verbal morphology has also received considerable attention in second-language research. Differences in coding practices and terminology make exact comparisons between studies difficult. However, in second-language research, as in first-language acquisition research, studies of learners from a variety of first-language backgrounds acquiring English as a second language, of Chinese speakers acquiring Japanese, and of English speakers acquiring Spanish indicate that aspect has a strong influence on the acquisition of second-language verbal morphology (Andersen, 1991, 1993; Bardovi-Harlig, 1992, 1998, 1999, 2000; Bayley, 1994; Robison, 1990, 1995; Shirai & Kurono, 1998).

Andersen proposed a prototype account of the role of aspect in first- and second-language acquisition (Andersen, 1991; Andersen & Shirai, 1996). This model, which has been tested on first-language acquisition of Japanese and English (Shirai, 1993; Shirai & Andersen, 1995) and second-language acquisition of Spanish (Andersen, 1993) and Japanese (Shirai & Kurono, 1998), predicts that language acquirers will initially use tense endings with verbs that are prototypical examples of their aspectual class. For example, learners of Spanish as a second language will first mark the preterit of punctual verbs such as *partirse* ("to break in two") and the imperfect of stative verbs such as *tener* ("to have").

Only fairly late in acquisition will they use the imperfect form of a punctual verb such as *partirse* or the preterit of a stative verb such as *tener* (Andersen, 1991).

In our analysis, we extend the prototype account to language shift at the level of the community. We report on a test of the prototype account on the Spanish of the focal children. Specifically, we examine the extent to which the loss of tense/aspect forms in the speech of bilingual children of widely varying degrees of Spanish proficiency mirrors the acquisition of such forms reported in Andersen's studies (1991, 1993) of the acquisition of Spanish by second-language learners. The results, based on analysis of elicited narratives from children aged 10 to 12, suggest that the prototype account of tense and aspect also predicts the loss of morphological distinctions in communities undergoing language shift. The pattern of tense-aspect marking in the Spanish of Mexican-origin children undergoing language shift to English is the reverse of the pattern predicted for acquisition. Moreover, the preservation of tense/aspect distinctions (or the acquisition of such distinctions) is tied to the amount of Spanish used in the home. All of the children whose narratives exhibit the full range of tense/aspect distinctions that we investigated used Spanish extensively in interactions with at least one parent and other caretaker.

Grammatical Aspect and Lexical Aspect

Two types of aspect are usually distinguished: grammatical aspect and lexical aspect.[1] Grammatical aspect refers to those distinctions that are explicitly marked by linguistic devices, such as the English progressive, marked by the suffix *-ing,* or the distinction between the imperfective and the perfective in the Romance languages.

Lexical aspect is also referred to as "inherent lexical aspect" (Shirai & Andersen, 1995) or "situational aspect" (Smith, 1983). In contrast to grammatical aspect, lexical aspect refers to the inherent properties of the verb, or in some cases the entire predicate. For example, the verb *live* is inherently stative, whereas *reach,* as in *reach the summit of the mountain,* is inherently punctual (Comrie, 1976, p. 47). In this chapter,

---

[1]For fuller discussions, see Andersen and Shirai (1996), Comrie (1976), Shirai and Andersen (1995), and Bardovi-Harlig (2000).

following Andersen (1991) and Andersen & Shirai (1996), we adopt the categories proposed by Vendler (1967): states (e.g., *amar* "love," *querer* "want"), activities (e.g., *correr* "run," *pescar* "fish"), accomplishments (e.g., *correr un kilómetro* "run a kilometer," *dibujar un dibujo* "draw a picture"), and achievements (e.g., *caer* "fall," *morder* "bite"). As Shirai and Andersen (1995) noted, Vendler's categories are characterized by different combinations of the features stative/dynamic, telic/atelic, and punctual/durative.[2]

Stative verbs are –punctual, –telic, and –dynamic (+ indicates presence of a feature; – indicates absence). That is, the states they describe occur over a perceptible period of time, they have no inherent endpoint, and they require no continuing input of energy to continue, as in the following examples from the narratives produced by the focal children:

> (1) *Un día había un niño y un perrito y una rana.*
> (One day there was a boy and a dog and a frog.)

> (2) *y creía que estaba muerta.*
> (and he believed that it [the turtle] was dead.)

Activity verbs, like statives, are –punctual and –telic. However, they are +dynamic; for example,

> (3) *y él estaba pescando.*
> (and he was fishing.)

> (4) *el perro está hablando con el sapo.*
> (the dog is talking with the frog.)

Telic, or accomplishment, verbs are –punctual and +dynamic. They are also characterized by an inherent endpoint, for example,

> (5) *el niño se quitó la ropa.*
> (the boy took off his clothes.)

---

[2]Vendler's terms, although widely used, are somewhat opaque, particularly the distinction between accomplishment (+dynamic, +telic, –punctual) and achievement (+dynamic, +telic, punctual) verbs. In an effort to avoid terminological confusion, we refer to accomplishment verbs as telic verbs and achievement verbs as punctual verbs because it is the feature +/– punctual that distinguishes between the two classes. Although this solution is not entirely satisfactory, it does have the virtue of distinguishing between the three types of nonstative verbs, activity verbs, which have no inherent endpoint (–telic), accomplishment verbs, which have an inherent endpoint, and achievement verbs, which have an inherent endpoint and do not occupy perceptible time.

(6) *se la llevó pa' su casa.*
(he brought it [the turtle] home.)

Finally, punctual, or achievement, verbs are –durative (or +punctual), +telic, and +dynamic. They are distinguished from accomplishment verbs by the fact that the actions they describe have no perceptible duration; for example,

(7) *se cayó el niño al agua.*
(the boy fell in the water.)

(8) *y luego la rana se despertó.*
(and then the frog woke up.)

The Primacy of Aspect in L1 and L2 Acquisition

As applied to L1 (first language) acquisition, the primacy of aspect (POA) hypothesis, which states that language learners tend to use their available verbal morphology to encode aspect rather than tense, may be divided into four interrelated predictions:

1. Children first use past marking (e.g., English) or perfective marking (e.g., Chinese, Spanish) on achievement and accomplishment verbs, eventually extending its use to activity and stative verbs.
2. In languages that encode the perfective–imperfective distinction, imperfect past appears later than perfective past, and imperfective past marking begins with stative verbs and activity verbs, then extends to accomplishment and achievement verbs.
3. In languages that have progressive aspect, progressive marking begins with activity verbs, then extends to accomplishment or achievement verbs.
4. Progressive markings are not incorrectly overextended to stative verbs (Andersen & Shirai, 1996, p. 533).

Andersen and Shirai (1996) summarized a wide variety of studies of first and second languages that confirmed these predictions. As concerns second languages, although terminology varies across studies, work carried out on the acquisition of L2 (second language) English, Spanish, and Japanese indicates that learners tend initially to use their available past-tense morphology to mark punctual and telic verbs. Only later is the past tense generalized throughout the system (Bardovi-Harlig, 1992, 1998; Bardovi-Harlig & Reynolds, 1995; Bayley, 1994; Robison, 1995; Shirai & Kurono, 1998). Andersen (1991) proposed an eight-stage model for the acquisition of L2 Spanish past-tense morphology. In this model, the acquisition of the preterit begins with punctual verbs, the prototypical case, and gradually spreads to stative verbs. In a second stage, the acquisition of the imperfect begins with stative verbs and gradually spreads to punctual verbs. Acquisition is complete when learners are able to use both the preterit and the imperfect with verbs of all lexical classes.

Language Loss in the Individual and in the Community

The prototype model provides a means of achieving powerful generalizations concerning reduced language systems, including the language of children acquiring their first language, children and adults acquiring a second language, and speakers of incompletely acquired minority languages who are shifting to the language of the dominant community. In part, the model has the potential to allow for such generalizations because the research to date has focused on basic functions of human language—situating events or states in time and in relation to one another. However, the particular characteristics of communities that are undergoing shift from a minority to a majority language also allow for generalizations about the underlying processes of language acquisition by the individual and language loss in the community. The nondominant language of many individuals in language minority communities is best characterized not in terms of attrition, but in terms of incomplete acquisition before shifting to the majority language.

Three siblings in the Baez family, described in chapter 3, provide an instructive example elucidating incomplete acquisition. Their Spanish proficiency was described by their mother as resembling a staircase, with the oldest child having near-native Spanish oral proficiency, the middle child considerable receptive ability but little active proficiency, and the youngest neither active nor receptive ability. Extensive ethnographic observations and interviews with the children confirmed the mother's description. The differences in the children's Spanish proficiency were most likely a consequence of the time they had spent with their nearly monolingual Spanish-speaking grandmother before moving to a predominantly English-speaking neighborhood and entering an English-medium child-care facility. In such circumstances, which are quite common, we may expect the incompletely acquired minority language to share many characteristics with early child language and the systems of second language learners. That is, minority language attrition may mirror first- and second-language acquisition because, at the level of the individual, language attrition is in fact incomplete acquisition (Andersen, 1982; Wong Fillmore, 1991).

Methods for Studying Tense and Aspect

In an effort to obtain comparable data from all of the focal children, we asked each child to retell the stories of two wordless picture books, *Frog, Where Are You?* (Mayer, 1969) and *A Boy, a Dog, a Frog, and a Friend* (Mayer & Mayer, 1971). (The first of these books has been widely used as an elicitation device in studies of language development.[3]) Children were asked to recount one story in English and the other in Spanish.[4]

The analysis in this section is based on 27 Spanish narratives elicited with the "Frog" stories. Included are narratives from the participants who had maintained sufficient productive ability in Spanish to produce a minimal narrative.[5] Thus, we include narratives from participants representing the full range of Spanish retention and loss, from fully proficient native speakers, as illustrated by (9), to children who had developed very little active proficiency in Spanish, as illustrated by (10). The narrators in both cases were 10-year-old residents of San Antonio.

(9) *Había una vez*
    un niño pescó una rana
    y se fué pa' su casa feliz
    porque había pescado una rana
    y luego le- hechó a la rana en un frasco
    y el perro le gustó la rana.

---

[3]See Berman and Slobin (1994, pp. 665–678) for a full list of studies using the "Frog" stories.

[4]We used two "Frog" stories to avoid the impression that we were testing participants by having them tell the same story in both languages. At the same time, the use of two different but closely related stories allowed for the collection of comparable English and Spanish data.

[5]In one family, "Frog" narratives were not elicited because the family objected to fictional stories on religious grounds.

luego esa noche el perro y el niño se fueron a dormir
y la rana se salió del frasco.
mañana el perro despertó al niño
y encontraron el frasco solo sin la rana
el niño buscó en todos lados
y no lo pudo encontrar.

(Once upon a time
a boy fished up a frog
and he went back to his house feeling happy
because he had caught a frog
and then he put the frog in a jar
and the dog liked the frog
then at night the dog and the boy went to sleep
and the frog left the jar
the next day the dog woke up the boy
and they found the jar empty without the frog
the boy looked everywhere
and he couldn't find him.)

The child told the remainder of the story in a similar manner, with use of Southwest Spanish forms (e.g., *pa'* as just shown), but without resort to English. The degree of Spanish retention represented by the opening narrative section just given contrasts sharply with the following narrative told by Alyssa Baez, whom we met in chapter 3:

(10) *había una vez un muchachita y un perro y* a frog *estaba*
fishing *en un* lake.
un un muchachita un perro y un lana [sic] *estaba* fishing
y luego la muchachita cotar un fish.
La fish- *la* fish uhm grabbed *la la muchachita into la agua.*
Y lo perro y lo lara, la la rana y la l- rana went into *la*
agua o- otra vez con la muchachita.
(Once upon a time a boy and a dog and a frog were
fishing in a lake.
A a boy a dog and a frog were fishing
and then the boy caught a fish.
The fish- the fish uhm grabbed the the boy into the water.
And the dog and the frog, the the frog and the frog went
into the water again with the boy.)

Coding for Tense and Aspect. After the narratives were transcribed in standard orthography, verbs were coded according to the standard Spanish tense system. They were then stripped of all verb endings and coded for lexical aspect. The following tests, from Shirai and Andersen (1995, p. 744), were used to classify verbs as state, activity, accomplishment (telic), or achievement (punctual):

Step 1: State or nonstate.
>   Does it have a habitual interpretation in simple present tense?
>> If no → State (e.g., *I love you*).
>> If yes → Nonstate (e.g., *I eat bread*) → Go to Step 2.

Step 2: Activity or nonactivity.
>   Does "X is Ving" entail "X has Ved" without an iterative/habitual meaning? In other words, if you stop in the middle of Ving, have you done the act of V?
>> If yes → Activity (e.g., *run*).
>> If no → Nonactivity (e.g., *run a mile*) → Go to Step 3.

Step 3: Accomplishment (telic) or achievement (punctual).
>   [If test (a) does not work, apply test (b), and possibly (c).]
>   (a) If "X Ved in Y time (e.g. 10 minutes)," then "X was Ving during that time."
>> If yes → Accomplishment (e.g., *He painted a picture*).
>> If no → Achievement (e.g., *He noticed a picture*).
>   (b) Is there ambiguity with *almost*?
>> If yes → Accomplishment (e.g., *He almost painted a picture* has two readings: he almost started to paint a picture/he almost finished a picture).
>> If no → Achievement (e.g., *He almost noticed a picture* has only one reading).
>   (c) "X will VP in Y time (e.g., 10 minutes)" = "X will VP after Y time."
>> If no → Accomplishment (e.g., *He will paint a picture in an hour* is different from *He will paint a picture after an*

hour, because the former can mean that he will spend an hour painting a picture, but the latter does not).

If yes → Achievement (e.g., *He will start singing in two minutes* can have only one reading, which is the same as in *He will start singing after two minutes,* with no other reading possible).[6]

Analysis of Tense and Aspect. We undertook two types of analysis of tense and aspect. The first involved comparing the range of tenses used by children representing different levels of Spanish retention and loss. The second involved a comparison of the use of past tense marking by lexical aspect in both the preterit and the imperfect. We used implicational scales for this comparison because our concern was to find whether children used their past tense morphology to mark the full range of lexical aspect forms rather than a quantitative analysis of the likelihood of their use of past forms belonging to particular aspectual categories. Non-prototypical forms (e.g., imperfect punctuals and preterit statives) are relatively rare. Given the small amount of data for each child and the limitations imposed by our elicitation procedures, we expected to find no more than a few tokens belonging to non-prototypical categories, even from children who had maintained a high level of Spanish proficiency.[7]

Children's Performance on Tense and Aspect Marking

The 27 narratives yielded a total of 1,339 verbs, of which 137 were in the present tense (including present indicative, progressive, subjunctive, and

---

[6]To assure reliability, Robert and a native Spanish-speaking research assistant coded approximately 200 tokens from several different narratives, resulting in an interrater reliability rate of .96. Coding disagreements were resolved through discussion, with coders going through the steps outlined here together.

[7]A number of researchers have noted that the frequency of tense–aspect morphology is not evenly distributed across aspectual categories in fully proficient native speech (Andersen & Shirai, 1996; Robison, 1995). Thus, according to what has become known as the Distributional Bias Hypothesis, children acquiring their first language and adults acquiring a second language do not receive nearly equal amounts of input of verbs of all aspectual classes. In our study, the Distributional Bias Hypothesis also accounts for the fact that not all of the children who had developed native proficiency in Spanish used the imperfect or the perfect in all aspectual classes, even though the "Frog" stories provided occasions for them to do so. In some cases, children chose not to recount in detail an episode that would have called for an unusual tense–aspect form, such as a stative preterit.

conditional), 1,170 in the past (including imperfect, preterit, and past perfect), and 32 belonged to other categories, including future periphrastic, future perfect, and bare progressive. The results of analysis by aspectual category show a weakening in the tense–aspect system among children who have shifted to English as their main language. Moreover, for 24 of the 27 children, the past was the dominant tense. Crucially, the results of implicational scaling support the POA hypothesis as applied to children undergoing language shift. That is, the children whose narratives are examined here exhibit a pattern of past marking by aspectual class that is the reverse of the pattern predicted for acquisition by the POA hypothesis.

Dominant Tense.   The past tense predominated in the narratives of the children in our sample. In the "Frog" narratives examined here, 54.14% of the verbs were in the preterit and 32.26% in the imperfect. Only 10.24% were in a present tense. The distribution by verb tenses is shown in Table 5.1.[8]

Past Marking by Lexical Aspect.   Our results for the analysis of past-tense forms by aspectual category suggest that the POA hypothesis applies to communities undergoing language shift as well as to children acquiring their L1 and children and adults acquiring an L2. Children who regularly interact in Spanish with a parent or primary caregiver exhibit past marking on the majority of aspectual categories, in both the preterit and the imperfect. Thus, 17 of the children who regularly used Spanish at home marked six or more past tense–aspect categories (out of a possible eight). Four of the five children who marked four or fewer past tense–aspect categories did not use Spanish on a regular basis in the home. Moreover, the one child who spoke Spanish regularly at home but who nevertheless marked fewer than three different past tense–aspect categories produced only a minimal narrative. Crucially, as shown in Tables 5.2 and 5.3, there is an implicational relationship in the order in which past marking of nonprototypical aspectual forms is absent. For preterits, the pattern is state, activity, telic, punctual; for imperfect

[8]These results for the dominant tense differ greatly from Sebastián and Slobin's (1994) results for Spanish children and adults and call into question their contention that the present is "the prototypical verb form for telling a story in Spanish" (p. 245). For a more detailed comparison between the results for the children in this study, as well as several other groups of Mexican-origin children, and Sebastián and Slobin's results, see Bayley (1999) and Bayley, Alvarez-Calderón, and Schecter (1998, pp. 221–230).

TABLE 5.1

Distribution of Verb Forms in Mexican-Origin Children's Narratives

Tense	n	%
Present indicative	96	7.17
Present progressive	29	2.17
Present subjunctive	8	0.60
Present conditional	4	0.30
Preterit	725	54.14
Preterit progressive	5	0.37
Imperfect	270	20.16
Imperfect progressive	153	11.43
Imperfect subjunctive	9	0.67
Past perfect	8	0.60
Periphrastic future	11	0.82
Future perfect	8	0.60
Bare progressive	13	0.97
Total	1,339	

forms, the pattern is the reverse, that is, punctual, telic, activity, state. Twenty-six of the 27 narrators used preterit forms to mark punctual verbs, the prototypical case, and 22 used the preterit forms of telic verbs. Turning to the nonprototypical instances of the preterit, only 9 children used the preterit forms of activity verbs, and 11 used stative preterits in their narratives.

The situation is similar in the case of imperfect forms. All 27 narrators used the imperfect form of a stative verb, the prototypical case, at least once; 25 children used at least one imperfect form of an activity verb. However, only 18 of the narratives contain one or more imperfect telic verbs. Even fewer, just 13, contain one or more examples of imperfect punctuals. Finally, the implicational relationships in Tables 5.2 and 5.3, with indexes of reproducibility of .954 for the preterit and .982 for the imperfect, are statistically significant at $p < .05$ (Pavone, 1980; Rickford, 1991).

TABLE 5.2

Preterit Tense by Aspectual Class in Mexican-Origin Children's Spanish Narratives

Subject	Narrative	Punctual	Telic	Activity	State
SF03*	Friend	+	+	+	+
SF05*	Friend	+	+	+	+
SF12*	Frog	+	+	+	+
SF13*	Friend	+	+	+	+
SF15*	Friend	+	+	+	+
SF15.2*	Friend	+	+	+	+
SF07*	Friend	+	+	(–)	+
SF08*	Frog	+	+	(–)	+
SF09*	Frog	+	+	(–)	+
SF17*	Friend	+	+	(–)	+
SA03*	Friend	+	+	(–)	+
SF02*	Frog	+	+	+	–
SF06*	Frog	+	+	+	–
SF10*	Frog	+	+	+	–
SF01	Friend	+	+	–	–
SF16*	Frog	+	+	–	–
SF18*	Frog	+	+	–	–
SA01*	Frog	+	+	–	–
SA04*	Friend	+	+	–	–
SA09	Friend	+	+	–	–
SA15.1*	Frog	+	+	–	–
SA21*	Friend	+	+	–	–
SF11	Friend	+	–	–	–
SF19*	Friend	+	–	–	–
SF20*	Frog	+	–	–	–
SA16	Friend	+	–	–	–
SA02	Frog	–	–	–	–

Notes. IR = .954; cells that do not scale are in parentheses. SA, San Antonio; SF, San Francisco. Participants marked with an asterisk regularly used Spanish in home interactions with one or more primary caregivers.

TABLE 5.3
Imperfect Tense by Aspectual Class in Mexican-Origin Children's Spanish Narratives

Subject	Narrative	State	Activity	Telic	Punctual
SF06*	Frog	+	+	+	+
SF07*	Friend	+	+	+	+
SF08*	Frog	+	+	+	+
SF10*	Frog	+	+	+	+
SF15*	Friend	+	+	+	+
SF16*	Frog	+	+	+	+
SF18*	Frog	+	+	+	+
SF19*	Friend	+	+	+	+
SA03*	Friend	+	+	+	+
SA15.1*	Frog	+	+	+	+
SA15.2*	Friend	+	+	+	+
SA21*	Friend	+	+	+	+
SA01*	Frog	+	+	(−)	+
SF01	Friend	+	+	+	−
SF02*	Frog	+	+	+	−
SF03*	Friend	+	+	+	−
SF13*	Friend	+	+	+	−
SA04*	Friend	+	+	+	−
SF09*	Friend	+	(−)	+	−
SF05*	Friend	+	+	−	−
SF11	Friend	+	+	−	−
SF12*	Frog	+	+	−	−
SF17*	Friend	+	+	−	−
SF20*	Frog	+	+	−	−
SA09	Friend	+	+	−	−
SA16	Friend	+	+	−	−
SA02	Frog	+	−	−	−

Notes. IR = .982. Cells that do not scale are in parentheses. SA, San Antonio; SF, San Francisco. Participants marked with an asterisk regularly used Spanish in home interactions with one or more primary caregivers.

Tense and Aspect: Implications

Our results provide further evidence of the role of lexical aspect in reduced language systems, including child language, interlanguage, and the incompletely acquired language of speakers who are in the process of shifting to a socially dominant language. The amount of data from each child analyzed here is clearly too small to judge adequately the full range of the child's Spanish proficiency. Hence we explore other measures later. Nevertheless, a clear pattern emerges from the narratives, a pattern that supports the POA hypothesis. That is, the results suggest that past marking of verbs of different aspectual classes is lost in the reverse order in which it is acquired, until the use of the preterit has been restricted to punctuals and the imperfect to statives.[9]

To summarize, the children who provided the Spanish "Frog" stories here demonstrated great variability in the extent to which they have acquired and/or maintained the minority language. Although this variability might be seen in a great many linguistic features, including, for example, vocabulary, the variety and type of discourse markers used, linguistic devices used to mark simultaneous action, and command of sophisticated syntactic structures, we have focused on one such feature, the use of tense/ aspect marking to describe past events. The focus on tense/aspect marking has allowed a comparison with the extensive body of work on first- and second-language acquisition and with a growing body of work on language shift. Two major conclusions emerge from our examination of tense–aspect morphology in the "Frog" stories. First, the pattern of tense/aspect marking seen in the narratives of some of our participants closely parallels the patterns seen in child language and in relatively early second language acquisition. Such a pattern is characteristic of incomplete minority language acquisition before shifting to the majority language. Second, the participants whose narratives

---

[9]The results reported here generally agree with Silva-Corvalán's (1994) work on change in Los Angeles Spanish across the bilingual continuum. Silva-Corvalán (1994) studied the verbal systems of Mexican-background adolescent and adult residents of Los Angeles in great detail. She found that United States-born speakers and those who had immigrated before age 6 had neutralized the preterit–imperfect distinction in favor of the imperfect with a small group of frequently occurring stative verbs, including *estaba* "was" (infin., *estar*), *era* "was" (infin., *ser*), *tenía* "had" (infin., *tener*), and *sabía* "knew" (infin., *saber*) (p. 44). This reduction of the verbal paradigm, moreover, could not be attributed to the greater regularity of the imperfect inflectional pattern. Speakers who had lost the preterit–imperfect distinction with frequently occurring statives continued to use the preterit forms of a variety of nonstative irregular verbs.

exhibit a broad range of tense/aspect distinctions, including use of non-prototypical forms, are those who regularly engage in extensive home interactions in Spanish.

In the next section, we turn from the examination of a specific aspect of language in Spanish and its relationship to language maintenance, loss, or incomplete acquisition and focus on the structure of the children's written narratives in both Spanish and English.

WRITTEN DISCOURSE

Narrative Development in English and Spanish

Narratives are a primary means by which human beings make sense of their experience (Hymes, 1982). Moreover, narratives are the earliest written form that children are expected to master at school. In this section, we explore children's narrative development in English and, where children had developed at least minimal writing ability in Spanish, in Spanish as well. The analysis allows us to examine, at least with respect to one genre, the relationship between children's developing literacy in the majority and the minority language. As noted at the beginning of this chapter, we report on analyses based on two different rating methods. The first is an examination of narrative structure; the second is based on an assessment rubric devised by practicing bilingual teachers. We obtained writing from focal children by means of the following essay prompts:

English:
Could you tell us about something that happened *in school* that you will always remember? An event or an incident that happened in school that you will never forget. It could be something really exciting, or happy, or scary. Remember ... something that happened in school.

Spanish:
¿Puedes escribir sobre un evento muy memorable que tú tuviste "afuera" de la escuela? Algo que nunca se te olvidará: Puede ser algo muy emocionante, o felíz, o miedoso. Recuerda ... algo que pasó afuera de la escuela.
(Can you write about a very memorable event that happened *outside of school*? Something that you will never forget. It can be something exciting, or happy, or scary. Remember ... something that happened outside of school.)

In most cases, children were asked to respond to one prompt after the first interview and the other after the second. Our elicitation resulted in 71 compositions, 41 in English (in one family two brothers participated) and 30 in Spanish. Essays ranged from fully developed and elaborated narratives in English and Spanish to minimal lists of the few words that the child was able to recall in Spanish.

Narrative Structure Analysis. Our analysis of narrative structure is based on Labov's framework (Labov, 1972b; Labov & Waletsky, 1967/1997). Although a number of more fine-grained analytic schemes have been proposed in the years since Labov and Waletsky's seminal essay (see, e.g., Gee, 1986; McCabe & Peterson, 1991; Peterson & McCabe, 1983), Labov's general scheme proved best suited to our purpose. Within this scheme, a minimal narrative is defined as two temporally ordered clauses in the past tense (Labov, 1972b, p. 360). The main sections into which narratives may be divided are an Abstract (one or two clauses that summarize the story), an Orientation (setting the stage for the narrative, providing background information), at least one Complicating Action (what happens that makes it a narrative), a Resolution (how the issue, question, or problem got resolved or what the outcome was), an Evaluation (the narrator's reflections on the meaning of the event, providing the purpose of the story), and a Coda (a final clause or series of clauses closing off the series of complicating actions and often bridging the gap between the time of the story and the present). In addition, the flow of the narrative may be interrupted on one or more occasions by a Suspension— additional information about participants in the action, for example, that is not part of the story line.

Using this general framework, the research team devised a scale to measure the degree to which children's written narratives made use of the sections outlined by Labov.[10] Because the ordering of sections, as well as the amount of emphasis given to each, may well be affected by cultural differences (McCabe, 1995), essays were rated only on whether they used the elements just outlined, not on whether the elements were used in a particular order or in the amount of emphasis given to each.[11] The Narrative Assessment Scale is shown in Table 5.4.

---

[10]The Narrative Assessment Scale was developed by Ann Robinson in cooperation with Adriana Boogerman.

Although the majority of scores clustered around 3 or 4 on this scale, the results illustrated the full range of scores. The following English example, one of the most elaborate narratives in our data, received a top rating of 6. (In the interests of space, the line divisions used in the coding have not been retained here.)

Abstract

Boy, I will never forget the time someone at school when we were

TABLE 5.4
Narrative Assessment Scale

Organization
a.   Abstract = summary
b.   Orientation (= who, when, what, where; often characterized by past progressive clauses; often placed at strategic points, not just at the beginning)
c.   Complicating action (= then what happened)
d.   Suspension (= additional information, not part of the story line)
e.   Evaluation (= the point of the narrative; why it is told; answers question "so what?")
f.   Result/resolution (= what finally happened)
g.   Coda (= signal that the narrative is finished)

Rating Scale
6   Has 6 of the above; must have action; action is detailed and clear; must have evaluation or resolution
5   Has 5 of the above; must have action; action is somewhat detailed and clear; some evaluation or resolution
4   Has 4 of the above; must have action; action has minimal detail and clarity; minimal evaluation or resolution
3   Has 3 of the above; must have action; action borders on minimal
2   Has 2 of the above; must have minimal action
1   No action = not a narrative

[11]Prior to rating, essays were entered into a computer in order to minimize distractions arising from extraneous matters such as handwriting. The original orthography and punctuation, however, were maintained. The essays were then divided into clauses. Line divisions were made at every discourse marker, such as *and, then, because, so, also, but, while, suddenly, boy!, well, you know, y, y luego,* and *entonces,* and at every sentence ending, whether or not it had a period. The narratives were then divided into sections and rated by two project assistants. Ratings were reviewed by Robert. In the very rare cases where ratings diverged by more than a point, the two closest scores were used.

playing on the structor at lunch time and one of my friends fell off and an ambulanc came to the school to take him to the hospital.

Orientation

It was about a month ago when this happened. Joel, Jetta, James, Vincent and me were standing on a concreat tube while the other kids tride to pull us down. We played this fore a long time. But we grew tired and stopped playing that game and left, except for James and the kids at the bottom of the tube. We went to the upstares part of the yard And played tag there.

Action

Suddenly kids started running down to the lower yard. We followed them. At the bottom we saw a crowd of people around some police who were knelt down over someone. When we got down there, we saw James on his back crying.

Suspension

Someone had pulled him off and he wasn't expecting it when he fell.

Action

Then they took him away.

Evaluation

I felt real bad because I could have saved him from herling him self. And if I had stayed there, it could have bin me moneing and growning on my way to the hospital.

Resolution

Later on that day, people said Mardin [another 6th grader] who was down on the lower year [sic] playing the game with James, was responsibal for James, and they wouldn't beleav him that he didn't. Then I felt sorry for Mardin because he was crying.

Evaluation

That was a realy skary experience. My stomach felt sick. I hope never to have a expereance like that again.

Fin
P.S. James was fine

The following narrative, also in English, represents a more typical example. It was rated a 3 on the narrative assessment scale:

Orientation
Wen I met my frinds at shool one is leslei she was the first And esmeralda was the second Mary is the thir and Katy the forth I didn't feel loenly anymoer in that shool it hapend in 1992 and 1993

Action
they shode my arunde the shool and we wen't to the same clasrom and we yousto play novels Katy alwas yous to be Plar and I ider was Fernanda or Maria Mersedes Sometimes leslei was Fernanda we played that we wantes to be atris and we new how to sing good but they said we waer to yung and we yousto say *Pastas de sanaoria y Care de bruja* to the Lady

Evaluation
I mis leslei she was the won that alwas made me lafe and I remember me and my friends yousto bring maykup to shool and we yous to get in trubel. Katy was the last so I hade to show her arunde.

Finally, we show a mid-range narrative in Spanish. The following account of a visit to Mexico to attend a cousin's wedding was rated a 3.

Orientation
a mi me justo cuando fui a la boda de mi primo se caso en Culiacan Sinaloa toda mi familia de mexico y todas nosotras estavamos vien feliz

Action
I me diverti vien mucho porque fuimos muchas a la misa I era muy vonita porque no mas vi a toda my familia. Y me sentí muy feliz I me dio muchas ganas de yorar y todas fuimas a la fiesta estabamos vailando y comienda todas feliz y mi familia ayudando a todas y uvo muchas personas vailanda

Evaluation
me divertí porque mi ermana se dio al casada un viveron de vino en su boca Y era en navidad y conosi a muchas de mis primas trana [?] mas omtes [?] I me divertimos mucho

Orientation
(I liked it when I went to my cousin's wedding. He got married in Sinaloa. My whole family went.)

Action
(And I enjoyed myself a lot because we went to the Mass a lot And it was very beautiful because I had never seen my whole family. And I felt

very happy And I really felt like crying and we all went to the party and were were all happily dancing and eating and my family was helping everyone and there were a lot of people dancing.)

Evaluation
(It amused me because my sister gave the bride [?] a bottle of wine in her mouth And it was Christmas and I met many of my cousins [?] And we had a lot of fun.)

Focal Children's Performance on the Narrative Assessment Scale. Here we compare Spanish and English results on the narrative assessment scale for children who were able to produce at least a minimal essay in Spanish. We then examine the English narratives separately, including narratives from children who were not able to write in Spanish.

Overall, there was very little difference in the narrative structure ratings for the English and Spanish essays, although, as we might expect given the wide range of proficiency represented in the Spanish essays, the standard deviation was greater in this task. The mean on the English essays was 3.65 ($SD = 1.33$). On the Spanish essays, the mean was 3.40 ($SD = 1.89$). Moreover, although there was a significant correlation between performance in English and Spanish as measured by the Narrative Assessment Scale, the correlation was not particularly strong ($r = .3111, p < .05$). Finally, when the English essays written by participants who were unable to produce an essay were included along with the essays by children who produced essays in both languages, the mean changed only slightly, decreasing from 3.65 to 3.51. Although the ability to write in two languages may not convey an advantage in English writing, this result suggests that language maintenance certainly does no harm, at least as measured on this dimension of language proficiency.

We turn now to the results from the Teachers' Assessment Rubric to see how well they correlate with the results for narrative development.

Teachers' Assessment Rubric

Beyond our interest in children's development of narrative structure, we wished to know how teachers would react to the types of essays our participants produced. We therefore brought together four experienced bilingual teachers to develop the Teachers' Assessment Rubric.[12] The teachers were recorded while they examined and rated a number of sample essays. They were asked to describe as fully as possible their reasons for rating the essays as they did. Subsequently, their discussion was summarized and the Teachers' Assessment Rubric was developed. The instrument went through a number of revisions as a result of the teachers' responses to the various iterations. The instrument consists of 10 separate categories ranging from organization and narrative content to breadth of vocabulary to handwriting and spelling (including correct use of accents in Spanish). The full list of categories follows:

Organization

Cohesion: has a "beginning, middle, end"

Maintains topic: "revisits" opening point/s at end of narrative

Paragraphing: sense of transition between subsections

Sentence transitions: appropriate and varied use of discourse markers to mark next point (e.g., *entonces, siempre,* but)

Description

Clarity: all points are clearly stated

Elaboration: develops point further, provides evidence, substantiates, provides details

Use of detail: "paints the evidence"

Narrative content

Setting: specifies setting

Character development: includes descriptive information that will help reader understand the characters' motives

Plot: includes evidence of plot development (e.g., movement toward statement of problem and its resolution)

Message: includes moral or stance on issue

Choice of language

Rich and varied vocabulary; *"vocabulario amplio"*

Non-redundance: does not overrely on same words

---

[12]The Teachers' Assessment Rubric was developed by Sandra Schecter in cooperation with Lucinda Pease-Alvarez.

> Verb tenses: uses different verb tenses to develop narrative
> and to make sequence clear
>
> Presentation
> Handwriting: includes legibility
> Appearance on paper: for example, use of indentation,
> location of writing on page
>
> Spelling
> Spelling
> Appropriate word segmentation, such as *"no sé"* vs. *"nose"*
>
> Mechanics
> Punctuation
> Appropriate use of accents for Spanish
> Capitalization
>
> Syntax
> Complete sentences
> Appropriate sentence segmentation, for example, "no run-on
> sentences"
>
> Creativity
> Sense of author: for example, personality, maturity
> Original content: for example, interesting "twists"
>
> Emotion/tone
> Creates a feeling or mood, such as sorrow, suspense, humor

These categories were rated on a 5-point scale that took into account the age of the writer: 1, not at all developed (for this age group); 2, somewhat developed; 3, average; 4, well developed; 5, very well developed. In accordance with the preferences expressed by the teachers with whom the Teachers' Assessment Rubric was developed, all categories were weighted equally.

The essays were read and assessed by two practicing bilingual teachers, one of whom had been involved in developing the rating instrument. In cases where ratings on any category diverged by more than a point, the essays were read by a third teacher and the two closest (usually identical) scores were used.

Focal Children's Performance on the Teachers' Assessment Rubric. The results for the ratings with the Teachers' Assessment Rubric generally show a high degree of correlation with the results of narrative structure analysis. Thus, the correlation between the English essay ratings according to the Teachers' Assessment Rubric and the Narrative Assessment Scale was .7685 ($p < .001$). The correlation between the ratings of the Spanish essays on the two measures was even higher, .8352 ($p < .001$). Like the Narrative Assessment Scale, the Teachers' Assessment Rubric shows a correlation between children's performance in the English and Spanish essays that, while significant at the .05 level, is rather weak, at only .3347. However, although the means for the Spanish and English essays did not differ significantly on the Narrative Assessment Scale, a two-tailed paired t test indicated that the mean rating for the Spanish essays according to the Teachers' Assessment Rubric was significantly lower than the mean rating for the English essays ($p < .005$). On the latter measure, the mean score for the Spanish essays was 1.97 ($SD = 1.05$), indicating that the teachers who rated the essays judged that the participant's Spanish writing, on average, was "somewhat developed for this age group." (Recall that 3 is defined as "average for this age group.") The mean rating of the English essays was 2.67 ($SD = .86$), indicating that, overall, participants' writing was judged by the teachers who rated the essays as only slightly below average for their age group. Finally, as with the ratings on the Narrative Assessment Scale, the inclusion of essays by English-dominant participants who were unable or unwilling to produce a Spanish essay had only a negligible effect on the mean rating for English essays according to the Teachers' Assessment Rubric. Table 5.5 compares the descriptive statistics for all measures of writing. Table 5.6 summarizes the correlations among both oral and written measures.

The results just summarized lead to several conclusions. First, the magnitude of the correlations between our two measures for the English and Spanish essays respectively suggests that when rating the essays, teachers using the Teachers' Assessment Rubric attended more closely to questions of structure and organization than they did to details of punctuation and spelling. In fact, the instrument is structured to promote just such an outcome. Although each main heading was worth an equal number of points in determining the overall score, only 3 of the 10 main categories deal with prescriptive grammar, mechanics, and presentation, areas that the Narrative Assessment Scale does not cover. Seven categories in the Teachers' Assessment Rubric are concerned with higher level questions of organization, description, and so forth. Second, as indicated in Table 5.6, acquisition of the Spanish grammatical system, or at least the morphological system used to mark tense and aspect, is not sufficient for writing a clear narrative. Rather, written literacy and oral proficiency are different dimensions of language

TABLE 5.5

Comparison of Results of Measures of Writing: Descriptive Statistics

Instrument	Mean	SD	Minimum	Maximum	n
TAR, Spanish	1.97	1.05	.00	3.80	30
Narrative, Spanish	3.40	1.89	.00	6.00	30
TAR, English	2.67	.86	1.00	4.30	30
Narrative, English	3.65	1.33	.00	6.00	30
TAR, English (all)	2.63	.83	1.00	4.30	41
Narrative, English (all)	3.51	1.32	.00	6.00	41

Notes. TAR, Teachers' Assessment Rubric; Narrative, Narrative Assessment Scale. TAR, English and Narrative, English include essays from participants who attempted to produce essays in both Spanish and English. TAR, English (all) and Narrative, English (all) also include the English essays from participants who were unable or unwilling to attempt a Spanish essay.

TABLE 5.6

Correlations Among Measures of Language Proficiency

	Narrative English	Narrative Spanish	TAR English	TAR Spanish	Tense Aspect
Narrative English	1.000				
Narrative Spanish	.3111*	1.000			
TAR English	.7685***	.3104*	1.000		
TAR Spanish	.3106*	.8352***	.3347*	1.000	
Tense Aspect	.0918	.2092	.0627	.2160	1.000

Note. Tense–aspect categories for preterit and imperfect were combined in the correlations reported in this table. Thus, the highest possible score was 8, indicating use of both the preterit and the imperfect in all lexical aspectual categories. TAR, Teachers' Assessment Rubric. Narrative, Narrative Assessment Scale. *p < .05. ***p < .001.

proficiency and show no significant correlations in our study. Finally, participants who have acquired sufficient Spanish literacy to at least attempt to produce a Spanish essay did as well (or slightly better) on the English essays as children who lacked sufficient written Spanish to attempt an essay. On this measure, then, we can make the argument that the participants who have acquired at least some writing ability in Spanish have indeed outpaced their peers because, in addition to doing as well in English writing, they have acquired a second writing system (cf. Krashen & Biber, 1988).

THE STORY THE STORIES TELL

Let us now cautiously review what we have learned from our analyses of the stories the focal children produced both orally and in writing. First, in reference to oral production, it is clear that children who on a regular basis interacted in Spanish in the home had access to close to the full tense–aspect system in that language. That is, they were able to express distinctions about the nature of states and actions and to situate those states and actions in time and in relation to one another. Thus, they could recount experiences in rich detail in Spanish, as well as understand the nuances of the experiences of others.

Second, with respect to those who would insist on hypotheses based on an "oral–written continuum," we found no correlation between the oral and written production of our focal children. On the contrary, we found these to represent distinct dimensions of language proficiency that are separable and situated in localized practices linked to the roles that English and Spanish played in children's lives. Children who were not taught to read and write Spanish either at home or at school did not develop proficiency in Spanish literacy from exposure to oral Spanish. In short, we found that reading and writing are not acquired; they are learned.

Third, we found a correlation, albeit not a strong one, between our measures of written production for Spanish and English. We have reason to believe that writing ability in fact does transfer across languages, although there are others who have made a more forceful case for this argument than the one we have been able to provide (see, e.g., Cummins, 1985, 1996).

Fourth, we found a strong correlation between the results on the different writing assessment measures, suggesting that good linguists and good teachers are not only developmentally and cross-culturally sensitive, but also in agreement about the attributes that constitute good writing. The four teachers who participated in developing and applying the Teachers' Assessment Rubric organized their assessments to privilege content, overall structure, and coherence over more surface and mechanical features such as handwriting and punctuation.

Fifth, we suggest that the difference in the results between the English and Spanish essays on the Teachers' Assessment Rubric (the Spanish writing was rated lower) may be attributed to patterns of language use in schools and to policies that encourage children to shift to all-English classes at the earliest opportunity. Considering that many of our participants had received no formal Spanish literacy instruction at school and that even those who did receive such instruction were usually transitioned to English by third grade, it is not surprising to see that the ratings for the Spanish essays on the Teachers' Assessment Rubric were lower than they were for the English essays, written in the language in which most of our participants had received the greater part of their formal literacy instruction. Further, many of the focal children were from homes where the parents had never had the opportunity to acquire literacy in Spanish. These children exhibited varying degrees of oral proficiency in Spanish. Some, like Marta Torres (chap. 4), could decode Spanish texts. However, few were able to engage in operations that require readers to extract core meaning from text or engage critically with text.

Finally, although the Spanish essays were rated significantly lower than were the English essays, it is instructive that those children who felt sufficiently confident to write in Spanish did as well on their English essays as children who could not or would not write in Spanish.[13] Some of our colleagues have interpreted similar results to mean that Spanish maintenance is not beneficial for children, because children who read and write in Spanish perform no better on measures of English language literacy than those who do not. But we would interpret the same statistics in a different way. Bilingual children who do *as well* as their monolingual coun-

---

[13]Results similar to those reported here have also been found in large-scale studies. Recently, for example, Yeung, Marsh, and Suliman (2000) used the broadly representative National Education Longitudinal Study of 1988 database to study the effects of home language maintenance on academic achievement. They found that "bilingual students' proficiency and use of first language did not have substantial negative impacts on subsequent English proficiency or English achievement" (p. 1023).

terparts on measures of English language proficiency, especially on measures which assess reading and writing ability, have, in our view, considerably benefitted from Spanish language maintenance. Given our idealized (and, admittedly, transformative) vision for the role of language in this society at this historical juncture, on which we elaborate in the concluding chapter, it is far better to have both than just one.

6

Doing School at Home

In this chapter we move from a focus on specific forms and narrative development to explore the impact of schooling on patterns of language socialization in the homes of Mexican immigrant families. Having witnessed multiple, complex facets of the relationship between the implicit—sometimes explicit—requirements of formal schooling and family socialization practices, we are struck by the broad range of strategies adopted by language-minority parents as they attempt to resolve the contradictions arising from their desire to preserve linguistic and cultural continuity while preparing their children to succeed in a school system that often evaluates children solely on the basis of their academic performance in English (Valdés & Figueroa, 1994). Equally striking, however, are the force and directionality of the family–school relationships we observed. Although the families differ in their approaches to defining their work in relation to school-based learning, overwhelmingly they acquiesce to the ideological framings through which professional educators—teachers, administrators, policy-makers—understand and seek to practice the family–school relationship (Griffith & Schecter, 1998; Wagonner & Griffith, 1998). In fact, in many of the homes we visited, the school's agenda serves as primary organizer of the educational work of caregivers and, in particular, mothers. Specifically with regard to extent and nature of involvement in language activities, the main order of business is how the pedagogical work that family members do at home, involving interactions with texts, fits with and supports the work of the classroom in promoting school literacy. And although we are in a position to provide some excellent illustrations of participants' engagement in reading and writing for instrumental purposes (e.g., deciphering information on promotional coupons, completing forms related to various social services and benefits), we would at the same time note that in the main the school academic agenda dominates home literacy activity (cf. McDermott, Goldman, & Varenne, 1984).[1]

In the portraits that follow we describe how members of four Mexican-immigrant families organize their caregiving in relation to their perceptions of the role of schooling as well as of their own and significant others' roles in their children's linguistic and academic development. We have encountered three of the families—the Gómezes, Esparzas, and Villegases—in earlier chapters, and we already have some idea about how individual members of these families envision the role of schooling in supporting the aspirations they maintain for their children's futures. Into this company we introduce a family about whom we have not previously written—the Ríos family. Since immigrating from Mexico more than a decade ago, the Ríoses have managed to survive at the margins of a thriving Bay Area economy.

In representing family members' experiences with school literacy and learning, we focus primarily on parent–child and sibling–sibling interactions in typical school-related and school-like activities—such as assistance with homework and reading to a preschooler. However, our discussions are not confined to these examples. For by attending to a broader range of family interactions around texts, we also derive insights into the ways in which cultural practice informs the pedagogical stances assumed by language-minority parents as they organize their children's engagement with schooling.

We show that notwithstanding family members' concerns with and attentiveness to the expectations of professional educators, their performances do not always coordinate with the agendas of schools, for a number of reasons. First, not all language-minority parents possess the necessary proficiency in the dominant language to be in a position to support the school's agenda in a manner their children's teachers deem

---

[1]Our results lead us to question whether perhaps researchers have made too much of isolated examples of family members' uses of literacy for instrumental and pragmatic purposes that they have found.

beneficial for their students' development. Second, for language-minority families the ordinary work of parents in constructing the relationship between the family and the school is embedded in another equally ordinary process, which, on a daily basis, entails thousands of routine decisions concerning language choice (Griffith & Schecter, 1998). This process often problematizes the relationship between home caregiving and schooling by introducing the additional important element of language maintenance or loss into the determination of educational priorities. Third, immigrant parents who are not native speakers of English are not always aware of the expectations of schools with regard to family support or the significance attached by professional educators to the various curricular programs to which children are assigned. Indeed, in our study a significant minority of immigrant parents find the terminology used in home–school communications—terms such as *primary language program* and *mainstream*—to be obfuscating.[2] Thus, they are not in a position to assist their children with school activities that foster the development of text-based, academic literacy consistent with educators' notions of successful student identities; nor are they able to seek out and acquire essential information that would allow them to be effective advocates for their children's learning needs.

FAMILIES AND SCHOOLS

Adapting the School Agenda for Spanish Maintenance: The Gómezes

We met the Gómezes, the ranch family who reside in rural south Texas, in chapter 4. We saw how intergenerational transmission of Spanish remains the highest priority for Sr. and Sra. Gómez, with this goal dictated both by the pragmatic requirements of parent–child communication (both parents are Spanish-dominant) and María and Esteban's unwavering commitment to cultural maintenance. Understandably, almost all of

---

[2]For example, one mother who was informed that her child had been placed in a primary language program was unclear as to whether the term *primary language* was intended to denote the child's native tongue, in this case Spanish, or English. In four cases, parents who had believed that their children were enrolled in either a regular English program or a Spanish–English bilingual program later discovered that the children actually had been placed in a special English as a second language class. In two of these cases, parents did not appreciate the implications of these distinctions for their children's academic development until the children had completed several years of primary school.

the informal interaction in the Gómez home, including communications among siblings, takes place in Spanish. In addition, in this family there is considerable sibling interaction focusing on school-related tasks that takes place in Spanish as well, notwithstanding that Ernesto, Carlos, and Antonio attend English-medium schools.

Among the many responsibilities he exercises as the oldest son, Ernesto, who is very successful in his school work, is often charged with assisting middle brother Carlos with homework. In the excerpt that follows, recorded during one of our after-school observations, Ernesto volunteers to help Carlos to review his assigned spelling words. Although the subject, English spelling, is one that would seem most likely to favor the use of English, the main language of the interaction is Spanish.

Ernesto:	*Te ayudo con la, para para que estudies diciéndote las palabras, a Carlos.*
Carlos:	*¿Cuáles palabras?*
Ernesto:	*Pos las palabras que tienes para Mrs. Lamar … las palabras aquí están. A ver. ¿Las palabras que tienen estrella?*
Carlos:	Yeah.
Ernesto:	*A ver. Listo a ver …* "bargain."
Carlos:	b-a-g-a-i-n.
Ernesto:	*Carlos mira, fíjate, dijiste … OK. bien nomás que te faltó una letra* b-a-r. *No* b-a-g-a-i-n.
(Ernesto:	I'm helping you with the [word list] so, so that you can study while I read you the words, OK Carlos?
Carlos:	What words?
Ernesto:	Well the words that you have for Mrs. Lamar … the words are here [points to a sheet of paper with spelling words]. Let's see. The words that have an asterisk?
Carlos:	Yeah.

Ernesto:	Let's see. Ready, let's see … "bargain."
Carlos:	b-a-g-a-i-n.
Ernesto:	Carlos look, pay attention, you said … OK. well, the only thing that's missing is a letter b-a-r. Not b-a-g-a-i-n.)

Although Ernesto often assumes the role of tutor for his younger brothers, Sra. Gómez is also heavily involved with her children's school work, even though she is not fluent in the language of the school. Frequently, her participation involves the two older boys' preparation for spelling tests. During several of our visits, she drilled the boys on word lists and checked the correctness of their written answers by orthographic matching with a master list from their school. Moreover, as illustrated by the following exchange between María and Ernesto, recorded during a weekday afternoon observation, she also monitors their progress closely.

María:	*No me dijiste cuánto te sacaste.*
Ernesto:	*Un treinta y dos.*
María:	*¿Por qué?*
Ernesto:	*Porque eran treinta y tres palabras, treinta y tres cosas. Y cada uno valía un punto y nada más me faltó una palabra.*
María:	*O sea te equivocasté en una …*
Ernesto:	*De todo el examen nada más me saqué una mala.*
María:	*¿De todo el examen qué?*
Ernesto:	*Nada más me saqué una mal. Una.*
(María:	You didn't tell me how you did.
Ernesto:	A thirty-two.
María:	Why?
Ernesto:	Because there were thirty-three words, thirty-three things. And each one was worth a point, and I only missed one word.

María: So you were wrong on one …

Ernesto: On the whole exam I only got one wrong.

María: Of the whole exam, what?

Ernesto: I didn't get any more wrong. Just one.)

María sees her role in her sons' schooling, however, as going beyond monitoring their progress as measured by test scores, or making sure that they are prepared for tasks like spelling quizzes that are accomplished primarily by rote memorization. Although her lack of proficiency in English prevents her from playing an active role in some curricular areas such as writing, she is a highly involved participant in many of the boys' school projects. For example, Ernesto, the oldest brother, spent the greater part of one weekday afternoon observation working on an assignment to construct a rather large and elaborate floor plan, with metric measurements, based loosely on the Gómezes' modest residence. María was quickly enlisted in the activity. Throughout the process, during which she pointed out the need to include various objects of furniture and commented on her son's choice of colors, María engaged in an extended series of questions in an effort to focus Ernesto's attention on missing details (e.g., an entrance to a bathroom) or to clarify the function of the various rooms:

María: *Bueno, espérame, por ejemplo esta recamara-*

Ernesto: *Hmm ¿cuál?*

María: *Uno y dos. Yo no veo baño.*

Ernesto: *Es el que está con la recámara tres, fíjate aquí en se- en seguida.*

María: *A que bue- entonces hay que entrar por el pasillo.*

Ernesto: *Tienes que salir de la recámara uno y dos, y: entras.*

María: *¿De dónde? O sí sí sí.*

Ernesto: *Eso tiene aquí.*

María: *Falta una recámara Ernesto.*

Ernesto:	*¿La de quién?*
María:	*¿Tú con quien vas a dormir?*
Ernesto:	*Recámara uno.*
María:	*¿Y en la dos?*
Ernesto:	*Papá y mamá.*
María:	*¿Y en la tres?*
Ernesto:	*Es la recámara de invitados.*
María:	*¿Y Carlos y Antonio?*
Ernesto:	*Ellos quedan cada quien en su casa.*
(María:	Good, wait a minute, for example, this bedroom-
Ernesto:	Hmm which?
María:	One and two. I don't see a bathroom.
Ernesto:	It's the one that's with bedroom three, look right here.
María:	Ah good- then you have to enter from the hallway.
Ernesto:	You have to leave bedroom one and two, and enter [the bathroom].
María:	From where. O yes, yes, yes.
Ernesto:	This has it here.
María:	It's missing a bedroom, Ernesto.
Ernesto:	Whose?
María:	Who are you going to sleep with?
Ernesto:	Bedroom one.
María:	And in the second?
Ernesto:	Father and mother.
María:	And in the third?
Ernesto:	It's the guest bedroom.
María:	And Carlos and Antonio?

Ernesto: Each of them can stay in his own house.)

We see that Sra. Gómez's questions, although brief and requiring equally brief responses, are genuine requests for clarification and information. For example, María has no way of knowing that her oldest son intends to evict his younger brothers from his idealized version of the family's living quarters. In this respect, they are typical of the discourse patterns observed elsewhere in Latino and other minority communities (Heath, 1983; Pease-Alvarez & Vasquez, 1994; Philips, 1983). Indeed, as concerns this family's interactions, aside from instances in which parents or older siblings were quizzing children about rote tasks such as memorizing lists of spelling words, we seldom observed instances of the initiation, response, evaluation pattern that remains the most common sequence of teacher–student interaction in mainstream classrooms (Cazden, 1988; Mehan, 1979; Tharp & Gallimore, 1989).

As a result of Esteban and María's commitment to a strategy of Spanish-language maintenance, Ernesto has retained native-speaker proficiency in Spanish. Moreover, he has learned to read and write in Spanish as well. Nor has the relationship of the Gómez family with Ernesto's teachers suffered as a result of the family's calculated decision not to exempt school-related activities from the Spanish-only policy that prevailed in this household. Ernesto has developed native-like proficiency in English as well, and his superior performance in all-English classes (a result supported by his writing samples, and by his performance in an extended English interview with one of the English-dominant members of the research team) has secured his good standing with school personnel.

However, Carlos, the middle child, while also retaining native proficiency in Spanish and near-native proficiency in English, has experienced frequent difficulties in his school work. María is willing to expend a great deal of time and energy to ensure that her sons meet school requirements and, as illustrated earlier, she often enlists Ernesto in her efforts to provide the additional help that her middle child sometimes requires. However, in the final analysis María and Esteban's priority is that their children acquire and maintain Spanish. Although María, especially, is aware that Carlos's teachers attribute his lackluster academic performance to insufficient exposure to the English language in the home environment, she does not agree with their position:

> *Yo he tenido problemas con sus maestras- porque las maestras me dicen que tienen que dejar un poco atrás el español para que vayan más rápido en las clases. Y yo digo que no, que las clases pueden seguir siendo en inglés y todo y que los niños sigan en español como- como hasta ahora.*

> (I've had problems with their teachers- because the teachers tell me that they have to forget about Spanish a bit so that they can progress more rapidly in their classes. And I say no, that the classes may continue in English and everything and that the children may continue in Spanish as- as they have until now.)

Where possible, however, in interactions with school personnel she steers clear of the topic. Part of her motivation for this minimalist strategy is to avoid a fractious relationship with the school, and partly, given her and her partner's priorities, she considers the issue moot.

Academic Literacy as a Home and School Language: The Villegases

We met Mariana and Enrique Villegas and their daughter Diana (age 11) and son Luis (age 5) in chapter 3. We witnessed the evolution of the parents' resolve to maintain the mother tongue and avert cultural loss, and saw how this commitment led to their decision, from the time Diana entered third grade, to interact with their daughter in Spanish, and to require the use of Spanish in return. In addition, Mariana, with the help of books sent from Mexico by her mother-in-law, began a formal program of teaching her daughter to read and write in Spanish. At the same time we noted Mariana and Enrique's preoccupation with securing a quality formal education for their daughter and saw how this concern led them to enroll Diana in St. Mary's Academy, a private Catholic school.

Despite the official Spanish-only policy that governs the Villegas household, Diana speaks a considerable amount of English with her parents when the topic centers around homework activity. Because in this household a high value is placed on academic achievement, Mariana makes an exception to her Spanish-only policy for the purpose of assisting her daughter with academic subject matter. She reasons that content understanding is primary, and because Diana's stronger language in the school domain is English, she would be undermining her own purpose by introducing a new vocabulary in Spanish. The following example, recorded during a weekday afternoon, is from a tutorial session focusing on a math homework assignment with which Diana is having difficulty.

Diana:	Um, OK. I didn't get that one ...
Mariana:	OK/I had trouble./
Mariana:	OK. What does it- the Wulf family uses an average of three hundred, ninety-one, point four kilowatt hours each month, so they pay this each month. What could you do- what's the equation, *qué- qué ecuación hiciste ahí?* (what- what equation did you write here?)
Diana:	XX multiply this XX.
Mariana:	*No:, por qué multiplicas? Si ellos pagan esto al mes, es lo que ellos pagan al mes, digo, e:r por hora, por cada kilowatt, déjame tú mi calculadora.* (No, why do you multiply? If they pay this much a month, it's what they pay each month, say, er, per hour, for each kilowatt, give me my calculator.) [Diana returns with the calculator. Mariana starts making the calculation.] *Trescientos noventa y uno, punto cuatro, cero punto diez y ocho, mamita, sí multiplicaste,* (Three hundred and one point four, zero point eighteen, my little one, yes, you multiplied) it's absolutely right. *Te acuerdas que te dije* (Remember what I told you), when you see these words "per"/Diana: uhhum/it's the same as saying "times," remember? How come, when you multiply this by this, gives you this? No way! The answer is seventy point forty-five!

Diana:	How did you get that?
Mariana:	I multiplied three ninety-one, point fi- er four, times- *¡a ver!* (Let's see!) Do it! *¡Hazlo!* (Do it!)
Diana:	Three ninety-one- *¡No! ¡Yo lo sé, yo lo sé!* (No! I've got it, I've got it!) Oops! Three ninety-one.

We see that in some cases Spanish is used for emphasis, as in Mariana's repetition of the question "what's the equation?" first in English and then in Spanish. A similar emphatic use of Spanish can be observed in Mariana's command to Diana to perform the required calculation, "Do it! *¡Hazlo!*" In these examples, as in her command to her daughter to fetch a calculator, Mariana appears to use Spanish to emphasize the seriousness of the directives. Moreover, the commands themselves provide Diana with no relevant information that is not already available in English or they are extraneous to the solution of the math problem on which mother and daughter are working. However, Mariana also uses Spanish for explanations that are crucial to the solution of the problem, such as *"Si ellos pagan esto al mes ..."* ("If they pay this much a month ...") This explanation of the relationship between the monthly utility bill and the amount per kilowatt hour is not repeated in English elsewhere in the discourse, and, judging from her comment (*"¡Yo lo sé!,* I've got it!"), Diana's understanding is not impeded by her mother's code alternation.

Tutorial sessions of the type illustrated occur frequently in the Villegas household, where "doing school," as Diana puts it, is an integral part of family routine. Unlike the large majority of families with whom we worked, the Villegases also "do school" for recreational purposes, that is, at times where activities involving academic literacy are not explicitly required by school personnel. In the following interaction, Diana, seated at the family computer, is pretending to be a receptionist in a medical office, while young Luis, for whom the household language policy is relaxed, plays the role of a new patient. In the exchange, revealing initiation, response, evaluation sequences representative of formal schooling environments (Cazden, 1988; Mehan, 1979), Luis speaks entirely in English. Diana uses mostly English as well, with only a few formulaic Spanish phrases:

Diana:	Hold on, yes? O.K. U:rm, we need you to fill out this form, your name is Luis what?
Luis:	Villegas.
Diana:	Luis Villegas. Let's put you on the computer. Er Villegas?
Luis:	Uhhum [he makes engine noise while she types].
Diana:	Villegas, O.K. *¿Cuántos años tienes?* (How old are you?)
Luis:	Five years.
Diana:	Your age is five. Erm, *¿dónde vives?* (Where do you live?)
Luis:	Five, five, five.
Diana:	No.
Luis:	Fifty, fifty, six, six.
Diana:	Ma- di- son [reads as types]. O:h, Lincoln City?
Luis:	Aha.
Diana:	Lincoln- City?
Luis:	Uhhum.
Diana:	Lincoln City, California, what is your zip code? Nine, four, one, two, three. O.K. well, we just want you to fill out this form, er, I want you to put your name, er, where you live, erm, the problem you're having ....[3]

The flexibility shown by Diana's parents with regard to language choice for the performance of school literacy has been extended to other school-related topics that do not involve instructional discourse. In these instances, however, the English phrases tend to be of the formulaic variety normally associated with the protocols of schooling, which, given the school's monolingual character, would have been is-

---

[3]The address given here is, of course, fictitious.

sued in English. Here, for example, on a Wednesday evening, Mariana elicits some information from Diana that she needs in order to organize her laundry:

Mother:	*¿Diana, el viernes vas a llevar uniforme?* (Diana, are you going to wear your uniform on Friday?)
Diana:	*¿El viernes? ¿Este viernes?* (Friday? This Friday?)
Mother:	Yeah.
Diana:	Uhm. No.
Mother:	*¿No?*
Diana:	*No.*
Mother:	It's free dress?

In general, Diana has been able to navigate the changes in the language environment that have characterized her life at home and at school. Before her family moved to California, she was well on the way to full acquisition of Spanish as her primary language. After the move, she adjusted to the new environment of an all-English day-care program. During her preschool years in Lincoln City, Spanish remained the language of home interactions. However, the home language environment changed abruptly to English when Diana entered St. Mary's, and then just as abruptly changed back to Spanish a few years later as the parents attempted to avert cultural loss. Throughout these changes, Diana developed native-like command of English without losing oral proficiency in Spanish. Her private speech is characterized by frequent code alternation, and she has developed appropriate sociolinguistic rules for dealing with interlocutors and domains. In conversations about school or school-like texts, she uses English primarily, both with her parents and when she assumes an adult, teacherly role with her younger brother. However, she does not experience problems when her parents use Spanish in explanations of school-related tasks: Academic literacy is a code that Diana engages comfortably both at home and at school and in both Spanish and English.

English Literacy as a Second Language: The Esparzas

We want to return briefly to the case of the Esparza family, in which the daughter, Marcella (age 11), attends a private, Catholic school with Diana Villegas. Marcella's mother, Teresa, it will be recalled, relied on recordings of English children's books to prepare her preschool daughter for a private English-medium school. Using audio cassettes in conjunction with printed materials, she taught herself to understand and speak English as she pretended to read to her baby daughter. Thus, mother and daughter's acquisition of English language and literacy proceeded simultaneously.

When we meet Marcella, now in sixth grade, Teresa's decision to place her daughter in a private, English-medium school appears to have produced successful results. Until recently Marcella has been receiving straight A's on her report card, and Teresa is generally satisfied with her daughter's academic achievement. With increasing difficulty, Teresa has managed to facilitate Marcella's academic learning at home. Notwithstanding that Teresa's proficiency in English has improved considerably since she decided to modify her monolingual Spanish lifestyle to prepare her daughter for an English-medium school program, in the upper elementary grades the appearance on Marcella's report card of several B's in math and science has been of concern. Both mother and daughter attribute the drop in grades to the fact that the academic subject matter has by now surpassed the mother's abilities, and consequently, she can no longer assist Marcella with homework. Asked whether her mom helps her with her homework, Marcella explains,

A veces sí cuando estaba más chiquita sí pero como ya voy a grados más altos y ya no me ayuda porque ella no- no fué a la escuela mucho porque ella vivía en ranchos.

(Sometimes yes when I was littler yes, but since now I go to higher grades and now she doesn't help me because she didn't, didn't go to school much because she lived on ranches.)

However, Teresa, ever resourceful, has found a strategy to compensate for what she perceives to be the limitations of her own educational background with regard to her daughter's academic development: She has enlisted the aid of Mariana Villegas (see earlier description), the most highly educated of the parents of Marcella's friends, as a tutor. Because her level of education and her English proficiency are considerably higher than most of the parents of Diana's Mexican-background school friends, Mariana often takes an active role in instructing these children. These informal pair or group tutoring sessions, normally conducted in English, involve a range of school subjects. During our late-afternoon observations, we recorded Mariana preparing Diana, Marcella, and another friend—either as a cohort of three or a team of two—for language arts, social studies, and math tests. Mariana sat at the kitchen table with the girls and quizzed them on spelling/vocabulary, providing corrections and rule explanations, or guided them to the solutions to word problems assigned as math homework.[4] Here we find Mariana coaching Marcella and Diana for an upcoming math exam:

Mariana: [to Marcella, pointing to an error on Marcella's worksheet] *¿Cómo se llama esto?* (What is this called?)

Marcella: Proper fractions.

Mariana: Oh, I know what you did. You just subtracted six minus one. You forgot about the whole process eh?

Marcella: Uhuh. [pointing elsewhere on her worksheet] I forgot about the whole process there too.

In this manner, that is, with the aid of extended support networks, Marcella's English literacy has developed to the point where her uses of reading and writing for academic purposes are indistinguishable from those of native speakers.

Academic Literacy as an Inaccessible Language: The Ríos Family

Manuel and Emilia Ríos were born, raised, and married in a small village in the central Mexican state of Michoacán. In 1986, they emigrated to the

---

[4]Mariana's role as academic mentor to her daughter's friends is valued in the community, although it often seems to entail heavy responsibilities. During one visit, Mariana complained about a call she had recently received from Teresa Esparza, Marcella's mother. Marcella had been less successful than her mother believed she should have been on a math test for which Mariana had been helping her to prepare, and Teresa held the tutor accountable.

United States with their three older children, Moises (17), Manuel (15), and Belinda (11). Belinda was 2 years old at the time. Her two younger siblings, Amy (8) and Higinio (6), are United States-born. The Ríoses reside in a cold-water, two-bedroom tenement flat in San Ignacio, California. By pragmatic necessity, the language of parent–child interaction in the home is Spanish. Both Emilia and Manuel, Sr., speak little to no English (Manuel: *"muy poquito, lo mínimo, nada"*), and their receptive capacities are similarly minimal (Emilia: *"muy poco entiendo"*). Manuel explains matter-of-factly: *"Si mi hablan en inglés no voy a entender."* ("If they speak to me in English, I won't understand.")

When it was time for Belinda to begin her formal education, the district board assigned the child to Cesar Chavez Elementary, a local bilingual school, even though neither parent had requested that their daughter be placed in a bilingual program. According to Belinda's parents, had they been consulted they would have elected to send their daughter to an English-medium school: *"Que aprendan bien el idioma del inglés, estamos en este país, que lo hablen bien"* ("They need to learn to speak the English language well, we're in this country, they need to speak it well").

During the period of our intensive involvement with the family, Belinda attended sixth and seventh grade at Mark Twain Middle School, an English-medium school in her local district. On recommendation of school personnel, who determined that bilingual instruction had not contributed sufficiently to Belinda's academic development, the child was transferred out of a bilingual and into a regular English program at the end of fifth grade. After completing sixth grade, Belinda was promoted to seventh grade but transferred once again, this time into a special class for ESL students within the same school. The fact that their daughter was receiving special instruction within an ESL framework came as a surprise to Belinda's parents when we inquired about the reasons underlying the school's decision to place their daughter in a class where the curriculum was designed for nonnative speakers of English. Although the Ríoses doubted that Belinda was receiving an adequate education in the bilingual program and supported her transfer to English-medium instruction, they remained under the impression that their daughter continued to be enrolled in a "regular" English class. Nor could they recall being informed of a change in her placement.

For her part, Belinda is sanguine about the recent change in her status, explaining that she was "switched into ESL because I didn't know how to read" and also had *"dificultades en escritura"* ("difficulties with writing"). Asked whether she had not been taught to read and write in her regular English class, she responded without hesitation, "No, you're supposed to know how." In the following exchange with Sandra, Belinda expresses her optimistic view that the most recent placement change has started to produce positive results:

Belinda:	Since last year, I choose the books that got more pictures than this year.
Sandra:	Yeah, because you were younger, during-
Belinda:	-No, because I didn't know how to read last year.
Sandra:	So last year you couldn't read but this year you *can* read. So how did *that* happen?
Belinda:	We always read in the ESL class, so I=
Sandra:	=So in the ESL class they teach you how to read but don't they teach you how to read in regular English class?
Belinda:	I don't got English, you see.
Sandra:	You didn't learn English?
Belinda:	I don't know why. That's what the teacher told me, that I jus- I need to have English, because I didn't know how to write- I don't know how to write well and I don't know how to read well.
Sandra:	Oh, so they put you in ESL, so that they can teach you.
Belinda:	Since last year.
Sandra:	Well you know how to read now, that's great! Does it feel good?
Belinda:	Uh huh. Now I will read- I wanna read a who:le chapter book.

At home with her parents and siblings, Belinda speaks almost exclusively Spanish, although her talk is peppered with common English politeness forms: *"Llámale a Higinio,* please, *dile que se venga"* ("Call Higinio, please, and tell him to come"). Although Belinda's parents are not in a position to evaluate their daughter's English-language proficiency, they did volunteer an informal assessment of her bilingual language usage: *"Hay ciertas cosas que="* ("There are some things which=") Manuel began; *"= no sabe en español y no lo dice en inglés tampoco"* ("she doesn't know in Spanish and she can't say in English either"), his partner Emilia completed his thought. They then provided an example of their daughter attempting to describe a frightening event she had experienced but lacking the necessary vocabulary in either code. Only months later, when Belinda showed them a photo she had come across in a magazine, did Sr. and Sra. Ríos realize that their daughter had been caught in a lightning storm, or *relámpagos.* In a separate interview, Belinda volunteered a similar assessment of her bilingual language proficiency, asserting that she speaks neither Spanish nor English well, but that in her view Spanish is her stronger idiom. She attributed this dilemma to confusion caused by the simultaneous presence of two codes: "Sometimes I mix the words in Spanish and English," "I'm too mixed up with the words."[5]

Most Ríos family interactions take place in the living room, which houses the family's television set. The majority of programs watched are on the English-medium channels, although the Ríoses watch considerably more Spanish television than almost all of the families we worked with both in California and in Texas.

On weekend mornings, Belinda is responsible for a variety of household chores—dusting, cleaning, tidying—while one or both of her parents work outside the home and her siblings are otherwise engaged. At those times she produces almost no oral language. Later in the day she is most often found in the presence of a peer cohort—shooting baskets on a makeshift court in the alley behind her apartment house, participating in rehearsals for cousins' or friends' *quinceañeras,*[6] hanging out and listen-

---

[5]In the professional literature, the phenomenon that Belinda describes here is sometimes referred to as *semilingualism,* a theoretical construct that has been seriously challenged (see, e.g., Romaine, 1995).

[6]The *quinceañera,* the fifteenth birthday party, is a major event in Mexican and Latin American families generally, and often involves years of planning and saving. For young women, it is the occasion for the family and community to mark the transition from childhood to young adulthood.

ing to music. In this company, she speaks Spanish predominantly, albeit with many observed instances of code switching. The following example, where Belinda is discussing plans for her upcoming birthday party, demonstrates the influence of the school milieu on Belinda's code-switching practices: *"Porque yo voy a hacer- voy a invitar puras* girls, *de- de- de* seven graders, *puras* seven graders" ("Because I am going to make- I am going to invite only girls, seventh graders, only seventh graders"). However, with her peers, as in the home, code mixing and lexical borrowings are important components of Belinda's linguistic repertoire. Here she is identifying a classmate to whose birthday celebration she is invited: *"Los* chores *cuadrados con la camisa blanca, ella es la que los cumple"* ("The one with the plaid shorts and white blouse, that's whose birthday it is").

On weekdays, returning from school in the late afternoon, Belinda watches television in the company of her younger siblings. Beside her, on either the floor or sofa, lie her two backpacks—the black one she uses for school and the stylish brown one we purchased for her (and the other focal children) as a present and also to protect the recording equipment used over many months of observations. Often her school pack remains undisturbed through the duration of our observation (4 to 5 hours); at other times she unzips the pack and removes papers and notebooks. One day Sandra noticed a group of (a dozen or more) three-by-five index cards lying in pick-up-sticks, random distribution on the floor. Gathering them up, Sandra saw that on one side appeared a single lexical item, in Belinda's print; on the reverse side, also in Belinda's hand (halfway between print and cursive), were lengthier, dictionary-style definitions. She began to ask Belinda the meanings of the various lexical items she had written on one side of the cards and, conversely, to elicit the lexical item that corresponded to the dictionary definitions she had recorded on the other side. An increasingly attentive Belinda abandoned the television screen to fix on Sandra and the cards she pulled from between her fingers. Younger sister Amy, also present in the room, watched intently, mouthing responses to queries directed to Belinda. Several minutes into this activity, Sra. Ríos entered the room from the adjacent kitchen where she had been preparing the family's dinner. For the duration of this quasi-instructional sequence, approximately 10 minutes, she remained standing, silently observing.

When the sequence had ended, as Belinda and her sister resumed their television watching (and Sandra her note-taking), Sra. Ríos asked Sandra whether she had been to see her daughter's teacher. No, of course not, we reassured, we would never presume in such a way (unless a host family specifically requested our assistance in advocating with school personnel). Then how, asked Belinda's mother, her mind working a scenario very different from the one we thought she was considering, did Sandra know what to do with the cards?

When it comes to assisting their children with homework, Belinda's parents are out of their element, although Sra. Ríos tries to assist with math and science to the extent that her English-language proficiency permits:

Belinda:	*¡No, siete!*
Mother:	*¿Por qué siete?*
Belinda:	*Mira, amá- porque tenemos que ver el- el- cómo se dice, el* pattern.
Mother:	*¿Pero* "pattern" *es?*
(Belinda:	No, seven!
Mother:	Why seven?
Belinda:	Look, Mom- because we have to see the- the- how do you say, the pattern.
Mother:	But the "pattern" is?)

Neither is academic support forthcoming from Belinda's siblings: One of her older brothers has already dropped out of school; the other works for wages while not at school and is rarely seen in the company of his siblings. Another obstacle to Belinda's doing school-related work at home is that the family's circumstances do not permit the purchase of a calculator, newspapers, and other required resources, a predicament that encourages Belinda to try to complete her math and current events assignments hurriedly in class. Apparently these circumstances are known to Belinda's teacher and the compensatory strategy is sanctioned: *"Nos dijo la maestra, 'XX ahora la pueden acabar horita,' porque dijo la maestra, 'si no tienen calculadora, no se pueden acabar mañana,' mejor la acabo en la clase"* ("Our teacher told us, 'You can finish it now,' because our teacher said, 'If you don't have a calculator you can't finish tomorrow,' I better finish it in class"). Moreover, unlike Teresa Esparza, Belinda's family does not have access to a community network where academic support can be provided by a school-educated adult familiar with the expectations and routines of formal learning environments. Also, although Belinda's parents are, in fact, able to read and write Spanish, they are not literate in the ways of American schooling. At a systemic level, they are unaware of their options with regard to their daughter's formal education, and they have no idea how to access the system to find this crucial information. At a discourse level, they are unfamiliar with the text-based conventions associated with academic literacy—at least with the performance of activities associated with school-based reading and writing. Moreover, they are unlikely to encounter these conventions and codes through the normal conduct of their daily lives. For the Ríoses, reading and writing represent awkward, imposed practices that do not mediate the central social relations in their lives. To the extent that it is not used for intentional, real-life purposes, written language is not an important part of their worlds. In fact, this code serves few functions other than to render them invisible to those for whom practices associated with academic literacy constitute the key agenda of child socialization (cf. Gee, 1990; Graff, 1987).

HOME LANGUAGE PRACTICES, SCHOOL LITERACY, AND LITERACY ABOUT SCHOOLING

As with the families we have profiled, both in California and Texas, the majority of Mexicano parents we spoke with are significantly involved with their children's schooling, and many have developed creative strategies to compensate for what they perceive to be their own limitations. The parents with whom we worked, whose strongest or only language differs from that of the school, have adopted a wide range of strategies to assist their children with school-related tasks. These strategies include using audio recordings of children's books to teach a child to read in English, using the cooperative social networks that characterize Latino immigrant communities to find assistance for a child when the level of schoolwork surpasses the mother's educational attainment, and providing at home tutorial and review sessions in English and/or Spanish when children experience difficulty with particular subjects. For the most part, moreover, these strategies are expressions of well-formed ideologies—about factors that parents believe foster their children's language learning and academic development.

Interacting with this first set of beliefs concerning orientation to school-based learning is a second constellation of values concerning the relative importance of minority-language maintenance and the extent to which attention to related goals can be adapted to complement, rather than undermine, the agenda of school-based learning. Here, however, caregivers differ in their ability and willingness to alter their home language practices to match those of the schools their children attend. As in this chapter, in about half the families parents have modified their home language practices (sometimes repeatedly) to fulfill the often conflicting requirements of school success for the children, the expectations of family members who wish to see Spanish transmitted to the next generation, and the pragmatic requirements of communication with Spanish monolingual members of the household. The Villegas and Esparza families illustrate the dilemmas faced by parents who attempt to alter patterns of home language use to meet what they perceive to be the expectations of the schools. However, the Villegases possess far greater linguistic and cultural capital than the Esparzas, in English proficiency, particularly on the part of Mariana, and in access to both Spanish and English literacy in the form of books and other (than textual) mass media discourses on current events and the arts. Thus, they have greater facility in meeting the conflicting demands that originate from the school and their own family members and, when the scales tip, in altering their home language practices accordingly.

The case of the Gómez family demonstrates the persistence required by parents who wish to maintain a minority language as the language of the home while fostering their children's academic development in the dominant language. María and Esteban's insistence that their children use only Spanish at home, including in sibling–sibling interactions, is facilitated by the relative isolation of the ranch on which they live as well as by their frequent visits with the Mexican relatives who form their primary social networks. Insistence on the use of Spanish in home interactions, however, does not preclude parental involvement in the school's activities. María

Gómez's lack of proficiency in the language of the school does prevent her from working with her sons in some areas of the curriculum. Nevertheless, she is actively engaged in areas where she can be of help and closely monitors her children's progress in other areas as well. Interestingly, in the case of the Gómezes' older son, who excels in school, although Ernesto's teachers fail to recognize the value of the Spanish input from family members, neither do such discourse practices appear to have elicited negative reactions. However, educators involved with the Gómezes' middle son, Carlos, for whom academic learning has proved a struggle, have been quick to seize on the family's practice of using only Spanish in the home language environment as a significant causal factor underlying the child's difficulties in school. None of the schools—neither those serving focal children who are successful academically nor those serving focal children who are not— have expressed a transcendent commitment to "parent involvement in education" by showing interest in parents' views concerning the concurrent versus complementary roles of home and school in relation to Spanish maintenance and the acquisition of the societally dominant language.

For the most part, however, families are not without support in their efforts to implement the decisions they have arrived at concerning their children's language development. Of the families discussed in this chapter, for example, both the Gómezes and the Villegases have considerable support from their extended families for their decisions to pursue Spanish-language maintenance, the Gómez family from relatives with whom they visit frequently and the Villegas family from Enrique's mother, who not only visits her son and daughter-in-law in California but regularly sends Spanish-language reading materials from Mexico. Moreover, despite their very different circumstances, both the Gómez and Villegas families possess considerable educational capital. Unlike Enrique and Mariana Villegas, neither María nor Esteban Gómez has ever attended a university in Mexico, or even the university preparatory schools that are the Mexican equivalent of U.S. academic high schools. However, as graduates of Mexican *secundarias,*[7] their education ex-

---

[7]The Mexican public educational system is divided into three levels: primary (6 years), secondary (3 years), and university preparatory (2 to 3 years). The preparatory schools are normally attached to public universities. At the time the immigrant parents in our study were attending school in Mexico, 6 years of education were compulsory, although this was not always observed, particularly in rural areas.

tended 3 years beyond the mandatory schooling required in their country, and in María's case also included a 1-year paraprofessional course.

With regard to family resources and educational capital, the Esparza and the Ríos families present a striking contrast to the Gómez and Villegas families, as well as to each other. When they arrived in the United States, neither Sra. Esparza nor Sr. and Sra. Ríos had family members who could support their children's acquisition of literacy in any language, nor did they themselves have the educational backgrounds that would have facilitated the task of literacy instruction. As we have seen, however, Teresa Esparza did have a clear vision of the future she desired for her daughter and was able to use the limited resources available—primarily children's books and cassettes. She later was able to enlist the aid of Mariana Villegas to assist her daughter with school work.

Finally, the case of Belinda Ríos provides a dramatic illustration of the implicit assumptions underlying the position of mass compulsory schooling with regard to "parent involvement" by showing the disconnect that can ensue when families do not anticipate, support, and extend the issues and agendas of schools. Belinda's parents do not do—indeed, they do not know *how* to do—educational work that fits with and supports the ordinary activities of their daughter's classroom, nor do they have access to the resources that would enable them to acquire such knowledge. They do not understand reading and writing as cultural, as well as schematic, practices that constitute an essential component of their roles and responsibilities as caregivers (Purcell-Gates, 1995). Rather, they have entrusted their child's academic development and, by extension, longer term interests, to an educational system that assumes a shared construction of the "partnership" it enjoys with Belinda's family. In addition, like a significant minority of immigrant parents who participated in our project, the Ríoses report confusion about the nature of the school programs in which their children are enrolled.

These findings are, indeed, no different from that what we have observed in other societal contexts. Certainly they are understandable, given the continuing gap between Latino school performance and the performance of members of the majority group (August & Hakuta, 1997). Nevertheless, we view as unsettling the increasing tendency on the part of contemporary schooling—as reflected in curricular reform efforts at the state and local levels—to link parents' performance of activities that support and extend the school's agenda to children's educability. It is, moreover, troubling that what most distinguishes Belinda's family from the others we have presented as representative of a larger cohort is not that they lack proficiency in English, or that they speak predominantly Spanish in the home, or even that literacy does not occupy a central place in their daily lives. It is, rather, that Belinda's parents, and more particularly her mother—for in this society it is women who are primarily entrusted with the work of supporting the educational agenda of schooling and who are held accountable for their children's inadequacies—did not know what to do with the three-by-five index cards. This stark image embodying Belinda's school failure provides the most compelling testimony that these tacit norms and implicit expectations, in addition to contributing to the stressful nature of parenting for many linguistic minority parents, do little to address the gaps and disjunctures in the unequal relationship between low-status families and mainstream schools.

7

Language Socialization
in Theory and Practice

We met Nilda Quintana in the summer of 1992, through an acquaintance who worked in a California state community college.[1] At the time, Nilda was 29 years old, a single mother who was raised in a Latino farm worker community by Mexican immigrant parents who spoke Spanish at home. However, as we discovered, Nilda's own decisions regarding her child's language socialization reflected the ebb and flow of her adult life, a life in which, as she came to terms with it, she had lived in "two worlds."

For reasons we could not fully articulate—or did not have full access to—we found Nilda's story immediately compelling. As we began to design a research agenda that would make a contribution to understanding of the relationship between family language environment and the development of bilingual abilities, we sought to reconcile Nilda's account with our own knowledge about the language socialization of children and youth. As should more often be the case when researchers attempt to get on with their agendas by reducing individuals' complex, recalcitrant trajectories into well-formed, theoretically rationalized scenarios, this process of reconciliation was not easily negotiated; throughout the design and fieldwork stages of the project, Nilda's narratives hovered in

---

[1]The "we" here refers to Sandra and Diane Sharken-Taboada, then a doctoral student at University of California, Berkeley, and research assistant for the pilot study, "Bilingual by Choice" (Schecter et al., 1996).

the virtual spaces where composing themes flicker and recede—a taunting refrain.

SHIFTING LOCATIONS: A DIACHRONIC PERSPECTIVE

In the text that follows, we have edited Nilda's narrative to highlight the junctures at which she chose to turn away from, or enter anew into, a commitment to Spanish language maintenance for herself and her son, Jaime, age 13. Nilda's decisions were not only about language; nor was language necessarily at all times Nilda's primary consideration. From Nilda's account we might conclude that at certain junctures language was of primary concern; at others, it was a complicating factor in the influences that bore on decisions regarding the direction of her life and the definition of her personhood.

We join Nilda's narrative at the point where she located and assumed responsibility for her own actions in matters of importance, including language choice.

> (1) When I left home, I was fifteen. I ran away from home. And that's when I got married. And I got pregnant, and it seemed inconceivable to me that I would teach my son anything else but Spanish. Because I *knew* that if he went into the school system, he'd learn English. And I spoke English, so I could always help him out in that way. But to think that my son would lose out on all that I had learned and all that was me. There was too much of me to say, "Well now you learn English so you can get ahead." Well the world that we learned gets you ahead is an alien world. And is a non-family world. So the family is- the core culture ... And I married a Mexican man who only spoke Spanish, and he wanted his son to speak Spanish so when we went to Mexico his son could speak with his father.

At this juncture, Nilda's decision to pursue a Spanish-dominant home language use strategy appears to have been based on both cultural identity and pragmatic considerations. Clearly, Nilda's decision to speak Spanish with her son was motivated by her desire to maintain Mexican cultural values that she considered an integral component of her identity. However, from a practical perspective, Jaime also needed to acquire Spanish to communicate with his monolingual Spanish-speaking father and with his father's relatives who resided in Mexico.

We next encounter Nilda several years into what may appear on the surface a traditional marriage. At this point she was troubled by what she perceived as the inhibiting nature of her primary relationship.

> (2) So for seven years I did. I scrubbed, I cleaned ... and this [points to head] was going wild! I wanted to read, I wanted to write, I wanted to learn, and it seemed that my only world was my husband. When I told my husband, "You know I think I wanna do this," "I wanna go to the library," "I went to the library today," "I bought books," well that became kind of threatening for my ex-husband because he felt, "Well, what's in the books?" "Oh just things." "Well, what things?" "Well- just things." Well I- I- I had to stop reading novels, I had to stop reading history, I had to bring down- What is this guy's name? Doctor-Dodson or Doctor, I don't know, I bought all these baby books. And I'd bring six- six baby books and then one book of a novel or something and hide the novel inside. I ended up hiding all my books. I ended up hiding magazines. I ended up hiding anything that brought another culture or another world view into my home. Because that would be stepping outside- of what I had learned.

Predictably, a time came when Nilda decided she could no longer sustain the inauthentic persona she saw represented by her role in the partnership, and she sought a divorce. In the following excerpt, Nilda describes the compromise she arrived at in an attempt to gain her young son's acceptance of this decision, a compromise with implications for language use in the Quintana household.

> (3) I divorced my ex-husband, and I went to school, and it was too painful to communicate with my son in Spanish. If I said, *"M'hijo, todo va a estar bien"* ("My son, everything will be OK"), I knew that within that world- I had broken with that world when I left my ex-husband. So, I would say in English, "You know what, sweetheart, things change." And- I- I thought if I said it in English- he

LANGUAGE SOCIALIZATION   **169**

could understand on *that* level. Because um the traditional pattern is so strong you must not break it. You-
you just must not.

Over time, English asserted a position of dominance in the Quintana
household. Certainly it required minimal effort to use English. Both
mother and son were United States-born, and spoke the language fluently. Moreover, English did not resonate with the painful personal bag-
gage that Nilda and Jaime associated with Spanish. However, as the
traumatic effects of the divorce subsided, Nilda decreasingly viewed the
use of English in her home as a necessary accommodation strategy. She
began rather to associate it with a reductionist attack on her identity,
which she saw the need to resist.

> (4) It was in the sixth grade where I'd say, "Jaime," and he
> seemed not to want to speak Spanish with me, although
> he continued to speak only Spanish with his father. And
> that felt insulting and alienating, a way to keep me out
> of his father's world which was really one of my worlds
> too. So I forced my son, in different ways, to begin to
> speak the language to me again … Now he identifies
> with the core culture. *"Soy Mexicano, soy Chicano."*
> ("I'm Mexican, I'm Chicano.")

But Jaime's rededication to his cultural heritage proved short-lived,
and when we next spoke, Nilda was experiencing some difficulty in her
efforts to maintain Spanish with her son. She attributed the change in
Jaime's attitude to a recent move. Within the preceding year they had re-
located to a neighborhood closer to the community college where Nilda
was resuming her studies. Since that time Nilda had observed a tendency
on Jaime's part to use English in the home. She also reported feeling
somewhat helpless to affect this shift, in the face of her teenage son's
growing autonomy.

> (5) [Recently] we moved away from the community that he
> belongs to and that I was raised in, where most of the
> households are Mexican American, and it's been a very
> trying year. He decided this year that he didn't want to
> take Spanish in school, he was gonna take French … It

> was a great struggle, to belong, to not, who do I belong
> to, who am I ... And I want him to continue to learn
> Spanish, and to see it as enriching, as the door to his
> other world.

In the final analysis, however, the bilingual status of the Quintana household, and in particular Nilda and Jaime's code-switching abilities, were proving useful to mother and son in reconciling the cultural traditions to which they remained attached with the complexities presented by modern life in the multicultural community in which they found themselves. In this final excerpt, Nilda provides a compelling example of resourceful use of her own and Jaime's bilingual skills.

> (6) I don't want my son to have sex until he's ready to. I
> don't want him to have sex before he's eighteen when he
> can make a responsible decision. I would not discuss it in
> Spanish with my son. But in English I know. "You, if- if
> anything were to happen, use a condom." If my son were
> to contract AIDS just for some adventure with his friends,
> I would die. And drugs, no drugs. And drugs in Spanish,
> well I don't say *"No tomes drogas"* ["don't use drugs"]. It's
> a- it would be an insult to offend my son to say *"No usas
> drogas."* In Spanish it's assumed that my son has a behav-
> ior that will be responsible to me as his MO:ther.

Let us now revisit our original research goals. Our main agenda was to explore in depth the relationship between family language environment and bilingual development, in societal and situational contexts where individuals may encounter—to greater or lesser extents—both the dominant and minority languages. We viewed this inquiry as contextualized in and by a tradition of research on language socialization, especially those studies that focused on the acquisition of language abilities on the part of children in bilingual and multilingual settings. We were interested in investigating children's developing abilities (or, conversely, the atrophy of these abilities) in various speech and literacy events as well as in changes in the symbolic meanings that family members attached to the uses of Spanish and English. Because we envisioned our research as contributing to a growing body of work that explores choice of language practices in fluid social contexts, in the planning stage we were especially influenced by research that looked at language socialization throughout the life cycle and that addressed variation in the choice of practices made by individuals in different societal contexts.[2]

However, disposed as we were to interpreting our findings within a sociohistorical and developmental framework, Nilda Quintana's account compelled us to revisit several of the premises we regarded as central. First, although recent sociolinguistic work on language shift and obsolescence has contributed in important ways to our understanding of the social and linguistic processes involved in choice and change at the individual and societal levels, Nilda's testimony heightens our sensitivity to the ephemeral quality of the bilingual persona in fluid societal and situational contexts. In such environments, despite what official characterizations may imply, identity is not a fixed category. Thus, support for a strategy of maintenance may well ensue not from a one-time decision on the part of caregivers regarding family language practice but rather from a series of choices that constitute affirmations and reaffirmations of a commitment to the minority language. Admittedly, this state of existential revisionism regarding the valorization of certain language practices (and the concomitant devaluation of others) does not fairly characterize the experiences of all the families we spoke with. A significant number of respondents, however, contextualized the historical progression of family language practices in a manner that underscored the tenuous nature of any claims we might have wished to make regarding dominant or subordinate status of a given variety for a specific individual.

A second complication: Consistent with a relatively long tradition of research on child language acquisition, we began by conceptualizing language socialization as a unidirectional process, that is, as a process by which adults socialize children into the cultural framework and linguistic repertoire of their society or social subgroup. However, this dy-

---

[2]This work is in contrast to the majority of research reports of parent–child interaction in homes where two or more languages were used which were available in the early nineties. Typically, such reports were based on synchronic descriptions, documenting observations in a number of home settings over a relatively short, circumscribed period. Descriptions tended to follow a patterned format that delineated the language strategy used by each caregiver. Examples are: (a) One parent speaks a nondominant language, one parent speaks the dominant language; (b) both parents speak a nondominant language; and (c) one parent speaks both languages, one parent speaks a nondominant language. Clearly, such synchronic descriptions were not sufficiently responsive to the findings of our pilot study, since they could not account for intragenerational changes in patterns of language use reported by respondents.

namic of directionality is not so straightforward, and developmental factors clearly play a role, as the testimonies of parents of older children revealed.[3] For example, when we examine the more recent portions of Nilda's account, if it could be claimed that one member of the Quintana household were acting in the role of facilitator of the other's socialization to and by language, this facilitator role could not easily be ascribed to the mother. Arguably, by the age of 13, Jaime was exercising a more forceful influence than Nilda on language choice in the Quintana household. Clearly, interpretations of patterns of variation and choice within a framework where language socialization is a one-way process in which mothers, teachers, and other caregivers inculcate the values, knowledge, and linguistic repertoire of their culture *into* children are increasingly problematic in reference to contemporary Western settings where adolescents, and even preadolescents, exercise a fair amount of autonomy within family units. Rather, through their participation in interactions, children also contribute to shaping the process, and caregivers, as we have seen with Nilda, are often changed as a result. In addition, as our research progressed, we became aware of a number of recently published studies that focus on older children's socially influenced understandings around the empowering and disempowering functions of language and other markers of personal identity such as dress, music, and group affiliation (see, for example, Hoyle & Adger, 1998; Mendoza-Denton,

---

[3]Kulick's (1992) study of language socialization practices in the remote village of Gapun in Papua New Guinea illustrates the interactive nature of language socialization practices. His focus was on the loss of the village language, Taiap, and the shift by children to Tok Pisin, an English-lexified contact language that serves as the main *lingua franca* and official language in a country with more than 700 languages. Kulick showed how parental beliefs about the nature of children and the relative difficulties of Taiap and Tok Pisin, as well as the practice of giving older siblings much of the responsibility for child care, resulted in children's receiving much more input in Tok Pisin than in Taiap. In interactions with children, adults frequently received no response when they spoke in Taiap. In such cases, they shifted to Tok Pisin. Children thus had no need to acquire Taiap. They only had to wait to receive the message in Tok Pisin.

A similar situation arose in our own fieldwork in the case of the Sierra family of San Antonio (see Schecter & Bayley, 1998, for a full account). When first interviewed, Alicia Sierra recounted how, with the support of another mother with a child of the same age, she had managed to resist the urgings her own parents and her in-laws, as well as her own inclination, that she use only English with her oldest daughter. She recounted with pride how her daughter had excelled in Spanish classes. Although Alicia regretted that youngest child Larry, age 10, had only minimal productive ability in Spanish, she also spoke about how she usually addressed the boy in Spanish. However, when we later interviewed Larry, we asked him what he did when his mother spoke to him in Spanish. He answered, "I just say 'What?' and she tells me in English." Like the children in the vastly different world of Gapun, Larry felt no need to acquire Spanish because any information that he needed would be forthcoming shortly in English.

1997). Given the cumulative effect of these acts of self–other demarca-
tion, "Who is socializing whom?" is a question we needed to consider
seriously as we sought to account for the complexity of individual language behaviors observed over years and across a spectrum of family
contexts.

The third and perhaps most disorienting complication for a language
socialization framework was the extent to which accounts such as
Nilda's troubled the foundation of the organizing metaphor undergird-
ing this research, the core narrative to which explanatory hypotheses are
fitted. From her story it is clear that Nilda's socialization in the home of
monolingual Spanish-speaking parents predisposed her predominant
use of Spanish as a child. It is equally clear that her acquiring a monolingual Mexican partner predisposed the socialization of her son Jaime to
these same patterns of mother-tongue use and maintenance. Also, it
makes good sense that English would acquire an increased prominence
in the Quintana household during and after Nilda's divorce from her
ex-husband, for reasons—well explained by Nilda—related to degree of
cultural congruence, or incongruence, of given social practices. However, can socialization account for all the various events and turns in
Nilda's life that have consequences for language? Presumably other
Latinas with monolingual Spanish-speaking partners have retrieved
English-language literary works from the library without this activity
being perceived by either them or their partners as provocative and sub-
versive. Presumably other Latinas who speak, read, and write Spanish
fluently have engaged with English-language material while remaining
within the regulatory practices of gender coherence (cf. Butler, 1993,
1999). To what extent does ascribing patterns of language attitude and
choice to the respective socializations of Nilda, her ex-husband (who to
this day remains nameless), and Jaime, as opposed to their wills, obscure the complexity of the perspectives from which they have acted?
Where, and to what degree, might we locate their language attitudes and
practices in their own subjectivities, albeit embedded within a cultural
frame of reference with evolving participation frameworks?

MULTIPLE SUBJECTIVITIES: A SYNCHRONIC PERSPECTIVE

With this appreciation of dialectical tensions in play in the relationships
among language attitudes, situational circumstances, and personal

agency, we return for a final visit to the Villegas household. This time, rather than concentrate on the language practices of our focal child, Diana, we turn the spotlight to focus on her mother, Mariana Villegas, whom we met in chapters 3 and 6. If the case of Nilda Quintana serves to problematize the notion of socialization as a key explanatory factor in relation to linguistic identification that changes over time, the case of Mariana Villegas, which we recount synchronically, reveals another source of difficulty.

To recap: Mariana lives with her husband Enrique, daughter Diana, and young son Luis in Lincoln City, California, close to the *barrio* that contains Lincoln City's majority Mexican-origin population. Both Mariana and Enrique are from professional families in central Mexico. The couple moved to northern California so that Enrique could pursue a business degree, and subsequently made the decision to remain permanently in the United States.

Although the Villegases were concerned about Spanish-language loss on the part of their children, they could not see their way to placing their daughter in a bilingual program in a local public school, where they found the quality of Spanish to be appalling. Further, it is not only in the public schools that the Villegases encountered what they regarded as *"un español muy pobre"* (an impoverished Spanish), but all around them—in the community and in the media as well. In fact, the Villegases see a direct link between the varieties of Spanish common in the United States and lower-class Mexican values and mores. For the Villegases, the main drawback of living in the United States is the absence of the kind of cultural activity they associate with their life in Mexico—museum exhibits, concerts, and media resources where one could depend on *"un buen español, un español estándar"* ("a good Spanish, a standard Spanish").

Diana's teachers at the English-language private school she attends counseled Mariana against teaching Spanish literacy to her daughter and advised the parents to speak English wherever possible in the home, so as not to "create a conflict" that would cause the child to experience problems in school. This advice, they clarified, was not based on any deficits they identified in Diana's learning abilities, but was being offered to "all Mexican parents." Mariana and Enrique elected, nonetheless, to use, and to require Diana to use, Spanish in the home and to teach their daughter to read and write in Spanish. However, as we have seen, Mariana made an exception to her Spanish-only policy for the purpose of assisting her daughter with school-related work, reasoning that because the language of instruction is English, they should follow through in the home in English as well. Mariana's decision to facilitate her daughter's school learning in English was predisposed by another subject position she occupies within the small community of Mexican families whose children attend the private school—that of educated mediator between the Latino community and the academic culture represented by the school. Thus Mariana, proficient in both Spanish and English and literate in the ways of schools, plays a central role in tutoring the cohort of three Latina girls in Diana's class.

We have touched on three subject positions identified with Mariana—that of bilingual, well-educated member of the Mexican professional elite, that of respected literacy mediator, and that of marginalized, immigrant parent (within an acquired deficit perspective). Let us expand briefly on the third. During the course of our field work, Mariana and Enrique were informed that young Luis, age 4, had performed poorly on his entrance exam for kindergarten and would not be accepted as a student at the private school.

According to Mariana, school officials attributed Luis's "cognitive deficit" to the fact that the couple had unwisely ignored their advice to speak only English in the home. Although with us Mariana expressed anger at an elite that sought to consolidate its position of privilege by defining her son as marginal ("I never imagined that a child going into kindergarten would be expected to know how to write his name"), at the same time the incident was catalytic in her appropriating the subject position of minority, given increasing familiarity with a dominant culture where overt descriptors such as race and language are stronger indicators than less visible ones such as class.

Moreover, Mariana came to see it as useful to assume this one-down position: "If they put us with the rest of the Mexicans it's easier." Easier for what? Sandra wanted to know. To get a break on tuition, for one. The Villegases are of Mexican origin; technically they live within the boundaries of Lincoln City, a large ethnic *barrio*. Enrique's earned income is low (as incomes tend to be for graduate students). No one associated with the school thought to ask whether the couple had access to means, and Diana's tuition is subsidized largely through various philanthropic activities coordinated by the school's board of directors.

Two other subject positions that can be associated with Mariana deserve mention. One may be subsumed under the heading "social coordinator." For social gatherings that include extended family and friends, Mariana orchestrates all the preparations, such as food and decor; she is, as well, the family member who appears most bound by etiquette conventions associated with hosting. It is, for example, Mariana who will coordinate the house decorations for family festivities and holiday gatherings, attend to the ice for the *sangría*, and exhort children to stand so that adults might sit.

However, another subject position, in some tension with the more traditional role invoked by the preceding one, is that of equal partner in the domestic realm. In the nuclear family unit, responsibilities for house and child care are more or less evenly divided between Mariana and Enrique, or if they aren't, Mariana will seek before long to reconcile the ledger: "I stayed with them two nights already this week, it's his turn." In this society (and others), such performatives are not consonant with the production of a gendered identity, with the exception perhaps of that associated with an upper-middle-class professional stratum.

MULTIPLE CHARACTERS IN SEARCH OF A THEORY
OF SOCIAL DIFFERENTIATION

We have seen, within a diachronic perspective—that is, by looking at variation or change in language use practices and their signifying functions across time—how with Nilda Quintana the explanatory value of socialization (as opposed to that of agency) can be problematic. The case of Mariana Villegas, viewed synchronically—that is, where we are looking at multiple subjectivities in play at more or less the same time—raises further questions about the notion of socialization. Here, however, the main issue is not so much its explanatory force as the validity of the framework as a measure in ethnographic inquiry. Specifically, which subject positions would descriptions of language socialization patterns in Mariana's history and current home environment be summoned to "explain"? Are there certain subject positions for which these explanations might, arguably, be gratuitous?

From feminist, from postcolonial, and from recent sociolinguistic writings we learn that defining categories are not given a priori but rather produced through people's interactions in particular zones of contact, and that, subsequently, they are subject to shift over time (Bhabba, 1994; Butler, 1999; deCerteau, 1997; Eckert, 2000; Gupta & Ferguson, 1997; Mendoza-Denton, 1997; Pratt, 1987; Spivak, 1993). Our agenda has been more specific than those of many of the authors just cited: It has involved elucidating processes of language maintenance and shift both within and across time. In pursuing this inquiry, we have discovered that various enabling or constraining factors do not necessarily have the same effects for different actors, or for the same actors at different times in their evolutions. Although some of these processes have proven responsive to sociolinguistic hypotheses, we have also learned that in some situations when people have choice, there is a limit to how accurately one can predict how they will choose. Variability implies systematicity, and the controls provided by such structure (Labov, 1971). However, our contention is that in situations of language and dialect contact, or what Pratt (1987) has described as the "contact zone," a fair amount of "online" decision making takes place that is not circumscribed by schematic behavior related to who speaks what language to whom. To be sure, this decision making is ideologically motivated, but ideology, we must insist, is not impervious to individuals' immediate best interests—to factors such as whether the kindly neighbors in the house to the left, as opposed to the mean-spirited ones to the right, speak Spanish or English, or to how weary or energized one finds oneself after work or school. Before continuing, however, we find it useful, at this point, to take up the notion of the construct *contact zone*, a term we used in the preceding paragraph and will use again before our argument is concluded.

The notion of the contact zone was proposed by Pratt (1987), in a critique of the common practice in linguistics of treating either the homogeneous community (in the Chomskyan tradition) or the tightly bounded albeit variable speech community (in the Labovian paradigm) as the norm, and relegating zones of contact to the margins. Pratt proposed instead

a linguistics that decentered community, that placed at its centre the operation of language *across* lines of social differentiation, a linguistics that focused on modes and zones of contact between dominant and dominated groups, between persons of different and multiple identities, speakers of different languages, that focused on how such speakers constitute each other relationally and in difference, how they enact differences in language. (1987, p. 60)

Pratt (1987) further argued that bilingualism should be studied "less as an attribute of a speaker than as a zone for working out social meanings and enacting social differences" (p. 62).

Although Pratt's call for a shift in the focus of linguistics has had considerable influence (see, e.g., Bizzell, 1994), some scholars have been critical. Guerra (1998), for example, voiced concern that Pratt's emphasis on zones of contact may lead to the neglect of "those whose limited economic and educational options give them little choice but to make their homes in highly segregated racial and ethnic communities out of which some members rarely venture" (p. 5). We recognize, of course, that in the United States such communities are common. Labov and Harris (1986), for example, showed that African Americans in Philadelphia were less likely in the 1980s to come into contact with non-African Americans than in previous decades. However, as Santa Ana (1993) and Zentella (1997) showed in their respective analyses of Chicano and New York Puerto Rican communities in the United States, language contact is a defining feature of many Latino communities. Santa Ana's model, in particular, is relevant to the present discussion because he examines the relationships among the multiple language varieties that exist in Mexican-origin communities. He focuses on the many different types of speakers who exist in such communities, ranging from monolingual speakers of standard Mexican Spanish to monolingual speakers of standard varieties of English, with numerous degrees of bilingualism and combinations of language varieties in between. Moreover, as we have seen in our work, even within the same households in nearly exclusively Latino communities, we find household members with differing types of bilingualism and with very different linguistic repertoires. Furthermore, speakers position themselves in various ways, not only synchronically but also diachronically, with respect to the languages and dialects to which they have access and the social and familial groups with which they are affiliated. We thus find that there is no necessary opposition between a focus on the contact zone and a focus on the home front because, in many cases, the home front, whether conceived of as the immediate community or as the individual household, is also a contact zone, as attested by the cases of Nilda Quintana and Mariana Villegas.

Moreover, not only Nilda Quintana and Mariana Villegas, but a good number of other participants as well, displayed a reticence to stand still, as it were, for traditional notions of language socialization that assume a clear differentiation between home and community influences. (It is sobering that such traditional notions, to the effect that "People who speak this language and who are located in this social space and geographic place do this, so children who speak that language and are located in that social space and geographic place learn that," undergird most pedagogic practices and policies.[4]) We have decided not even to presume to count how many influences are present, or to specify a proportion, in deference to the ongoing, shifting circumstances of family members' lives as well as well as the shifting boundaries of their zones of contact. However, if language socialization theory, with its implied determinacy, may not be adequately responsive to the texts of participants' lives, as revealed through interviews and observed practices, then what are we to make of these same texts in terms of informing discourses, or theories, of "culture" and cultural practice? Does the "fractured reality of [their] linguistic experience," in Pratt's words (1987, p. 51), render futile such strategies for understanding?

Given the multiplicity of meanings ascribed to the term *culture,* we wish to be clear as to which of the term's possible meanings we are using in this discussion. Stuart Hall (1996) quite sensibly delineated two rather different senses in which culture is conceptualized in both literary and academic discourses. The first relates to "the sum of the available descriptions through which societies make sense of and reflect their common experiences" (p. 33). This conception of culture is more democratized than earlier variants that admitted only the ideas and artifacts conventionally associated with more refined dimensions of "high culture," such as classical art and music. Within the revised (or revisioned) definition, which may be read as an act of resistance to dominant understandings of what is moral and what has value (Eagleton, 2000), *culture* also includes in referential content ideas and artifacts commonly associated with dimensions of social processes that may be

---

[4]For an excellent elaboration on this state of affairs, see Dyson (1999).

subsumed under "popular culture." Examples drawn from U.S. society include such signifying practices as baseball caps worn backward, baggy pants (on youth), and the expression "wazzup?"

The second conception of *culture* is more deliberately derived from the discipline of anthropology and in turn places more deliberate emphasis on those aspects that refer to social *practices*. Within this definition, studying *culture* concerns the discovery and description of patterns of human organization as well as the analysis of (a) the relationships and interactions between elements within these patterns, and (b) differences in the practices and meanings that arise between social groups such that these groups are viewed as distinctive. Central to the project of inquiry within this framework is a concern with how these conditions and structures of relations are experienced by people, a concern that is reflected in the documentary tradition of ethnography. Implicit in the manner in which we now take up the implications of our findings for theories of culture (as well as the format we have selected for this book) is the framework suggested by this second conception.[5]

We continue, revisiting Nilda's and Mariana's texts with an eye to how they can theoretically inform discourses of culture, or group affiliation and boundedness. Immediately we are confronted with an intriguing paradox, for notwithstanding the liminality of Nilda's and Mariana's extant states with regard to the role of language in their own social locations and, by extension, cultural identifications, at the same time their testimonies reveal visions of a normative community that are as uncomplicated as any revealed through those of participants who inhabited relatively isolated situations, removed from the more fluid contact zone. Nilda no longer claims membership in the Mexican American community—at times she even appears to wear her disaffiliation as a badge of honor—but she has a clear understanding of how "real" members of the community behave. For example, female members stay at home. They

---

[5]There have been divisions—leading to differing foci—among scholars who work within this second conception of the study of culture. The most significant debate has been between two intellectual communities aligned with approaches (some call them *paradigms*; however, we view such nomenclature as overambitious) that have come to be known as *structuralism* and *culturalism*. The former hold that culturalists place a too-inclusive emphasis on the conscious awareness—represented in the articulations—of individual subjects; culturalists, for their part, affirm the specificity of different practices and critique the structuralists for their overreliance on the determinacy of social practices and relations (see Hall, 1996, for a more extensive discussion).

don't read novels. They don't get divorced. Moreover, this concept of the core attributes of Mexican American culture remains stable over time even as Nilda's own psychic positionings toward the definition of her personhood evolve and change.

Mariana, as well, operates with a clear prototype of Mexican core culture—or, more precisely, two prototypes; for she has experienced two distinct cultural conditions. Currently, she finds herself adrift in a Mexican American dystopia, with her family's material conditions no better than those of persons of the same ethnic heritage who speak a vernacular Spanish that she regards as substandard but that constitutes the dominant language of most working-class immigrants. At the same time, she clings to a vision of the glorious world of her youth, where as part of the privileged class she participated in Mexican "high culture," attending dramatic readings and other classical performances rendered in standard Spanish. Her identity, like Nilda's, is contained both in the persona she defines herself as inhabiting and in that of those she sets herself apart from.

We have known both Mariana and Nilda for more than 8 years now. We have witnessed their subject identities—as well as the roles they ascribe to Spanish and English in the practice of these identities—evolve, even as they continue to wrestle with some irreconcilable contradictions, both external and internal. Their expressions of ambivalence and loss are not especially unusual, it may be claimed; these states have been embodied by other immigrant women whose lives have undergone disruptions, or defining displacements (see Chaudhuri, 2001; Heilbrun, 1999; Hoffman, 1989). It is worthy of serious reflection, however, that their prototypes—we may even be entitled to call them "stereotypes"—of what they have left behind, or distanced themselves from, remain fixed. Indeed, Nilda's image of "traditional [Mexican American] culture"—these are *her* words—remains petrified in the moment of disavowal, in the final experience of being perceived to be part of it and sharing in its values. This image, which once made the leaving imaginable, then possible, now serves to make it bearable. From a functionalist perspective, maintaining the prototype is psychologically advantageous: It confirms the goodness of her decision to break ranks and strengthens her resolve to define herself in oppositional tension with an envisioned normative culture.

Mariana, for her part, keeps her two contrasting, imagined communities at hand as social referents. (We use the phrase *imagined community,* in the sense of Mary Louise Pratt [1987] and Benedict Anderson [1983] to denote a modern social entity where group boundaries are imagined, because individuals cannot know, nor will they have met, most of the constitutive, embodying members.[6]) Her experience is not comprehensible (not to us, and more importantly, not to herself) apart from the relationality of these two normative communities—one an idealization with which she has virtually no remaining contact, the other an infelicity with which she must negotiate daily. As she holds on to her place *in* the Mexican upper stratum, at the same time she negotiates her place *in relation to* an envisioned Mexican American, or Chicano, core community.

But although Mariana's and Nilda's images of these referential environments remain static, at the same time we have observed considerable changes in how the two women want to position themselves in relation to these "imagined communities." We have witnessed, for example, times when Nilda chose to turn away from the representation she has internalized of Mexican American culture, and we are aware, equally, of junctures where she has desired a rapprochement. We have noted, equally, how language has played a key role in her enactments of these different positionings, inside and outside this mythic realm. Similarly, we have witnessed how, when confronted with ignorant, reductionist hypotheses on the part of school personnel explaining the putative cognitive deficit of her young son, Mariana began to develop an empathy for the experience of immigrant minorities.

However, why do these women's positionings toward these referential groups, and the concomitant role of language within these positionings, change at all, when those of many other participants do not? We want to argue that this is because they have been confronted with, or have appropriated, situations requiring them to make important choices. These dilemmas provide opportunities for reevaluation of how they position themselves with regard to these imagined groups and cre-

---

[6]There are, of course, important differences in the entities Pratt and Anderson referred to. Pratt's object of study was the *speech community,* a concept used by sociolinguists to represent a group of speakers who share discrete communicative practices and norms for appropriate usage (Labov, 1972a). Anderson, for his part, was concerned with how the *nation community* develops and, in particular, how solidarity with this idealized entity is achieved, sustained, and represented.

ate a space for reassessment of the linguistic basis for enacting these social differentiations. Clearly, those family caregivers and children who participate in a variety of information and social networks are both presented with and required to make more decisions, to choose from a greater number of possible courses of action, than those who participate in fewer. And, because in the contact zone the circumstances and results of these decisions are not inevitable—indeed, implicit in the definition of contact zone is their contestability—in making these choices actors are positioned in relations that constitute them as agents. Increasingly aware of their own ability to influence outcomes, by observing the choices of others they also acquire insights into additional subject positions that they might inhabit and social realities that they can construct.

Yet, at the same time, ironically, even those who spend much of their lives negotiating in contested spaces continue to define themselves in relation to postulated subgroups that are homogeneous, that exert normative pressures, and that remain static. Nilda and Mariana persist in taking the part for the whole, even as they, and others like them who inhabit liminal spaces, are summoned as individual examples of the outmoded status of such mystifying practices. Thus, their ideologies of community remain stubbornly resistant to the decentering arguments contained in much postmodern, poststructuralist writing on culture and identity (cf. Storey, 1996). Further, their texts about relationality reveal an opposition to the reduction of important questions of dominance and hegemony to issues of language and textuality (cf. Foucault, 1977a, 1978, 1988).

Thus, although our findings lead us to reevaluate, or at least to refrain from asking an unreasonable amount of, the organizing framework of language socialization theory, by the same token we are not so quick to adopt a skepticism about the relationship between practices that constitutes "culture." Indeed, close observation of multiple, diverse family scenes over time would suggest that such an approach would obscure the perspectives from which individual family members have acted, perspectives that reveal actors positioning themselves in relation to one symbolic locus of meaning. Moreover, in theorizing on cultural identification we would caution against overreliance on a single empirical source, that is, information gleaned from interviews or conversations with informants on the subject of how they self-define. Certainly we want to consider these texts, but in tandem with other information, for example, about those putatively constitutive features that informants see themselves as *not* incorporating, and those imagined communities that they position themselves in relation to.

At this juncture, we are not in a position to—nor would we wish to—bring theoretical or empirical closure to what has proven a generative (although at times polemical) debate surrounding theories of and hypotheses about group boundedness. At the same time, we must conclude from the practices of self–other differentiation that we have observed in the course of our inquiry that *culture* remains a primary structuring principle for actors in making sense of the various relations that inhabit their social worlds. It remains, too, a responsive analytic framework for those who would presume to theorize these at times material, at times abstract categories, as well as the linguistic practices that inform their meanings.

8

Bilingualism in Time and Space

In previous chapters, we attempted to give some shape to the diverse, evolving landscapes of language practices of Mexican-descent families living in California and Texas. Here we pursue this effort, summarizing our findings in two key areas: first, the nature of intersections between sociocultural ecology, language practices, and identity, and second, the relationships among home language maintenance, literacy development, and schooling. Finally, with these summative texts in mind, we engage the implications of our findings for the work of educators, policymakers, and other advocates for linguistic-minority learners, concluding with a plea for a critical reformulation of the terms of debate over educational equity.

CALIFORNIA AND TEXAS: TWO SOCIOCULTURAL ECOLOGIES

We have seen in previous chapters that an overwhelming majority of our focal children, as well as their parents and siblings, define themselves in terms of allegiance to their Mexican heritage and view bilingualism as a positive attribute. Perhaps more importantly, nearly everyone we talked with accords an important role to Spanish in the formation of her or his individual identity; many view it as important in forming their collective identities as well. However, at the same time we noted wide variation in

185

the use of Spanish by and among family members and, hence, in the intergenerational transmission of the minority language.

Not surprisingly, we identified patterns in the alignment of these differential findings according to geographic locale; surprisingly, these trends did not correspond to our initial hypotheses. In chapter 2 we observed that the differences between the two locales had been shown by ethnolinguistic research to represent crucial factors in minority language maintenance. Indeed, the relatively high concentration of Latinos in San Antonio, the overwhelming majority of whom are of Mexican descent, as well as the relative proximity of San Antonio to the border and the historic ties between south Texas and northern Mexico, suggested to us that Spanish-language maintenance among the Texas families would be more prevalent than we actually found. Of course, we also expected that differences in population structure, with the majority of Mexican-background parents in Texas having been born in the state, would exert a countervailing force. Nevertheless, popular perceptions and the presence of Spanish in the public sphere, for example, on billboard advertisements, initially led us to expect that robust minority language maintenance in San Antonio would extend beyond the children of immigrants.

That, however, was not what we found. Indeed, in Texas, only two children of United States-born mothers were able to converse with ease in the Spanish portions of the interviews, and those children represent relatively unusual cases. One child, Ana Trujillo, whom we met in chapter 4, acquired Spanish as her first language because her Mexican-born and raised father and United States-born mother had made the conscious decision to use only Spanish during her infancy. Concerned to prepare their daughter for an English-medium school, however, the Trujillos eventually enrolled Ana in an English-medium preschool program and her mother, although not her father, began to use considerable English in interactions with their daughter. Gabriela Valdez, whom we also met in chapter 4, is the other child of a United States-born mother who has maintained a fairly high level of oral proficiency in Spanish. However, as we have seen, the circumstances of Gabriela's life differ greatly from those of most of the other San Antonio children. Gabriela is being raised by her grandparents, who have legally adopted her. Although they were born in the United States, Sr. and Sra. Valdez both grew up in the Río Grande Valley area of south Texas where Spanish was, and continues to be, the predominant language of the Mexican-origin community.

With regard to the role of schooling, approximately half of the California focal children are or have at one time been enrolled in bilingual programs, while only three of the Texas children have been in such programs. However, this difference is attributable partly to the ways in which the educational infrastructures of the two states interpreted the mandates of the federal Bilingual Education Act (Title VII), permitting the creation of bilingual programs providing mother-tongue instruction to linguistic-minority students in the early grades. Most of the Texas focal children have not attended bilingual classes because they are second- or third-generation U.S. citizens who speak English fluently. In Texas, although the situation is beginning to change, on the official level the role of "bilingual schooling" has generally been seen as entirely compensatory and hence these programs have not been available to children who are already proficient in English. Conversely, although the state of California has passed legislative restrictions on bilingual education (Crawford, 1998–1999), at the same time the state department of education has accorded a greater amount of latitude to professional educators and parents with regard to decision making about the placement of language-minority students.

Perceptions of the quality of bilingual programs also affected the schooling decisions of immigrant San Antonio families whose children were eligible for enrollment in classes where instruction was at least partly in Spanish. Indeed, one mother, raised in the Mexican state of Durango, who had chosen to enroll her two children in a bilingual program, commented explicitly on the negative perceptions of bilingual education, not only among adults, but also among children themselves:

> *Hemos sabido ... que hay niños que ... les hacen como burla porque estas en el bilingüe ... quiere decir que ... sabes menos o sea no tienes la misma capacidad que yo porque yo si hablo inglés y puedo aprender las clases ... con las personas que están hablando inglés. Pero yo pienso que el programa bilingüe es muy importante.*

> (We knew ... that there are children who ... make fun because you're in the bilingual program ... it means that ... you know less or that you don't have the same ability as me because I speak English and I can learn in classes ... with people who are speaking English. But I think that the bilingual program is very important.)

Although the California parents who elected to send their children to publicly funded bilingual classes have relied to a certain extent on the schools to assist with the maintenance of the minority language, California and Texas families essentially concur in the view that school is a place to acquire academic competence in the dominant societal language. They believe that responsibility for Spanish maintenance rests primarily with the family. However, California and Texas caregivers differ somewhat in how they see the idealized role of the school in relation to Spanish-language maintenance and cultural identity. At least some of the Texas parents believe that the public schools have an obligation to assist them in maintaining their language and ethnic heritage, and have been disappointed with the lack of support from public officials whom they have encountered. In the following excerpt, Elena Torres articulates a perspective shared by other Texas caregivers with whom we spoke. Sra. Torres, whom we also met in chapter 4, is involved with her children's education as an active member of the PTA (Parent–Teacher Association), as a volunteer in accompanying the children on field trips, and as a manager who oversees completion of homework assignments. In her view, she provides active support on a number of dimensions for the school system's agenda for her children. Thus, she has difficulty accepting that the schools her children attend do not provide any support for her efforts to transmit her language, especially because the family lives in an almost entirely Latino neighborhood in a city with a majority Mexican-descent population:

> I think that the attitude that the city has ... that they feel that this is the United States an ... this is an English speaking country. But I feel that it is wrong. I feel that they shouldn't just because they were born here does not mean that only English is the language that should be used. I believe that we have to hold to something and that something is my parents come from Mexico. And if I don't have something to hold on to- if we don't have something to hold on to then what is our culture- what do we teach our children? There is nothing there, if we have to give that up.

In large measure, the differences between the California and Texas participants may be attributed to the differences in the sociocultural ecologies of the two communities that the families represent. As is the case with the overall Mexican-origin population in the two states (Solé, 1995), the California and Texas families differ with respect to the depth of their ties to the United States. California parents are for the most part immigrants, having moved to the United States after the age of primary-language acquisition. In contrast, in 14 of the Texas families, both parents were born in the United States and speak fluent English. Moreover, unlike the California families, the majority of Texas families have their important relations close at hand. After-school and weekend visits by focal children to the homes of grandparents, aunts, uncles, and cousins, along with the large Mexican-origin population of San Antonio, create a perception of strength through numbers as well as the possibility for at least some Spanish interaction beyond the home. In contrast, the California parents frequently use diaspora metaphors in representing their social condition: Removed from a natural community of Spanish speakers, living in a metropolitan area in which Mexican culture is devalued, and perceiving the constraints on sustaining their sense of roots as numerous and oppressive, they feel they cannot "let up," as one parent put it. The home being the arena over which they exercise significant control, cultural identification is best achieved, they believe, through an aggressive Spanish-maintenance strategy.[1]

Several years ago, Zentella (1996) decried what she termed the "chiquitafication" of U.S. Latinos—the tendency of the popular media and, unfortunately, of much of the educational community to gloss over the highly diverse perspectives and backgrounds represented by the increasing numbers of U.S. residents who trace their roots to Mexico and the Spanish-speaking countries of Central America, the Caribbean, and South America. She challenged researchers to explore the diversity of discourse practices in Latino communities, ranging from newly arrived Dominicans in New York to the Mexicanos whose Southwestern settlements predate English colonization of the eastern United States, and to relate their findings to larger sociopolitical concerns. The research we have undertaken may be viewed as one response to that challenge. The

---

[1]Despite differences between the two states, however, the differing opinions among the families over the role of the schools in minority-language maintenance appear to depend largely on the circumstances of each family. We reported in chapters 4 and 6 on the Gómezes, the immigrant family living on a south Texas ranch. Sr. and Sra. Gómez insist that their children use Spanish exclusively in the home and expect their children to acquire English at school. Like the Villegas and Hernández families in California, the Gómezes view intergenerational transmission of Spanish as a task best accomplished by the family.

design of our project reflected our desire to probe the implications of the differing social and historical contexts of Spanish maintenance among groups of Mexican-descent Americans who live in geographically distinct areas. Indeed, although the families whose language practices we have described all share a single national origin, they present anything but a monochromatic picture. The parents and children whose stories we enlisted share a sense of belonging to a larger Mexican or Mexican American culture, and they all are aware that Spanish is tied to participation in that identity. However, the ways in which families have chosen to pursue the goal of intergenerational transmission of Spanish, if indeed they have chosen to pursue that goal, vary widely. Moreover, as we have seen, even the ideational and pragmatic meanings of Spanish "maintenance" vary among individuals who profess support for the goal of maintenance and report that they engage in practices designed to foster this outcome.

MINORITY LANGUAGE MAINTENANCE, LITERACY DEVELOPMENT, AND SCHOOLING

As specialists in the area of first- and second-language learning and as advocates for linguistic-minority students, we have throughout this journey acknowledged a dual professional responsibility to elucidate family members' definitions of language acquisition, maintenance, and loss within their own terms and to inform these various frameworks with our own intertextual expertise based on the historicity of research in these important areas. Regarding the latter, chapter 5 represents our efforts to probe specific relevant constitutive elements, by considering separately and holistically the results of different measures of the language proficiency of children in bilingual families. Toward this goal, we have devised and selected measures that are responsive to community criteria regarding narrative competence, that build on an extensive corpus of linguistic work on first- and second-language acquisition, and that are respectful of the pedagogic (including aesthetic) criteria of experienced bilingual teachers. From the different analyses, we concluded unequivocally that in both California and Texas, *use* of Spanish in the home is critical for minority-language maintenance; that is, children who on a regular basis interact in Spanish with caregivers and siblings demonstrate an ability to describe experiences and elaborate on emotional states in sufficiently nuanced detail that, assuming a bilingual interlocutor, communicative content would not be substantively affected by language choice.[2] However, this conclusion does not address the principal concern of many educators, policymakers, and caregivers—the relationship of minority-language maintenance and the development of academic competence.

For two reasons, our research cannot be used to substantiate claims to the effect that minority-language maintenance promotes school achievement. First, we did not deliberately collect the kind of information that would testify to language-minority children's relative success or failure in schools. For example, we did not seek to obtain copies of focal children's report cards, or to ascertain their results on standardized performance measures administered by the school. Second, and more importantly, our own results do not allow us to draw this conclusion. Thus, we found no evidence of an "oral–written continuum." Alone, speaking and being spoken to in Spanish do not demonstrably affect children's development of academic, that is, text-based, literacy either in the dominant or the minority language. Our findings, however, do support the claim that minority-language maintenance in no way impedes children's linguistic and academic development in the dominant language. We have seen that by our standards children who produced Spanish narratives did as well on their English essays as those who wrote only in English.

From our ethnographic inquiry we learn also that for children who report (or are reported as) being successful in school and who demonstrate relatively high levels of language proficiency on our measures, literacy in the home is the common, crucial factor. Here, however, we must add an important qualifier: a passive engagement with print (e.g., being read to as a young child) is not the most significant factor in children's development of literacy in either language. Rather, those children who evidence high rates of language proficiency on the measures of writing engage *actively* with text on a regular basis—decoding and translating

---

[2]Of course, this statement must be qualified to a certain extent, as the languages of the focal children described here are subject to domain-specific constraints. For example, although there is no question that she has maintained Spanish, as we saw in chapter 6, Diana Villegas is far more comfortable doing school work in English, the language of the school she attends, than in Spanish.

official documents and promotional ads, assisting in the completion of forms and other formatted materials, deciphering the meanings of road signs, food labels, and other semiotic communications, reading literature, and elaborating in talk about concepts encountered in written texts.

We are aware that we are not the first to report these findings, and we are sensitive to the equity issues that they raise for those among us who are committed to securing equal access for all students to the skills, knowledge, and opportunity the school curriculum is intended to promote. The (latent, but not innocent) disenfranchisement of the Ríos family (chap. 6) through their daughter Belinda's estrangement from the school curriculum provides compelling evidence that such misgivings regarding inequitable distribution of linguistic resources and access to the school curriculum are justified. However, at the same time we would not be disingenuous. Soberingly, if development of the kind of literacy valued by mainstream schools is what one cares most about in relation to decisions concerning bilingual language practices, then even reading to one's children—an enormous lifestyle commitment in the case of Teresa Ezparza, who did not speak English and could scarcely read at the time her daughter Marcella was born—is not a sufficient strategy to secure the most advantageous outcome.

BILINGUALISM AND POSSIBILITY

Our main agenda was not to investigate how well or poorly home language practices oriented linguistic-minority children to school literacy.[3] Rather, our intent was to examine the roles of Spanish and English in family members' lives and in the social worlds they aspired to. Before continuing to discuss the implications of our findings, however, we wish to underscore the complex issues involved in debates over the nature of bilingualism and to highlight recent changes in attitudes among members of both majority and minority groups toward the acquisition and maintenance of nonsocietally-dominant languages.

---

[3]Although discovering the relationship between the use of Spanish and English in the home and children's academic achievement was not our main goal, we are troubled by the misguided beliefs of many in education, including the officials of St. Mary's Academy in northern California, the school attended by Diana Villegas and Marcella Esparza, and the rural south Texas public school attended by Ernesto and Carlos Gómez, that use of Spanish at home is likely to cause problems for children in school.

Defining Bilingualism

The first of these sets of issues concerns the definition of the term *bilingual*. In popular discourse in the United States, the definition seems to veer between the view that a bilingual is someone who does not speak English very well or at all and the maximalist position that excludes all except those who have attained native-speaker proficiency in both of their languages. Thus, in many schools, the "bilingual kids" are those children from language-minority homes who have not yet achieved sufficient proficiency in English to enable them to benefit from instruction in mainstream classrooms rather than children who have proficiency in more than one language. Indeed, in our work encounters we have heard professional educators complaining about being behind in their syllabi because their classes contained "too many bilingual kids," a speech act that makes sense only if one accepts the equation of "bilingual" with "limited English proficient." On the other hand, when referring to themselves, many educators, as well as members of the general public, seem to accept the maximalist position articulated by Leonard Bloomfield (1933), the leading figure in American structuralist linguistics, who wrote:

> In the extreme case of foreign language learning, the speaker becomes so proficient as to be indistinguishable from the native speakers round him.... In the cases where perfect foreign-language learning is not accompanied by loss of the native language, it results in bilingualism, [the] native-like control of two languages. (p. 56)

The cases presented in this book, as well as the results of more than five decades of research on bilingualism, indicate that both of the positions just summarized are too narrow. Other less restrictive definitions, however, have been put forth. For example, Einar Haugen (1953), whose work on the Norwegian community in the Midwest is among the earliest studies of immigrant bilingualism in the United States that might properly be termed sociolinguistic, offered a developmental perspective that recognized different degrees of bilingualism:

> Bilingualism ... may be of all degrees of accomplishment, but it is understood here to begin at the point where the speaker of one language can produce complete, meaningful utterances in the other language.

From here it may proceed through all possible gradations up to the kind of skill that enables a person to pass as a native in more than one linguistic environment. (p. 7)

More recent work by Valdés & Figueroa (1994), based on research in Mexican-background communities in the United States, incorporates both developmental and social aspects into a definition of bilingualism. Like many recent researchers (e.g., Silva-Corválan, 1994), Valdés and Figueroa incorporated Haugen's developmental perspective into the notion of a bilingual continuum. They also distinguished between elective and circumstantial bilingualism.[4] Elective bilingualism is characteristic of individuals who "choose to learn a nonsocietal language and create conditions ... that help bring about such learning," whereas circumstantial bilingualism is characteristic of groups (e.g., Mexican immigrants to the United States) whose members must learn a second language because their first language is no longer sufficient to meet all of their needs (Valdés & Figueroa, 1994, p. 13). Generally, elective bilingualism is viewed by the larger society as prestigious, whereas circumstantial bilingualism has been considered a deficit.

With the exception of those who have remained monolingual in Spanish and the children who have not acquired Spanish, the great majority of family members we have written about here are circumstantial bilinguals who acquired English by necessity and in whose lives English and Spanish play different roles. Among the caregivers whose stories we have recounted in detail, only Louise Pollack and Jeffrey Pearson, the upper-middle class Anglo mother and stepfather who changed their home language practices to maintain the language of their son Alfredo's divorced Mexican father, and Mariana and Enrique Villegas, who acquired English as a foreign language in Guadalajara before they decided to journey to California, first as students and later as immigrants, could be considered elective bilinguals. And, with the exception of Alfredo Villafuerte, Louise Pollack's son, and possibly Ana Trujillo of San Antonio, whose middle-class family we also met in chapter 4, overwhelmingly, school authorities did not accord the bilingualism, of whatever

---

[4]As Valdés and Figueroa pointed out (1994, p. 11), other researchers (e.g., Paulston, 1977; Skutnabb-Kangas, 1981) suggested a similar distinction, using the terms *natural* and *elite/academic* bilingualism.

degree of accomplishment exhibited by the focal children with whom we worked, the status that normally accrues to elective, or elite, bilingualism. Rather, as we have seen, even in cases such as the Gómez family of rural south Texas, teachers attributed the middle child's lack of school success to the family's insistence on Spanish in home interactions, that is, to immigrant bilingualism, despite the fact that the oldest child, Ernesto, raised in the same linguistic milieu as his younger brother, consistently made the honor roll. And even though Enrique and Mariana Villegas of northern California might be regarded as elective bilinguals according to Valdés and Figueroa's (1994) classification, neither they nor, more importantly, their children were so regarded by the teachers and administrators at St. Mary's Academy, the school that Diana Villegas attended. As we saw in the previous chapter, school officials did not distinguish between upper-middle-class educated immigrants like Mariana Villegas and other "disadvantaged" Mexicans. Only in the case of Alfredo Villafuerte in northern California and Ana Trujillo in south Texas, both of whose families had achieved upper-middle-class or at least middle-class status, do we find positive responses to children's bilingualism from mainstream institutions. However, the case of Ana Trujillo, with her school's response to her bilingualism, highlights the question of dialects, norms, and bilingual maintenance, a question to which we now turn.

Language Norms and Bilingual Maintenance

As we have seen, some of the families we spoke with associated Spanish maintenance with what they conceived of as standard Mexican Spanish, as distinguished from the vernacular varieties spoken by immigrants and United States-born Latinos. Both Mariana Villegas and María Gómez were particularly insistent in this regard, as was Ana Trujillo's mother, Anita. In fact, Anita reported extensively on the comments of Sr. Baroja, Ana's fifth-grade Spanish teacher, who praised the child (and her parents) for the lack of Texas vernacular features in her Spanish.

Prescriptive attitudes such as those evidenced by the Villegas, Gómez, and Trujillo families have long affected minority language maintenance in immigrant communities such as those we have described here because they contribute to the process of "dialectalization." That is, the varieties of the minority language spoken by immigrants, who most often are members of the urban working class or the rural poor, come to be regarded as mere "dialects" rather than proper varieties of a language, and hence unworthy of preservation.[5] Reduced to the status of "dialects" (in the popular sense of the term), vernacular varieties become less worthy of being maintained, because they are not regarded, either by others or often even by their speakers, as "real Spanish." Moreover, they are interpreted by representatives of mainstream institutions as indicators of lower educational achievement, and therefore discouraged.

Despite deep-seated attitudes such as those just described, language norms do seem to be changing, at least among some groups in the United States. The increasing visibility and acceptance of code switching is perhaps the most obvious index of such a change (cf. Limón, 1991; Zentella, 1981). For example, code switching has been widely used in broadcast media since the early 1990s, including the most popular radio stations in San Antonio (Bayley & Zapata, 1993), and, at least some United States-born speakers have embraced both code switching and southwest Spanish forms as symbols of Tejano or Chicano identity (Santa Ana, 1993).

Moreover, even among non-Latinos, changes in attitudes toward Spanish are evident, although certainly not as widespread as we would hope. In San Antonio, for example, a Spanish immersion program, modeled on the successful French immersion programs for anglophones in Canada, has been in operation for several years in the largely Anglo Alamo Heights school district. In California, the Palo Alto School Board in the heart of Silicon Valley recently voted to extend its first primary-level Spanish immersion program, where Spanish and English native-language-speaking students learn to read, write, and converse fluently in both languages, through middle school. Close monitoring has shown that, in addition to having attained proficiency in both languages, the fifth-grade children who are graduating from the original program are

---

[5]The term *dialect* is used here in the popular sense of a nonstandard variety of a language, usually spoken by someone other than the person using the term. Of course, for linguists, any variety that is spoken by a definable social or regional group, and that can be described in terms of features that distinguish it from varieties spoken by other definable social or regional groups, is a "dialect." Thus, the Castillian Spanish of Madrid, the *norma culta* of the Mexican upper classes, and the Texas Spanish spoken in the *barrios* of south Texas are all dialects, and none has any claim on linguistic grounds to superiority over the others. Nevertheless, the speech of the upper classes of Madrid and Mexico City clearly enjoys more social status than the speech of the working class in the Texas *barrios*.

performing as well as peers enrolled in the regular programs in language arts and math.

REFRAMING THE DEBATE ON BILINGUALISM

In light of the preceding, we now address the terms of debate that have dominated the professional discourse about the educational needs of linguistic-minority children over the past half century. Our research showed that maintaining Spanish had many beneficial effects for the linguistic-minority children who participated in our study. We would not deny the importance of minority language or dialect status for children's developing self-concepts or the importance of academic achievement for language minority children. However, we would point out that for the children we worked with, questions of the status of different language varieties, attitudes of the dominant society toward their family's language, and even success in school were not the main issues. Rather, children who had maintained proficiency in Spanish most often provided affective rationales for wanting to continue to speak their families' traditional language. Indeed, the affective motivation for Spanish maintenance was clear even for developing Spanish literacy. Thus, one northern California child, when asked whether she wanted to continue to write in Spanish even though she lived in the United States, replied, *"si no escribo en español tengo que aprender más en escribir en español porque yo no sé escribirles a mis abuelitos en Mexico"* ("if I don't write in Spanish I['ll] have to learn more how to write in Spanish because I won't know how to write to my grandparents in Mexico"). Another child, in San Antonio, has a somewhat broader perspective that extends into the future. Ten-year-old Luis Guajardo not only spoke of communicating with members of his immediate and extended family, all of whom spoke Spanish, but also with members of the broader community as well: *"Quiero los dos ... porque en mi vida la gente va a andar hablando en inglés y español"* ("I want both ... because in my life people are going to continue speaking English and Spanish").

Parents and other family members, although many also emphasized the affective and broad communicative value of Spanish, provided a broader array of rationales for Spanish maintenance. Almost all of the caregivers who shared with us their aspirations for their children perceived knowledge of Spanish as an important part of their children's sense of Latino identity. For some the decision was largely pragmatic—their proficiency in the dominant language was not sufficiently developed and they were more comfortable using Spanish. Others privileged a developmental rationale. At a future time their children might wish to communicate in Spanish, and they would acquire the language more easily when they were young. Some explained their decision in terms of personal enrichment: They believed that their children's lives would be more rewarding intellectually as a result of their ability to participate fully in two cultures. Other frequently cited rationales included an aesthetic appreciation of the possibilities of the Spanish language and the desire for children to maintain and strengthen ties with non-English-speaking relatives and friends. Of course, instrumental rationales such as succeeding in school and getting an edge in the job market figured strongly as well.

We are not the first to underscore the positive and uplifting consequences reported by individuals in describing their personal experiences with minority-language maintenance (see, e.g., Bunge, 1992; Cummins, 1996; González, 1996; Tinajera & Ada, 1993; Tinajera & DeVillar, 2000; Wong Fillmore, 1996). However, scarcely any of these findings have been acknowledged or taken up by policymakers or the media as legitimate arguments for consideration in professional discussions and debates about educational programs for linguistic-minority students. Because of the obvious social policy implications that such a perspective would engender, policymakers have been reluctant to engage the needs of linguistic-minority groups to maintain their language, and through it their cultural traditions. Rather, they have sought to attenuate the scope of discussion—to consign mother-tongue maintenance to the domestic domain where individuals who are members of linguistic-minority groups are free to debate it as a private, individual matter—and to frame the societal issue in terms of the underachievement of minority students and what can be done about it. Thus, when the educational infrastructure entertains a bilingual education initiative, its members embed their arguments within the larger movement for "school reform," contextualizing such an approach as a curricular response for raising test scores. In this manner, the debate about the education of linguistic-minority students is constrained by a set of ideological premises in which measurable educational outcomes based on standardized norms are the only authorized goals.

Yet, as we have seen, the family members we spoke with did not abide by these discursive constraints in arguing in favor of Spanish-language maintenance and bilingualism. It would appear that as parents, we are entitled to advance the diverse arguments they gave voice to, but as professional educators and/or specialists in the areas of first- and second-language acquisition, we are not. Clearly, there is a gap between what is considered appropriate private and public discourse, based on assumptions about the individual and the social, that needs to be renegotiated if a more fruitful debate is to ensue. But here we would go further, and argue that it is important that we aggressively oppose this discursive formation. For we view these distinctions, not as an interstitial aspect of social reality, but rather as a political strategy to circumscribe the societal discourse about diversity to ensure that difference can be effectively managed (James & Schecter, 2000; Macedo, 2000).

Increasingly, it is difficult to locate monolingual societies, regardless of what official characterizations may specify. Immigration, or the transportation of people across national and local boundaries, is a logical consequence of globalization and the creation of global economies. For example, the demographic composition of California is undergoing rapid change: By the year 2020, Latinos and Asian Americans will comprise half of the state's population (Hajnal & Baldassare, 2001).[6] We see bilingualism, or multilingualism, as part of a larger vision that regards cultural pluralism as a desirable state, one with additive potential. Moreover, we see monolingualism as entailing high costs, not only in terms of the loss of a nation's linguistic and cultural capital, but also in terms of individual and societal development and possibilities (cf. Snow & Hakuta, 1989).

However, to prevail against those with homogenizing, "English Only" agendas, we must resist the imposed terms of debate about the education of immigrant minority students by refusing to engage the discussion within a deficiency framework. Who among us have maintained or learned a nonsocietally-dominant language in order to avoid failing in school? Who have found this a compelling argument in deciding to en-

---

[6]A more hawkish interpretation of this demographic trend views such migratory patterns as a process of repatriation, whereby immigrant groups are reclaiming their lands (see, e.g., Mukherjee, 1999).

courage *our* children in such linguistic practices? If such a jejune rationale does not suffice to motivate the decisions that we make about our
own lives or the better interests of our family members, then surely it is
no more acceptable a stance in the name of the empowerment of other
people's children.

   Instead, let us be proactive. Let us take up what as advocates for equi-
table educational practices and outcomes for linguistic minority students we know to be our two strongest arguments—first, that for
members of linguistic minority groups mother tongue maintenance represents a theoretically coherent and historically situated means for the
expression and affirmation of lived experience; and second, that support
for bilingual initiatives is grounded in a rich tradition of research that
documents the many empowering and emancipatory effects that the
mastery of two or more languages can have and has had for individuals
and societies. As our work—and that of many fine colleagues—has
demonstrated, academic success in the majority language is but one of
the many cognitive, affective, and instrumental benefits that strategic
momentum in the direction of individual and group bilingualism can anticipate and foster.

References

Acuña, R. (2000). *Occupied America: A history of Chicanos*. New York: Longman.

Allard, R., & Landry, R. (1992). Ethnolinguistic vitality beliefs and language maintenance and loss. In W. Fase, K. Jaspaert, & S. Kroon (Eds.), *Maintenance and loss of minority languages* (pp. 171–195). Amsterdam: John Benjamins.

Andersen, R. W. (1982). Determining the linguistic attributes of language attrition. In R. D. Lambert & B. F. Freed (Eds.), *The loss of language skills* (pp. 83–118). Rowley, MA: Newbury House.

Andersen, R. W. (1991). Developmental sequences: The emergence of aspect marking in second language acquisition. In T. Huebner & C. A. Ferguson (Eds.), *Crosscurrents in second language acquisition and linguistic theories* (pp. 305–324). Amsterdam: John Benjamins.

Andersen, R. W. (1993). Four operating principles and input distribution as explanations for underdeveloped and mature morphological systems. In K. Hyltenstam & Å. Viborg (Eds.), *Progression and regression in language* (pp. 309–339). Cambridge: Cambridge University Press.

Andersen, R. W., & Shirai, Y. (1996). The primacy of aspect in first and second language acquisition: The pidgin-creole connection. In W. C. Ritchie & T. J. Bhatia (Eds.), *Handbook of second language acquisition* (pp. 527–570). San Diego: Academic Press.

Anderson, B. (1983). *Imagined communities: Reflections on the origin and spread of nationalism* (rev. ed.). London: Verso.

Arias, M. B., & Casanova, U. (1993). Contextualizing bilingual education. In M. B. Arias & U. Casanova (Eds.), *Bilingual education: Politics, practice, research. 92nd Yearbook of the Society for the Study of Education* (Part 2, pp. 1–35). Chicago: University of Chicago Press.

Auer, P. (1984). *Bilingual conversation*. Amsterdam: John Benjamins.

August, D., & Hakuta, K. (Eds.). (1997). *Improving schooling for language minority children*. Washington, DC: National Academy Press.

Austin, J. (1962). *How to do things with words*. Oxford: Clarendon Press.

Bachman, L. (1990). *Fundamental considerations in language testing*. Oxford: Oxford University Press.

Baker, C. (1996). *Foundations of bilingual education and bilingualism* (2nd ed.). Clevedon, UK: Multilingual Matters.

Bardovi-Harlig, K. (1992). The relationship of form and meaning: A cross-sectional study of tense and aspect in the interlanguage of learners of English as a second language. *Applied Psycholinguistics, 13,* 253–278.

Bardovi-Harlig, K. (1998). Narrative structure and lexical aspect: Conspiring factors in second language acquisition of tense-aspect morphology. *Studies in Second Language Acquisition, 20,* 471–508.

Bardovi-Harlig, K. (1999). From morpheme studies to temporal semantics: Tense–aspect research in SLA. *Studies in Second Language Acquisition, 21,* 341–382.

Bardovi-Harlig, K. (2000). *Tense and aspect in second language acquisition: Form, meaning, and use*. Oxford: Blackwell.

Bardovi-Harlig, K., & Reynolds, D. W. (1995). The role of lexical aspect in the acquisition of tense and aspect. *TESOL Quarterly, 29,* 107–131.

Barrera, M. (1979). *Race and class in the Southwest: A theory of racial inequality*. Notre Dame, IN: University of Notre Dame Press.

Barrera, M. (1988). *Beyond Aztlán: Ethnic autonomy in comparative perspective*. New York: Praeger.

Barth, F. (Ed.). (1970). *Ethnic groups and boundaries: The social organization of culture difference*. London: Allen & Unwin.

Bayley, R. (1994). Interlanguage variation and the quantitative paradigm: Past tense marking in Chinese-English. In E. Tarone, S. Gass, & A. Cohen (Eds.), *Research methodology in second-language acquisition* (pp. 157–181). Hillsdale, NJ: Lawrence Erlbaum Associates.

Bayley, R. (1999). The primacy of aspect hypothesis revisited: Evidence from language shift. *Southwest Journal of Linguistics, 18*(2), 1–22.

Bayley, R. (in press). Linguistic diversity and English language acquisition. In E. Finegan & J. R. Rickford (Eds.), *Language in the USA: Perspectives for the 21st century*. Cambridge: Cambridge University Press.

Bayley, R., Alvarez-Calderón, A., & Schecter, S. R. (1998). Tense and aspect in Mexican-origin children's narratives. In E. V. Clark (Ed.), *Proceedings of the Twenty-Ninth Annual Child Language Research Forum* (pp. 221–230). Stanford, CA: Center for the Study of Language and Information.

Bayley, R., Schecter, S. R., & Torres-Ayala, B. (1996). Strategies for bilingual maintenance: Case studies of Mexican-origin families in Texas. *Linguistics and Education, 8,* 389–408.

Bayley, R., & Zapata, J. (1993). *"Prefiero español porque I'm more used to it": Codeswitching and language norms in South Texas*. Hispanic Research Center Working Paper WP-02. San Antonio: University of Texas at San Antonio.

Berman, R., & Slobin, D. I. (1994). *Relating events in narrative: A crosslinguistic developmental study*. Hillsdale, NJ: Lawrence Erlbaum Associates.

Bhabba, H. K. (1994). *The location of culture*. London: Routledge.

Billig, M., Condor, S., Edwards, D., Gane, M., Middleton, D., & Radley, A. (1988). *Ideological dilemmas: A social psychology of everyday thinking*. London: Sage.

Bills, G. B. (1997). New Mexican Spanish: Demise of the earliest European variety in the United States. *American Speech, 72,* 154–171.

Bizzell, P. (1994). Opinion: "Contact zones" and English studies. *College English, 56,* 163–169.

Blackwelder, J. (1984). *Women of the Depression: Caste and culture in San Antonio, 1929–1939.* College Station: Texas A&M University Press.

Blom, J. P., & Gumperz, J. J. (1972). Social meaning in linguistic structures: Codeswitching in Norway. In J. J. Gumperz & D. Hymes (Eds.), *Directions in sociolinguistics: Ethnography of communication* (pp. 407–434). New York: Holt, Rinehart, and Winston.

Bloomfield, L. (1933). *Language.* New York: Holt.

Bodgan, R. C., & Biklen, S. K. (1992). *Qualitative research for education: An introduction to theory and methods.* Boston: Allyn and Bacon.

Bourdieu, P. (1993). *The field of cultural production: Essays on art and literature.* New York: Columbia University Press.

Briggs, C. L. (1986). *Learning how to ask: A sociolinguistic appraisal of the role of the interview in social science research.* Cambridge: Cambridge University Press.

Brown, R. (1973). *A first language: The early years.* Cambridge, MA: Harvard University Press.

Bucholtz, M. (1995). From mulatta to mestiza: Passing and the linguistic reshaping of ethnic identity. In K. Hall & M. Bucholtz (Eds.), *Gender articulated: Language and the socially constructed self* (pp. 351–373). London: Routledge.

Bunge, R. (1992). Language: The psyche of a people. In J. Crawford (Ed.), *Language loyalties: A source book on the Official English controversy* (pp. 376–380). Chicago: University of Chicago Press.

Butler, J. (1993). *Bodies that matter: On the discursive limits of "sex."* New York: Routledge.

Butler, J. (1999). *Gender trouble: Feminism and the subversion of identity.* New York: Routledge.

Camarillo, A. (1984). *Chicanos in California: A history of Mexican Americans in California.* San Francisco: Boyd and Fraser.

Cárdenas, J. A. (1995). *Multicultural education: A generation of advocacy.* Needham Heights, MA: Simon and Schuster.

Cazden, C. (1988). *Classroom discourse: The language of teaching and learning.* Portsmouth, NH: Heinemann.

Chaudhuri, U. (2001). Theater and cosmopolitanism: New stories, old stages. In V. Dharwadker (Ed.), *Cosmopolitan geographies: New locations in literature and culture* (pp. 171–195). New York: Routledge.

Comrie, B. (1976). *Aspect.* Cambridge: Cambridge University Press.

Crago, M., Annahatak, B., & Ningiuruvik, L. (1993). Changing patterns of language socialization in Inuit homes. *Anthropology and Education Quarterly, 24,* 205–223.

Crago, M., Chen, C., Genesee, F., & Allen, S. E. M. (1998). Power and deference: Bilingual decision making in Inuit homes. *Journal for a Just and Caring Education, 4,* 78–95.

Crawford, J. (1992). *Hold your tongue: Bilingualism and the politics of "English Only."* Reading, MA: Addison Wesley.

Crawford, J. (1995). *Bilingual education: History, politics, theory, and practice* (3rd ed.). Los Angeles: Bilingual Education Services, Inc.

Crawford, J. (1998–1999). What now for bilingual education? *Rethinking Schools, 13*(2), 1, 4–5.

Cummins, J. (1985). The role of primary language development in promoting educational success for language minority students. In California State Department of Education, *Schooling and language minority students: A theoretical framework* (pp. 3–49). Los Angeles: Evaluation, Dissemination and Assessment Center, California State University, Los Angeles.

Cummins, J. (1996). *Negotiating identities: Education for empowerment in a diverse society.* Ontario, CA: California Association for Bilingual Education.

deCerteau, M. (1984). *The practice of everyday life.* Berkeley: University of California Press.

De León, A. (1982). *The Tejano community, 1836–1900.* Albuquerque: University of New Mexico Press.

Delgado-Gaitan, C. (1990). *Literacy for empowerment: The role of parents in children's education.* London: Falmer Press.

Donato, R. (1997). *The other struggle for equal schools: Mexican Americans during the Civil Rights era.* Albany: State University of New York Press.

Dorian, N. (1981). *Language death: The life cycle of a Scottish Gaelic dialect.* Philadelphia: University of Pennsylvania Press.

Dyson, A. H. (1999). Transforming transfer: Unruly children, contrary texts, and the persistence of the pedagogical order. In A. Iran-Nejad & P. D. Pearson (Eds.), *Review of research in education* (vol. 24, pp. 141–171). Washington, DC: American Educational Research Association.

Eagleton, T. (1991). *Ideology: An introduction.* London: Verso.

Eagleton, T. (2000). *The idea of culture.* Oxford: Blackwell.

Eckert, P. (2000). *Language variation as social practice: The linguistic construction of identity in Belten High.* Oxford: Blackwell.

Eisenberg, A. (1986). Teasing: Verbal play in two Mexicano homes. In B. B. Schieffelin & E. Ochs (Eds.), *Language socialization across cultures* (pp. 182–208). Cambridge: Cambridge University Press.

Faigley, L. (1994). *Fragments of rationality: Postmodernity and the subject of composition.* Pittsburgh: University of Pittsburgh Press.

Fairclough, N. (1995). *Critical discourse analysis.* New York: Longman.

Fishman, J. A. (1991). *Reversing language shift: Theoretical and empirical foundations of assistance to threatened languages.* Clevedon, UK: Multilingual Matters.

Fishman, J. A., Cooper, R. L., & Ma, R. (1971). *Bilingualism in the barrio (Language Science Monographs,* vol. 7). Bloomington: Indiana University.

Foucault, M. (1977a). *Discipline and punish: The birth of the prison.* New York: Vintage Books.

Foucault, M. (1977b). *Language, counter-memory, practice: Selected essays and interviews* (trans. D. F. Bouchard & S. Simon). Ithaca, NY: Cornell University Press.

Foucault, M. (1978). *The history of sexuality,* vol. 1: *An introduction* (trans. R. Hurley). New York: Pantheon.

Foucault, M. (1988). *Politics, philosophy, culture: Interviews and other writings 1977–1984.* London: Routledge.

Fox, R. G. (1991). For a nearly new culture history. In R. G. Fox (Ed.), *Recapturing anthropology: Working in the present* (pp. 93–114). Santa Fe, NM: School of American Research Press.

Gal, S. (1979). *Language shift: Social determinants of linguistic change in bilingual Austria.* New York: Academic Press.

Gambitta, R., Milne, R. A., & Davis, C. R. (1983). The politics of unequal educational opportunity. In D. Johnson et al. (Eds.), *The politics of San Antonio: Community, progress and power* (pp. 134–156, 232–237). Lincoln: University of Nebraska Press.

García, R. (1991). *Rise of the Mexican American middle class: San Antonio, 1929–1941.* College Station: Texas A&M University Press.

Garza, R., & Herringer, L. (1988). Social identity: A multidimensional approach. *Journal of Social Psychology, 127,* 299–308.

Gaskins, S., Miller, P. J., & Corsaro, W. A. (1992). Theoretical and methodological perspectives in the interpretative study of children. In W. A. Corsaro & P. J. Miller (Eds.), *Interpretative approaches to children's socialization* (pp. 5–23). San Francisco: Jossey-Bass.

Gee, J. (1986). Units in the production of narrative discourse. *Discourse Processes, 9,* 392–422.

Gee, J. (1990). *Social linguistics and literacies: Ideology in discourse.* London: Falmer Press.

Giles, H., Bourhis, R. Y., & Taylor, D. M. (1977). Toward a theory of language in ethnic group relations. In. H. Giles (Ed.), *Language, ethnicity, and intergroup relations* (pp. 307–348). New York: Academic Press.

Godfrey, B. (1984). *Inner-city neighborhoods in transition: The morphogenesis of San Francisco's ethnic and nonconformist communities.* Unpublished doctoral dissertation, University of California, Berkeley.

Godfrey, B. (1988). *Neighborhoods in transition: The making of San Francisco's ethnic and noncomformist communities.* Berkeley: University of California Press.

Gómez-Quiñones, J. (1990). *Chicano politics: Reality and promise, 1940–1990.* Albuquerque: University of New Mexico Press.

Gonzales, M. (1999). *Mexicanos: A history of Mexicans in the United States.* Bloomington: Indiana University Press.

González, N. (1996). Blurred voices: Who speaks for the subaltern? In C. Pearson Casanave & S. R. Schecter (Eds.), *On becoming a language educator: Personal essays on professional development* (pp. 75–83). Mahwah, NJ: Lawrence Erlbaum Associates.

Goodwin, M. H. (1990). *He-said-she-said: Talk as social organization among Black children.* Bloomington: Indiana University Press.

Graff, H. (1987). *The legacies of literacy: Continuities and contradictions in western culture and society.* Bloomington: Indiana University Press.

Griffith, A., & Schecter, S. R. (1998). Mothering, educating, and schooling. *Journal for a Just and Caring Education, 4,* 5–10.

Grumet, M. (1987). The politics of personal knowledge. *Curriculum Inquiry, 17,* 319–329.

Guerra, J. (1998). *Close to home: Oral and literate practices in a transnational Mexicano community.* New York: Teachers College Press.

Gumperz, J. J. (1982a). *Discourse strategies.* Cambridge: Cambridge University Press.

Gumperz, J. J. (Ed.). (1982b). *Language and social identity.* Cambridge: Cambridge University Press.

Gupta, A. & Ferguson, J. (Eds.). (1997). *Culture, power, place: Explorations in critical anthropology.* Durham, NC: Duke University Press.

Hajnal, Z., & Baldassare, M. (2001). *Finding common ground: Racial and ethnic attitudes in California.* San Francisco: Public Policy Institute of California.

Hakuta, K. (1986). *Mirror of language: The debate on bilingualism.* New York: Basic Books.

Hakuta, K., & D'Andrea, D. (1992). Some properties of bilingual maintenance and loss in Mexican-background high-school students. *Applied Linguistics, 13,* 72–99.

Hakuta, K., & Pease-Alvarez, L. (1994). Proficiency, choice, and attitudes in bilingual Mexican American children. In G. Extra & L. Verhoeven (Eds.), *The cross-linguistic study of bilingual development* (pp. 145–164). Amsterdam: Netherlands Academy of Arts and Sciences.

Hall, S. (1995). The question of cultural identity. In S. Hall, D. Hall, D. Hubert, & K. Thompson (Eds.), *Modernity: An introduction to modern societies* (pp. 595–634). Malden, MA: Blackwell.

Hall, S. (1996). Cultural studies: Two paradigms. In J. Storey (Ed.), *What is cultural studies?* (pp. 31–48). London: Arnold.

Haraway, D. (1991). *Simians, cyborgs, and women: The reinvention of nature.* London: Routledge.

Haugen, E. (1953). *The Norwegian language in America: A study in bilingual behavior.* Philadelphia: University of Pennsylvania Press.

Hayes-Bautista, D. E. (1992). *No longer a minority: Latinos and social policy in California.* Los Angeles: UCLA Chicano Studies Research Center.

Heath, S. B. (1981). English in our national heritage. In C. A. Ferguson & S. B. Heath (Eds.), *Language in the USA* (pp. 6–20). Cambridge: Cambridge University Press.

Heath, S. B. (1982). What no bedtime story means: Narrative skills at home and school. *Language in Society, 11,* 49–76.

Heath, S. B. (1983). *Ways with words: Language, life, and work in communities and classrooms.* Cambridge: Cambridge University Press.

Heilbrun, C. G. (1999). *Women's lives: The view from the threshold.* Toronto: University of Toronto Press.

Heller, M. (1988). Strategic ambiguity: Codeswitching in the management of conversation. In M. Heller (Ed.), *Codeswitching: Anthropological and sociolinguistic perspectives* (pp. 77–96). Berlin: Mouton de Gruyter.

Hill, J. H., & Hill, K. C. (1986). *Speaking Mexicano: Dynamics of syncretic language in central Mexico.* Tucson: University of Arizona Press.

Hoffman, E. (1989). *Lost in translation: A life in a new language.* New York: Penguin.

Hoyle, S. M., & Adger, C. T. (Eds.). (1998). *Kids talk: Strategic language use in later childhood.* Oxford: Oxford University Press.

Hurtado, A., & Rodríguez, P. (1989). Language as a social problem: The repression of Spanish in south Texas. *Journal of Multilingual and Multicultural Development, 10,* 401–419.

Hymes, D. (1982). Narrative form as a "grammar" of experience: Native Americans and a glimpse of English. *Journal of Education, 2,* 121–142.

James, C., & Schecter, S. R. (2000). Mainstreaming and marginalization: Two national strategies in the circumscription of difference. *Pedagogy, Culture and Society, 8,* 23–41.

Kondo, K. (1997). Social-psychological factors affecting language maintenance: Interviews with *shin Nisei* university students in Hawaii. *Linguistics and Education, 9,* 369–408.

Krashen, S. D., & Biber, D. (1988). *On course: Bilingual education's success in California.* Sacramento: California Association for Bilingual Education.

Kulick, D. (1992). *Language shift and cultural reproduction: Socialization, self, and syncretism in a Papua New Guinean village.* Cambridge: Cambridge University Press.

Labov, W. (1971). The notion of system in creole languages. In D. Hymes (Ed.), *Pidginization and creolization of languages* (pp. 447–472). Cambridge: Cambridge University Press.

Labov, W. (1972a). *Sociolinguistic patterns.* Philadelphia: University of Pennsylvania Press.

Labov, W. (1972b). The transformation of experience in narrative syntax. In *Language in the inner city: Studies in the Black English vernacular* (pp. 354–396). Philadelphia: University of Pennsylvania Press.

Labov, W., & Harris, W. (1986). De facto segregation of Black and White vernaculars. In D. Sankoff (Ed.), *Diversity and diachrony* (pp. 1–24). Amsterdam: John Benjamins.

Labov, W., & Waletsky, J. (1967). Narrative analysis: Oral versions of personal experience. In J. Helm (Ed.), *Essays on the verbal and visual arts: Proceedings of the 1966 annual spring meeting of the American Ethnological Society* (pp. 12–44). Seattle: University of Washington Press. Rpt. *Journal of Narrative and Life History, 7,* 3–38 (1997).

Landry, R., & Allard, R. (1992). Ethnolinguistic vitality and the bilingual development of minority and majority group students. In W. Fase, K. Jaspaert, & S. Kroon (Eds.), *Maintenance and loss of minority languages* (pp. 223–251). Amsterdam: John Benjamins.

Landry, R., & Allard, R. (1994). Diglossia, ethnolinguistic vitality, and language behavior. *International Journal of the Sociology of Language, 108,* 15–24.

Larrain, J. (1979). *The concept of ideology.* Athens: University of Georgia Press.

Le Page, R., & Tabouret-Keller, A. (1985). *Acts of identity: Creole-based approaches to language and ethnicity.* Cambridge: Cambridge University Press.

Limón, J. (1991). Representation, ethnicity, and the notes of a precursory ethnography: Notes of a native anthropologist. In R. G. Fox (Ed.), *Recapturing anthropology: Working in the present* (pp. 115–136). Santa Fe, NM: School of American Research Press.

López, D. E. (1982). *Language maintenance and shift in the United States today* (vols. 1–4). Los Alamitos, CA: National Center for Bilingual Research.

Luke, A. (1995). Text and discourse in education: An introduction to critical discourse analysis. In M. Apple (Ed.), *Review of research in education* (vol. 21, pp. 3–48). Washington, DC: American Educational Research Association.

Macedo, D. (2000). The colonialism of the English only movement. *Educational Researcher, 29*(3), 15–24.

Márquez, B. (1993). *LULAC: The evolution of a Mexican American political organization.* Austin: University of Texas Press.

Mayer, M. (1969). *Frog, where are you?* New York: Dial Books.

Mayer, M., & Mayer, M. (1971). *A boy, a dog, a frog, and a friend.* New York: Dial Books.

McCabe, A. (1995). *Chameleon readers: Teaching children to appreciate all kinds of good stories.* New York: McGraw-Hill.

McCabe, A., & Peterson, C. (Eds.). (1991). *Developing narrative structure.* Hillsdale, NJ: Lawrence Erlbaum Associates.

McCarthy, C., & Crichlow, W. (Eds.). (1993). *Race, identity and representation in education.* New York: Routledge.

McDermott, R. P., Goldman, S., & Varenne, H. (1984). When school goes home: Some problems in the organization of homework. *Teachers College Record, 85,* 381–409.

McDonald, D., & Matovina, T. (1995). *Defending Mexican valor in Texas.* Austin, TX: State House Press.

Mehan, H. (1979). What time is it, Denise?: Asking known information questions in classroom discourse. *Theory into Practice, 18,* 285–294.

Mendoza-Denton, N. (1997). *Chicana/Mexican identity and linguistic variation: An ethnographic and sociolinguistic study of gang affiliation in an urban high school.* Unpublished doctoral dissertation, Stanford University, Stanford, CA.

Michaels, S., & Collins, J. (1984). Oral discourse styles: Classroom interaction and the acquisition of literacy. In D. Tannen (Ed.), *Coherence in spoken and written discourse* (pp. 219–244). Norwood, NJ: Ablex.

Miles, M. B., & Huberman, A. M. (1984). *Qualitative data analysis: A sourcebook of new methods.* Beverly Hills, CA: Sage.

Montejano, D. (1987). *Anglos and Mexicans in the making of Texas, 1836–1986.* Austin: University of Texas Press.

Mukherjee, B. (1999). Imagining homelands. In A. Aciman (Ed.), *Letters of transit: Reflections on exile, identity, language, and loss* (pp. 65–86). New York: New Press.

Muñoz, C. (1989). *Youth, identity, power: The Chicano movement.* London: Verso.

Myers-Scotton, C. (1993). *Duelling languages: Grammatical structure in codeswitching.* Oxford: Oxford University Press.

Navarro, A. (1995). *Mexican American Youth Organization: Avant-garde of the Chicano movement in Texas.* Austin: University of Texas Press.

Nettle, D., & Romaine, S. (2000). *Vanishing voices: The extinction of the world's languages.* Oxford: Oxford University Press.

Nolasco, M., & Acevedo, M. L. (1985). *Los niños de la frontera* [Border children]. Mexico City: Centro de Ecodesarrollo, Ediciones Oceano.

Ochs, E. (1988). *Culture and language development: Language acquisition and language socialization in a Samoan village.* Cambridge: Cambridge University Press.

Ochs, E., & Schieffelin, B. B. (1995). The impact of language socialization on grammatical development. In P. Fletcher & B. MacWhinney (Eds.), *The handbook of child language* (pp. 73–94). Oxford: Blackwell.

Padilla, A. M., Fairchild, H. H., & Valadez, C. M. (Eds.). (1990). *Bilingual education: Issues and strategies.* Newbury Park, CA: Sage.

Paulston, C. B. (1977). Theoretical perspectives on bilingual education programs. *Working Papers on Bilingualism,* No. 13. Toronto: Ontario Institute for Studies in Education.

Pavone, J. (1980). *Implicational scales and English dialectology.* Unpublished doctoral dissertation, Indiana University, Bloomington.

Pease-Alvarez, L., & Vasquez, O. (1994). Language socialization in ethnic minority communities. In F. Genesee (Ed.), *Educating second language children: The whole child, the whole curriculum, the whole community* (pp. 82–102). Cambridge: Cambridge University Press.

Peterson, C., & McCabe, A. (1983). *Developmental psycholinguistics: Three ways of looking at a child's narrative.* New York: Plenum.

Phillips, S. U. (1983). *The invisible culture: Communication in classroom and community on the Warm Springs Indian Reservation.* New York: Longman.

Phinney, J. S. (1990). Ethnic identity in adolescents and adults: Review of research. *Psychology Bulletin, 108,* 499–514.

Pitt, L. (1966). *The decline of the Californios.* Berkeley: University of California Press.

Portes, A., & Hao, L.-x. (1998). *E pluribus unum:* Bilingualism and loss of language in the second generation. *Sociology of Education, 71,* 269–294.

Pratt, M. L. (1987). Linguistic utopias. In N. Fabb, D. Attridge, A. Durant, & C. MacCabe (Eds.), *The linguistics of writing: Arguments between language and literature* (pp. 48–66). London: Methuen.

Purcell-Gates, V. (1995). *Other people's words: The cycle of low literacy.* Cambridge, MA: Harvard University Press.

Rampton, B. (1995). *Crossings: Language and ethnicity among adolescents.* London: Routledge

Reed, D. S. (1995). *Democracy v. equality: Legal and political struggles over school finance equalization.* Unpublished doctoral dissertation, Yale University, New Haven, CT.

Reed, D. S. (1998). Twenty-five years after Rodriguez: School finance litigation and the impact of the new judicial federalism. *Law and Society Review, 32,* 175–220.

Rickford, J. R. (1991). Variation theory: implicational scaling and critical age limits in models of linguistic variation, acquisition, and change. In T. Huebner & C. A. Ferguson (Eds.), *Crosscurrents in second language acquisition and linguistic theories* (pp. 225–246). Amsterdam: John Benjamins.

Robison, R. E. (1990). The primacy of aspect: Aspectual marking in English interlanguage. *Studies in Second Language Acquisition, 12,* 315–330.

Robison, R. E. (1995). The aspect hypothesis revisited: A cross-sectional study of tense and aspect marking in interlanguage. *Applied Linguistics, 16,* 344–370.

Rogoff, B., Mistry, J., Göncü, A., & Mosier, C. (1993). *Guided participation in cultural activity by toddlers and caregivers* (Monographs of the Society for the Study of Research in Child Development). Chicago: University of Chicago.

Romaine, S. (1995). *Bilingualism* (2nd ed.). Oxford: Blackwell.

Ruskin, F., & Varenne, H. (1983). The production of ethnic discourse: American and Puerto Rican patterns. In B. Bain (Ed.), *The sociogenesis of language and human conduct* (pp. 553–568). New York: Plenum.

Sacks, H., Schegloff, E. A., & Jefferson, G. (1974). A simplest systematics for the organization of turn taking for conversation. *Language, 50,* 696–735.

Santa Ana, O. (1993). Chicano English and the Chicano language setting. *Hispanic Journal of Behavioral Sciences, 15,* 3–35.

Sánchez-Jankowski, M. (1999). Where have all the nationalists gone?: Change and persistence in radical political attitudes among Chicanos, 1976–1986. In D. Montejano (Ed.), *Chicano politics and society in the late twentieth century* (pp. 201–233). Austin: University of Texas Press.

Schecter, S. R., & Bayley, R. (1997). Language socialization and cultural identity: Case studies of Mexican-descent families in California and Texas. *TESOL Quarterly, 31,* 513–541.

Schecter, S. R., & Bayley, R. (1998). Concurrence and complementarity: Mexican-background parents' decisions about language and schooling. *Journal for a Just and Caring Education, 4,* 47–64.

Schecter, S. R., Sharken-Taboada, D., & Bayley, R. (1996). Bilingual by choice: Latino parents' rationales and strategies for raising children with two languages. *Bilingual Research Journal, 20,* 261–281.

Schieffelin, B. B. (1990). *The give and take of everyday life: Language socialization of Kaluli children.* Cambridge: Cambridge University Press.

Schieffelin, B. B., & Ochs, E. (1986). Language socialization. *Annual Review of Anthropology, 15,* 163–191.

Schmidley, D., & Alvarado, D. A. (1998). *The foreign-born population of the United States: March 1997 (Update).* Current Population Reports (P20-507). Washington, DC: U.S. Department of Commerce, Bureau of the Census.

Schmidt, A. (1985). *Young people's Dyirbal: An example of language death from Australia.* Cambridge: Cambridge University Press.

Scollon, R., & Scollon, S. (1981). *Narrative, literacy, and face in interethnic communication.* Norwood, NJ: Ablex.

Searle, J. R. (1969). *Speech acts: An essay in the philosophy of language.* Cambridge: Cambridge University Press.

Searle, J. R. (1975). Indirect speech acts. In P. Cole & J. L. Morgan (Eds.), *Syntax and semantics 3: Speech acts* (pp. 59–82). New York: Academic Press.

Sebastián, E., & Slobin, D. I. (1994). Development of linguistic forms: Spanish. In R. A. Berman & D. I. Slobin, *Relating events in narrative: A crosslinguistic developmental study* (pp. 239–284). Hillsdale, NJ: Lawrence Erlbaum Associates.

Secada, W. G., & Lightfoot, T. (1993). Symbols and the political context of bilingual education in the United States. In B. Arias & U. Casanova (Eds.), *Bilingual education: Politics, practice, research. 92nd Yearbook of the Society for the Study of Education* (pp. 36–64). Chicago: University of Chicago Press.

Shirai, Y. (1993). Inherent aspect and the acquisition of tense/aspect morphology in Japanese. In H. Nakajima & Y. Otsu (Eds.), *Argument structure: Its syntax and acquisition* (pp. 185–211). Tokyo: Kaitakusha.

Shirai, Y., & Andersen, R. W. (1995). The acquisition of tense–aspect morphology: A prototype account. *Language, 71,* 743–762.

Shirai, Y., & Kurono, A. (1998). The acquisition of tense-aspect marking in Japanese as a second language. *Language Learning, 48,* 245–279.

Silva-Corvalán, C. (1994). *Languages in contact: Spanish in Los Angeles.* Oxford: Oxford University Press.

Skutnabb-Kangas, T. (1981). *Bilingualism or not: The education of minorities.* Clevedon, UK: Multilingual Matters.

Smith, C. (1983). A theory of aspectual choice. *Language, 59,* 479–501.

Snow, C. E., & Hakuta, K. (1989). *The costs of monolingualism.* Bilingual Research Group Working Paper No. 89-06. Santa Cruz: University of California, Santa Cruz.

Solé, Y. R. (1995). Language, nationalism, and ethnicity in the Americas. *International Journal of the Sociology of Language, 116,* 111–138.

Sommer, G. (1997). Towards an ethnography of language shift: Goals and methods. In M. Pütz (Ed.), *Language choices: Conditions, constraints, and consequences* (pp. 55–76). Amsterdam: John Benjamins.

Spindler, G., & Spindler, L. (Eds.). (1987). *Interpretative ethnography of education: At home and abroad.* Hillsdale, NJ: Lawrence Erlbaum Associates.

Spivak, G. (1993) *Outside in the teaching machine.* New York: Routledge.

Stanford Working Group. (1992). *Federal education programs for limited-English-proficient students: A blueprint for the second generation.* Stanford, CA: Author.

Stewart, K., & De León, A. (1993). *Not room enough: Mexicans, Anglos, and socioeconomic change in Texas, 1850–1900.* Albuquerque: University of New Mexico Press.

Storey, J. (Ed.). (1996). *What is cultural studies?* London: Arnold.

Tharp, R., & Gallimore, R. (1989). *Rousing minds to life: Teaching, learning, and schooling in social context.* Cambridge: Cambridge University Press.

Tinajero, J. V., & Ada, A. F. (Eds.). (1993). *The power of two languages: Literacy and biliteracy for Spanish-speaking students.* New York: Macmillan/McGraw-Hill.

Tinajero, J. V., & DeVillar, R. (Eds.). (2000). *The power of two languages 2000: Effective dual-language use across the curriculum.* New York: McGraw-Hill.

U.S. Department of Commerce, Bureau of the Census. (1993a). *The foreign-born population of the United States.* 1990 Census of Population, CP-3-1. Washington, DC: Author.

U.S. Department of Commerce, Bureau of the Census. (1993b). *Public use microdata samples: A (5%) sample.* Washington, DC: Author.

Valdés, G. (1996). *Con respeto: Bridging the distances between culturally diverse families and schools.* New York: Teachers College Press.

Valdés, G., & Figueroa, R. (1994). *Bilingualism and testing: A special case of bias.* Norwood, NJ: Ablex.

Valencia, R., & San Miguel, G. (1998). From the Treaty of Guadalupe Hidalgo to "Hopwood": The educational plight and struggle of Mexican Americans in the Southwest. *Harvard Educational Review, 68,* 353–412.

Vasquez, O., Pease-Alvarez, L., & Shannon, S. (1994). *Pushing boundaries: Language and culture in a Mexicano community.* Cambridge: Cambridge University Press.

Veltman, C. (1983). *Language shift in the United States.* Berlin: Mouton.

Veltman, C. (1988). *The future of the Spanish language in the United States.* Washington, DC: Hispanic Policy Development Task Force.

Vendler, Z. (1967). *Linguistics in philosophy.* Ithaca, NY: Cornell University Press.

Verkuyten, M. (1995). Self-esteem, self-concept stability, and aspects of ethnic identity among minority and majority youth in the Netherlands. *Journal of Youth and Adolescence, 24,* 155–175.

Waggoner, K., & Griffith, A. (1998). Parent involvement in education: Ideology and experience. *Journal for a Just and Caring Education, 4,* 65–77.

Watson-Gegeo, K. A., & Gegeo, D. (1986). The role of sibling interaction in child socialization. In B. B. Schieffelin & E. Ochs (Eds.), *Language socialization across cultures* (pp. 17–50). Cambridge: Cambridge University Press.

Wiley, T. G. (1996). *Literacy and language diversity in the United States.* Washington, DC and McHenry, IL: Center for Applied Linguistics and Delta Systems.

Wong Fillmore, L. (1991). When learning a second language means losing the first. *Early Childhood Research Quarterly, 6,* 323–346.

Wong Fillmore, L. (1996). Luck, fish seeds, and second-language learning. In C. Pearson Casanave & S. R. Schecter (Eds.), *On becoming a language educator: Personal essays on professional development* (pp. 29–38). Mahwah, NJ: Lawrence Erlbaum Associates.

Woolard, K. (1985). Language variation and cultural hegemony. *American Ethnologist, 12,* 738–748.

Yeung, A. S., Marsh, H. W., & Suliman, R. (2000). Can two tongues live in harmony: Analysis of the National Education Longitudinal Study of 1988 (NELS88) longitudinal data on the maintenance of home language. *American Educational Research Journal, 37,* 1001–1026.

Zentella, A. C. (1981). "*Ta bien, you could answer me en qualquier idioma*": Puerto Rican code switching in bilingual classrooms. In R. Durán (Ed.), *Latino language and communicative behavior* (pp. 109–132). Norwood, NJ: Ablex.

Zentella, A. C. (1996, March). *The "chiquitafication" of U.S. Latinos and their language, or why we need a politically applied Applied Linguistics.* Paper presented to the American Association of Applied Linguistics, Chicago.

Zentella, A. C. (1997). *Growing up bilingual: Puerto Rican children in New York.* Oxford: Blackwell.

Zentella, A. C. (1998). Multiple codes, multiple identities: Puerto Rican children in New York City. In S. M. Hoyle & C. T. Adger (Eds.), *Kids talk: Strategic language use in later childhood* (pp. 95–112). Oxford: Oxford University Press.

Author Index

Note: Bold page numbers indicate complete citation information; parenthetical numbers show frequency of citation. The letter t refers to a table. Numbered footnotes, e.g., 13n6, 50n1, follow both their page numbers and the letter n.

Bunge, R., 198, **203**
Butler, J., 51, 173(2), 177, **203**(2)

C

Camarillo, A., 41(2), 42, 44(2), 45(2), **203**
Cárdenas, J. A., 38, 39, **203**
Casanova, U., 2n2, **201**
Cazden, C., 148, 151, **203**
Chauduri, U., 181, **203**
Chen, C., 13n6, 14, **203**
Collins, J., 58, **208**
Comrie, B., 115, 115n1, **203**
Condor, S., 50n1, **202**
Cooper, R. L., 12, **204**
Corsaro, W. A., 13, **205**
Crago, M., 8, 13n6(2), 14, 108, **203**(2)
Crawford, J., 2, 38, 187, 203(2), **204**
Crichlow, W., 51, **208**
Cummins, J., 138(2), 198, **204**(2)

D

D'Andrea, D., 8, 12, **206**
Daniels, R., **204**
Davis, C. R., 37, 38(3), **205**
deCerteau, M., 177, **204**
DeLeón, A., 32(2), 204, **211**
Delgado-Gaitan, C., 3, **204**
DeVillar, R., 198, **211**
Donato, R., 46(2), **204**
Dorian, N., 8, **204**
Dyson, A. H., 179n4

E

Eagleton, T., 50, 179, **204**(2)
Eckert, P., 51, 177, **204**
Edwards, D., 50n1, **202**
Eisenberg, A., 13n6, 14, **204**

F

Faigley, L., 51, **204**
Fairchild, H. H., 2n2, **209**
Fairclough, N., 53, **204**
Ferguson, J., 177, **206**
Figueroa, R., 113, 141, 194(2), 194n4, 195, **212**

Fishman, J. A., xi, 3, 4, 8, 12, 108, **204**(2)
Foucault, M., 51, 183(3), **204**(4)
Fox, R. G., 15, **205**

G

Gal, S., 8, **205**
Gallimore, R., 148, **211**
Gambitta, R., 37, 38(3), **205**
Gane, M., 50n1, **202**
García, R., 32(2), 33(3), 34(2), 35, 36(3), 37(2), **205**
Garza, R., 51, **205**
Gaskins, S., 13, **205**
Gee, J., 129, 161, **205**(2)
Genesee, F., 13n6, 14, **203**
Giles, H., 27, **205**
Godfrey, B., 42(2), 44(2), 45(3), **205**(2)
Goldman, S., 142, **208**
Gómez-Quiñones, J., 35, **205**
Göncü, A., 13, **210**
Gonzales, M., 34, 35, 36, 37, 41, 43, 44, 45, **205**
González, N., 198, **205**
Goodwin, M. H., 13, 13n6, **205**
Graff, H., 161, **205**
Grego, D., 13n6, **212**
Griffith, A., 141(2), 143, 205, **212**
Grumet, M., xvii, xix, **205**
Guerra, J., 178, **205**
Gumperz, J. J., 52(3), 203, **206**(2)
Gupta, A., 177, **206**

H

Hajnal, Z., 199, **206**
Hakuta, K., 2n2(2), 3, 8, 12, 108, 164, 199, **201**, **206**(3), **211**
Hall, S., 51, 179, 180n5, **206**(2)
Hao, L.-x., 8, **209**
Haraway, D., xix, **206**
Harris, W., 178, **207**
Haugen, E., 193, **206**
Hayes-Bautista, D. E., 47(2), **206**
Heath, S. B., 9, 13, 13n6, 17, 58(2), 148, **206**(3)
Heilbrun, C. G., 181, **206**
Heller, M., 52, **206**

Subject Index

Note: Bold page numbers indicate definitions. The letter t refers to a table. Numbered footnotes, e.g., 56n6, 172n3, follow both their page numbers and the letter n.